ISLAMIC THREAT
UPDATES
ALMANAC #1

5762

(OCT. 2001-SEPT. 2002)

By
Victor Mordecai

Direct inquiries to:

Victor Mordecai
P.O. Box 18209
Jerusalem, Israel 91181
Fax: 011 972 2 5355807

For reordering this book in the U.S.
1-800-540-0828

ISBN: 1-931600-48-1

www.vicmord.com
Email: vicmord2001@yahoo.com

First Printing
April, 2003 – Nissan 5762
10,000 copies
298 pages
Taylors, South Carolina

Second Printing
April, 2012 - Nissan 5772
5,000 Copies
336 pages
Taylors, South Carolina

Contents

PREFACE

As I write this preface to my third book, *Islamic Threat Updates Almanac #1 – 5762,* on the eve of the war with Saddam Hussein, I look back 12 years to when I began my work of speaking in churches, synagogues, on radio and TV.

It started out innocently enough. I had just completed my two-year stint in the Government Press Office of Prime Minister Yitzhak Shamir as senior editor and translator in the News Department and was traveling throughout the US to warn the American people then in November 1990 of the threat of Saddam Hussein!

At that time, I traveled light. I had no books, no audio tapes nor video tapes. I just had the beginnings of a message.

From the summer of 1991 to June 1994, I actually stopped most traveling and studied at the Jewish Theological Seminary (Jerusalem Branch) hoping to become a Conservative rabbi.

As fate would have it, God had other plans for me, and I never became a rabbi.

It was more or less during this time that I met a dear Christian woman, Barbara Richmond, who came to Israel frequently leading Christian pilgrimage groups to Israel. She invited me to speak before one of her groups, and I presented my usual presentation as I was so well taught to do in the Israeli Defense Forces Spokesman's Office as well as the Prime Minister's Office.

Barbara came up to me afterwards and said that the people in her group loved the presentation, but could not write down notes fast enough. Her solution was either to speak more slowly, which was impossible, or to prepare a written outline for the people in her group, maybe even a book.

Since I had never written a book, I viewed writing a book as nothing less than conquering Mt. Everest. But Barbara persisted and said, "I will help you." And she did.

My first book was indeed really more of just an outline of my message. The first edition of *Is Fanatic Islam a Global Threat?* appeared in January 1995 in 1000 copies. The first edition was a mere 63-page pamphlet.

By the time these were sold out in May 1995, I had accumulated more information which required revising my book. The second edition grew to 93 pages, still not really a book.

In January 1996, the 1000 copies of the second edition were all sold out. By now, the new information required a second revision and the third edition came out totaling 170 pages.

These 1000 copies all sold out in one month with the help of Dr. David Allen Lewis in Springfield, Missouri, and his son-in-law Neal Howell, who was to become indispensable for me in preparing the 3rd, 4th, and 5th editions. The book grew now to 200 pages in the 4th edition (10,000 copies) and 336 pages in the fifth edition (40,000 copies).

I thought: enough is enough. I made my contribution to world civilization with this book, and I could continue "traveling light."

Fortunately or unfortunately, US President Bill Clinton changed all of that. Even though I was accumulating more and more information on the threat of fanatic Islam, I did not want to be burdened down with "merchandise." But the bombing of the Serbs in April 1999 convinced me that something was very wrong with the United States of America, or at least with the administration in Washington. Moslems, on the other hand, could get away with murder, killing Jews, Christians, Hindus and Buddhists throughout the world, but no matter.

I saw Christians in Serbia being slaughtered and "sacrificed for a barrel of oil." This was something I had been writing about in my first book. I saw that the globalist agenda would then turn on Israel as soon as the war with the Serbs was over. Serbian president Slobodan Milosevic was described as a war criminal for killing 2,000 armed Moslem Albanian terrorists as part of his job of defending sovereign Serb territory. Yet Saddam Hussein had gotten away with the killing of over 2 million Moslems: Iraqis, Iranians, Kurds and Kuwaitis among others, but Clinton studiously avoided dealing with Saddam Hussein. Even the destruction of the US embassies in Africa in the summer of 1998 and the blowing up of the USS *Cole* in Yemen in 2000 went unanswered by President Bill Clinton. Shooting a few Tomahawk missiles into empty tents in Iraq or Afghanistan is not the answer.

I saw that Israeli prime ministers would be the next target for the War Crimes Tribunal in The Hague, Netherlands, after Slobodan Milosevic. It didn't matter if we were talking about Prime Ministers Benjamin Netanyahu (1996-1999), Ehud Barak (1999-2000) or Ariel Sharon (2000-2003). All Israeli prime ministers were liable to the War Crimes Tribunal if the globalists so desired. The same applies to Israeli army officers and even soldiers.

I was up in arms and realized that without a rebirth or revival of Israel's only friends, the Christian Bible believers, Israel was doomed by the Clintons and their bedfellows. So my second book appeared in the summer of 1999: *Christian Revival for Israel's Survival.*

In March 2001, I was ambushed by my two sons, who said I needed a website. I was a hard nut to crack and did not want to get near to a computer, because I was of the old school. Jodie Anderson of Texas, leader of the Battalion of Deborah (Christian women's group supporting Israel), together with my two sons convinced me that to better serve God, we needed to take advantage of this new technology and go hi-tech.

My constant research into the media was uncovering newspaper articles, radio and TV interviews as well as personal sources in the intelligence world. All this information had to be made readily available to the public and especially to those people who were hungering and thirsting after the truth. In Hosea 4:6 it says, "My people are destroyed for lack of knowledge."

Also, people who were looking for me needed an immediate connection to reach me. A website was the perfect solution. My sons also created a website bookstore where my books, audios and videotapes could be made readily available.

With the Islamic attacks on 9/11, I decided, or rather, we all decided on the birthing of a monthly newsletter which would update the public on the Islamic threat. After a few months of these newsletters which began immediately after 9/11 with October 2001, we all realized that 12 months of newsletters would easily fill up a few hundred pages, thus justifying my 3rd book, this book, *Islamic Threat Updates Almanac #1 – 5762.* The newsletters from the website were a free download, but the hard copy became a new product.

INTRODUCTION

As I said in the Preface, my work started out basically as an Israeli army spokesman in the reserves traveling around the US with a message focusing on the threat that Saddam Hussein posed to Israel in 1990. Indeed, already in 1986, Jonathan Pollard was arrested by the US government for sharing with Israel information about Saddam's biological warfare program plans to attack Israel. In April 1990, Saddam said he had enough biological and chemical weapons to burn half of Israel off the face of the map. (Jonathan Pollard was only giving Israel information that the US government promised it would share with Israel but reneged on its promise. Jonathan Pollard is still languishing in jail. He should be immediately released!)

My first trip to the States as a lecturer took place in November and December of 1990. Frankly speaking, I had information about Saddam's plans that I had received in Israel from Israeli media, military and government sources. When I came to the States, people were astounded at what I was saying because they had not this same information.

When the war took place in January to March of 1991, I was home in Jerusalem with my family, and then in April, I returned to the States for another two-month lecture circuit and was received as a hero and a prophet for having successfully predicted what would happen in "Desert Storm." My immediate response was: No, I was not a prophet. I just had the information which the Americans had not. But it became clear that there was a lack of information problem in the US and there was a great vacuum that had to be filled with the work of people like myself, Israelis and Americans – or Jews and Christians.

After a three-year hiatus from travels due to my studies in the rabbinical seminary, I was treated to the shock of seeing the rubbish which filled the TV screens in the US over the years such as the Lorena Bobbitt, Tanya Harding, and O.J. Simpson trials as well as the Elian Gonzalez custody case or the Gary Condit affair resulting from the Shandra Levy murder. These were a sampling of sick, "sexy," non-news coverage which dominated the media.

On the other hand, I had information about anti-aircraft missiles bringing down US airliners; the counterfeiting of US currency to destroy the US economy; Iraqi and Islamic involvement in the 1993 WTC terrorist attack, Oklahoma City bombing in 1995, the shooting down of TWA 800 in 1996 as well as a host of other incidents and plans to destroy Israel, the United States, the Judeo-Christian Western world as well as all the rest of the world which wasn't Islamic. This was the gist of my first book: *Is Fanatic Islam a Global Threat?* which first appeared in 1995 as described in the Preface and which has been self-printed in 53,000 copies in English, and 4,000 copies in German published by Haenssler Verlag in Germany.

Bill Clinton's administration turned its back on the genocide in Africa of two million blacks, the murders of almost two million Moslems by Saddam Hussein, and of course, the persecution and killing of Jews, Christians, Hindus and Buddhists by Islam worldwide. Yet Slobodan Milosevic was a mass murderer, just as bad as Adolph Hitler, for killing 2,000 armed Moslem Albanian terrorists in Kosovo. The US placed all its military might at the disposal of world Islam and at the expense of the Serbs. (By the way, the Serbs were the "good guys" in WWI and WWII. The Moslems were the "bad guys" who joined the ranks of Hitler's SS shock troops in WWII.)

The writing was on the wall of the Israeli leadership. The Palestinians, the Arabs and Moslems could target Israel and the Jews, but if the Israeli government did its job properly in defending Israel, these leaders and military men would now be considered war criminals. This was the reason for my writing my second book, *Christian Revival for Israel's Survival,* which has been self-printed until now in 20,000 copies.

Immediately after the appearance of my second book in the summer of 1999, I was treated to a horrific testimony (appearing in the first newsletter of October 2001) about Islamic plans to murder every Jew in Canada, the US, the Americas, Europe, and wherever Jews can be found.

With the decision by Palestinian terrorist leader Yasser Arafat to walk away from the most generous offer ever made by Israeli Prime Minister Ehud Barak in June 2000 at Camp David fulfilling 97% of Arafat's conditions, and the resulting Intifada Al Quds which has led to the deaths of thousands of Palestinians and Israelis, the stage was set, I believe, for a final showdown between Israel and the Palestinians. The so-called Oslo I & II peace process meant, basically, Israel gave and the Palestinians took. But the terrorism always continued.

A year after the Intifada began in September 2000 came the 9/11 attacks on the US. Now, the US was fighting for its survival just as Israel has had to do for a hundred years. In spite of all the proof that Saddam Hussein was aligned with Usama bin Laden and other international Islamic terrorist groups, the United States had to go it virtually alone in taking out Saddam Hussein.

For years, I have been documenting the infiltration along the porous borders of the US from Canada and Mexico of Islamic terrorists and illegal aliens. I have been revealing how oil money from Iraq, Iran, Saudi Arabia and Libya has been used to subvert the US and to empower the Moslems in the US to prepare for the Islamization of Judeo-Christian America. Meanwhile, the same has been apparent in every other country of the Judeo-Christian world in Europe, South America, Africa and Australia.

What many people don't understand is that five revolutions have taken place in the Islamic world since 1979:

1. The Afghanistan-Taliban-Al-Qaeda connection which prepared tens of thousands of terrorists to destroy the Judeo-Christian West.

2. The rise to power of the ayatollahs' regime in Iran in 1979 which has spread terror throughout the world as well as has squandered immense amounts of money in developing sleeper cell networks through North America, South America and Europe.

3. The metamorphosis of the Iraqi ally and savior in the war against Iran in 1980-88, Saddam Hussein, who stupidly enough attacked Kuwait and was repulsed by the entire world in 1991. Now Saddam has spent his oil money in attacking the US and spreading his sleeper cells throughout the US and the world in preparation for the final showdown with the Great Christian Satan, the United States.

4. Libya's spending of billions of dollars in its oil money to support the Nation of Islam and its leader, Louis Farrakhan, in the US plus the spending of billions of dollars in Islamizing the African continent.

5. Saudi Arabia has been notorious in its profligate, un-limited spending for Islamic missionary activities and the establishment of madrasa schools all over the world and particularly in the US. Johnny Walker Lindh, the Taliban of Marin County, California, is an example of a graduate of one of these madrasas.

If the world doesn't learn to deal with all of the above, it is the end for the United States, which will backslide into just another has-been leader, as predicted by Harvard Professor Samuel Huntington in his book *The Clash of Civilizations and the Remaking of World Order*, and of course, Islamic population growth will overtake the Judeo-Christian West, ending democracy, women's rights, minorities' rights, civil rights and basically destroying the earth.

So the purpose of this third book is to serve as a sequel and follow-up to my first two books and to show the patterns of Islamic cancerous growth throughout the world. We need to learn the nature of the beast in order to contend with and defeat it to save human civilization.

Chapter I
OCTOBER 2001 NEWSLETTER

Though there are indeed many newsletters out there, I have come to the conclusion that there is a need for a periodic news update with a particularly Judeo-Christian perspective on the threat of Islam to Western civilization in particular and the planet as a whole.

Victor Mordecai's Monthly Message

From January 1989 until October 1990, I served as senior editor and translator at the News Department of the Government Press Office in Jerusalem, under Prime Minister Yitzhak Shamir. A great part of my job included processing and translating from Israeli Military Intelligence translations of the Islamic Press into Hebrew and then into English for the English language foreign press. Unfortunately, the users of our services at the GPO were journalists either hostile to Israel at worst, or non-committal at best.

Since leaving the prime minister's office in November 1990, I have spent most of my time, up to eight months of the year for the last seven years, touring the US, teaching in churches and synagogues, speaking on radio shows and appearing on TV programs trying to create an awareness among Jews and Christians, especially the latter, about the need to be committed to Israel. One of the great challenges in this work has been to get out the information denied to world opinion, especially the Americans, by the mainline media. In addition to the current events denied you by the agenda media blackout, there will be military intelligence information included in this newsletter, as well as private investigation I have carried out abroad. All these will be brought to the attention of the reader.

With the very special experiences I have had with the Christian communities, of all denominations, I realized that a periodic newsletter with fresh information readily available in Israel, and directly primarily toward the Christians, especially pastors, would go a long way towards realizing the goal of mobilizing Christian support for Israel.

Conversely, failure to approach the Islamic threat from a clearly religious Judeo-Christian perspective would be missing the point. Before the terrorist attacks in the US on September 11th, 2001, it would have been considered politically incorrect to say that the world is definitely now in a conflagration of a religious nature, which is what I have been saying for more than a decade and is contained in my two books — *Is Fanatic Islam a Global Threat?* and *Christian Revival for Israel's Survival.* But the terrorist attacks unfortunately proved that though I was not politically correct, I was absolutely correct.

Professor Samuel Huntington of Harvard University writes in his book: *The Clash of Civilizations* that future wars will be without borders. They will not be between countries but between civilizations. Eastern pagan civilizations such as Islam, Mandarin China and India will modernize, but will not westernize, because westernization means Judeo-Christian Western civilization. Huntington shows how these three systems await the decline and demise of Western civilization during the coming 50 years.

The purpose of this newsletter will be to strengthen Israel, Western civilization, with the US as the vanguard, and finally the rest of the planet against what I consider the greatest threat from amongst the three civilizations Huntington is referring to — Islam.

Quoting from the Bible:

Hosea 4:6: *My people are destroyed for lack of knowledge.*

Ezekiel 33:6: *But if the watchman sees the sword come, and blows not the trumpet, and the people be not warned, and if the sword comes, and take any person from among them; he is taken away in his iniquity, but his blood will I require at the hand of the watchman.*

CURRENT EVENTS AND ANALYSIS

Italian Prime Minister Berlusconi on Islam

To kick off this newsletter, I thought it would be highly appropriate to quote the *Jerusalem Post* of Friday, September 28, 2001. Article by Susan Sevareid on p. 4.

Manama, Bahrain (AP) — Italian Prime Minister Silvio Berlusconi contends that Western Civilization is superior to Islamic culture. This compounded fears yesterday in the largely Muslim Middle East that the US war on terrorrism will be a war on Islam.

According to Amr Moussa, secretary general of the 22-nation Arab League, Berlusconi's remarks Wednesday in Berlin "crossed the limits of reason. We do not believe there is a superior civilization, and if he said so he is utterly mistaken."

The conservative Italian premier's comments were quickly condemned by other Italian politicians as the US is trying to build a coalition with Islamic countries to stamp out terrorism in the wake of the September 11th suicide jet strikes on America believed to have killed more than 6,000 people.

Coalition building with Middle East nations already is difficult because many have uneasy truces with homegrown Islamic extremists that easily could be shaken. Moderate

Moslems also could harden their views if they feel their faith is under attack.

Speaking at a news conference yesterday after talks in Berlin with German Chancellor Gerhard Schroeder and Russian President Vladimir Putin, Berlusconi said:

"We must be aware of the superiority of our civilization, a system that has guaranteed well-being, respect for human rights, and in contrast with Islamic countries, respect for religious and political rights." Berlusconi added he hoped the West will continue to conquer peoples, like it conquered Communism.

PRIVATE INVESTIGATION

The following is a testimony I received while visiting Edmonton, Canada, in August 1999. I am including this because it happened after the publication of my second book, *Christian Revival for Israel's Survival.* This testimony is in neither of my two books.

If someone is considered a radical and suggests a radical situation is possible, with radical repercussions, the non-radicals answer: "We will cross the bridge when we get to it." Well, we have reached the radical situation with the Islamic terrorist attacks in the US on September 11th, 2001. This following testimony deals with some radical repercussions that many of my readers will still find "too" radical. Judge for yourselves.

After speaking in a Baptist church in Edmonton Thursday night, August 19th, 1999, my Christian hostess in Edmonton sought out a synagogue for me in which to spend the Sabbath. The young rabbi and his wife were most gracious and took me in.

Saturday afternoon between Mincha and Maariv (afternoon and evening) services, the rabbi asked me to get up and share about my work with the Christians in building support for Israel. Instead of 9 hours, 3 hours, or 1 hour, the rabbi said: "You have 10 to 15 minutes"!

Telescoping my 9-hour message into 9 minutes is not easy.

I basically had to start with my conclusions that, again, are considered "radical" for someone who has not heard the full 9-hour teaching. And indeed after a very, very short introduction, I was cut short by some leftwing "liberals." (VM - I replace "liberals" with "totalitarians.") They heckled me and would not allow me to continue speaking, saying my message was a message of hatred. I said, "I don't hate Moslems. I love Moslems, but I do hate Islam because it is just another satanic system like Nazism."

To make a long story short, they were not going to allow me to speak. (VM: If you are not a "liberal" like they, then they are not going to be so "liberal" with you.) Finally, a young Christian woman who had come to the synagogue to hear me speak arose to her feet, and said, "I came to hear VM speak. If you are not going to allow him to speak, maybe you will allow me to share. You all know me."

And, indeed, they knew her and were willing to allow her to speak. This is the testimony:

"You all know that I am a social worker. I work at the family crisis center in Edmonton, Canada. I am a caseworker for an Egyptian Moslem woman doctor who just arrived in Canada from Cairo, Egypt."

It turns out she had her own private family clinic in one of Cairo's poorest neighborhoods. She really was kind of a Sister Teresa. She was a saint and healed many poor people. But indeed they had no way of repaying her. They paid her with bread, cheese, eggs, etc. They cleaned her house, cooked her meals and served her in many ways. But nobody had money.

Since she was in her 40's and was now concerned about the eventuality of retirement, she looked to Canada as a new place in which to live, work and accumulate some finances for that day of retirement. She applied for a visa. It was granted.

The next day, there was a knock on her door. It was three Moslem fundamentalists dressed in the appropriate attire. They said to her, "Mabruk" (congratulations). She answered: "Alai Barek Feek" which means, "You, too, should have congratulations. Why do I have congratulations?"

They answered her: "Because we know you're going to Canada." "How did you know?" she answered. "I only received the visa yesterday." They retorted: "We know everything about you. We have our people everywhere in the Egyptian administration. And yes, we also have congratulations in store for us because you are going to work for us. You are going to be our spy in Canada. Within a very short time, you will have your own family clinic. You will be in a position to know who the Jews are, who the Christians are, and anyone who opposes our Islamic agenda for Canada, and you are going to report back to us who they are, and we are going to kill all of them."

The woman doctor said to them: "I am a doctor. I swore to heal people and to save lives. I don't understand politics, am not interested in politics and am definitely not into killing people."

So they said to her: "So you don't want to work for us? That's OK." They then grabbed a young woman volunteer helping the doctor — her best friend from childhood — and they slit her throat. As the woman lay on the floor dead with her blood gushing out, the three Moslems of the Gama'a Islamiya said to her: "If you don't work for us, that's what we are going to do to you."

The next day, the woman doctor had political asylum in the Canadian embassy in Cairo. The Royal Canadian Air Force then flew in a private jet to spirit her out of Egypt to a safehouse in Canada.

And it was this Christian woman in the synagogue who was her caseworker. She is totally coordinated with the RCMP (Royal Canadian Mounted Police). The testimony continues:

"Don't understand from this testimony that Moslems in Canada are all like these terrorists. At least 90% of the Moslems in Canada are good peace-loving people. But perhaps up to 10% who get their salaries from the Middle East know what the plan is. And they follow orders. Churches in America or Canada grow little by little as the congregation grows and can afford increasingly larger facilities. But the Moslems have unlimited funds for building lavish mosques, economic infrastructures and finally housing for the troops who are later brought in. All of this is planned in advance, strategic planning from the Middle East to take over Canada in a few decades. The Islamic leadership, getting its funds from the Middle East, knows and must follow the orders from the fanatic leadership in Egypt, Saudi Arabia, Iraq, Iran, etc."

VM: My conclusions from this testimony are radical. Yes, we have reached the bridge and are presently crossing it. As the Islamic war against the world develops and as Israel inevitably will face a war of kill or be killed, the repercussions in the world will be that Moslems, who are in place and have the enemies of Islam totally computerized, will target Jews in their homes, cars, and places of work. There are no secrets. Jews and Christians will not be able to hide. Four or five million Jews are today outnumbered by up to 15 million Moslems in the US alone. These fanatic Moslems have shown they are not afraid to die. Will they be afraid to sit (picnic) in US jails? I don't think so. So the writing is on the wall for Jews and yes, for Christians as well, especially for those Christians who love Israel and stand by the Jews.

Yes, there will be massive killing of Jews and Christians by people who don't flinch at dying because their god, Allah, has promised them heaven as martyrs. Their god, Allah, has commanded them to kill the Jews on Saturday and the Christians on Sunday. But their god, Satan, is also a deceiver and a destroyer of the Moslems first just as Hitler deceived and destroyed his own German people. Moslems are created in the image of God just like the Jews and Christians, and Satan wants to see destroyed anyone created in the image of God. This includes the Moslem peoples.

The bottom line is, after the next war between Israel and its Islamic neighbors, there will be a tremendous homecoming of Jews and Christians to Israel. The Moslems say: "And now Allah is bringing home the Jews in large groups from all over the world to their mass graveyard in Palestine." (Sheikh Abdul Aziz Oudeh in Chicago at an Islamic conference in December 1990. From the Steven Emerson PBS video "Jihad in America.")

My response is: And now God is bringing home the Jews and the Christians to their home in Israel in expectation of the coming of the Messiah and the messianic era of peace. We Jews and Christians will receive the triumphant Messiah in Jerusalem at the

Mt. of Olives, and of course, Satan, Allah, will be relegated to the pits of hell for 1,000 years!

MILITARY INTELLIGENCE INFORMATION

The Iranian Nuclear Threat

Iran has long been considered the pioneer of the Islamic fundamentalism phenomenon in the 20th century. Reports from several intelligence sources and satellite pictures published in an Israeli newspaper, *Yediot Aharonot,* Sept. 26, 2001, show an increase in Iranian efforts to develop a nuclear plant for military purposes. In order to develop this kind of ability, Iran needs foreign know-how and aid.

In the past, Iran maintained contacts with the Chinese government and some European countries for nuclear aid, but after the US applied diplomatic pressure, these contacts were terminated. Recent satellite images prove the existence of Russian scientists in the "Bushehr" atomic complex near the Persian Gulf.

The Russians deny any connection to the project in spite of clear evidence that was handed over to Russian President Putin by American and Israeli intelligence. It appears that in the current economic situation in Russia, "money can buy everything," and the Iranians are paying Russian companies to send skilled Russian manpower to Iran with the necessary equipment.

Israeli intelligence estimates are that at the current rate of development, it will take 5 to 7 years until Iran will possess at least one nuclear bomb, but intelligence also warns that Iran is trying to obtain atomic components and equipment for the production of the bomb, a process that might shorten the above period to 2-3 years.

Iran is also developing ground-to-ground missiles with the ability to carry atomic, biological and chemical warheads with a range covering much of Europe and the Middle East.

In light of the terror attack on the World Trade Center and the Pentagon, Western countries (including Russia) should treat any Muslim fundamentalist country as a direct threat to its national security. When Israel attacked the nuclear plant in Iraq, many voices from the West in Western Europe and the US opposed the idea and condemned Israel for conducting the attack. Only ten years later, in the Gulf war, did the West understand how different the military and diplomatic conditions would have been had Iraq been allowed to obtain atomic capability.

The case of Iran is much more dangerous. Iraq's intentions in invading Kuwait were mainly economic and political. Iraq had, and still has, a dictatorial regime with a secular orientation and aims. Iran, on the other hand, is a fundamentalist Muslim country with hostile intentions towards the West, and is a supporter of international terrorism.

Chapter II
NOVEMBER 2001 NEWSLETTER

Victor Mordecai's Monthly Message

"Islamic Dominoes"

Following the terrorist attacks of September 11th, 2001 on NYC and Wash., D.C., President George W. Bush announced the planned mobilization of 50,000 military reservists.

My immediate gut reaction was, "This man is not serious." The Japanese attack on Pearl Harbor of December 7th, 1941, signalled the beginning of WWII for the US. At least 2,600 US servicemen were killed and the US mobilized all its strength for a war that was to last four years.

On September 11th, the Islamic terrorists struck in NY, Washington and Pennsylvania, killing over 3,000 people with many, many more probably going to die from asbestos lung poisoning when the twin trade towers fell.

So the Islamic attack was many times worse than the Japanese attack on Pearl Harbor. Is it over? Many people ask me, "What's going to happen now?" My answer is: Just as the Japanese followed up the attack on Pearl Harbor with the invasion of the Philippines, Malaya, Indochina, Burma, etc., so, too, do I believe that the Moslems have stages II, III, etc., in the pipeline.

As a matter of fact, as we speak right now, anthrax has begun to spread in the US and perhaps other countries as Islam goes right into stage II.

President George W. Bush thinks that by bombing Afghanistan and letting the Northern Alliance take over control from the Taliban that the bane of Islamic terrorism will be over. He has promised Pakistan that the US attacks in Afghanistan will end soon because Pakistan fears destabilization of its population should the US tarry or carry out attacks into other Arab or Islamic lands.

And indeed, my fear, or prediction, is that there will indeed be a remarkable rise of Islamic fundamentalism and radicalism throughout the world which may cause Arab and Islamic countries to succumb to fanatic Moslem revolutionary movements which will join Bin Laden and Saddam Hussein and Iran. There will be, I'm afraid, a domino effect in these countries, all of which will become Iran and Iraq type scenarios, hostile to the US and the West.

The solution is not in "nuking" them. The only solution is replacing the self-destructive and maniacal Islamic systems, which are anti-democracy, anti-women and anti-human civilization, with pro-Western, pro-Judeo-Christian democracy systems which will give these peoples in the Islamic world a chance to taste a good life, something they are denied in Islam.

Just as Nazi Germany was not nuked, so, neither should the Moslems be nuked. Just as Nazi Germany was replaced with a democratic Germany as a result of the British, French and American occupation zones, so too should Iraq, Iran and Afghanistan (to start with) be occupied by British, French, American, German, and other European democratic Western nations. The Moslems should be "retooled and reeducated" in the arts of democracy.

If the West fails to occupy these peoples, the inevitable result will be continuing wars and destruction both in the Islamic world as well as in the West. For this, President George W. Bush needs to mobilize more than 50,000 reservists. All of America and the West must mobilize to occupy the Islamic lands and purge those countries of their corrupt, inhuman regimes and replace them with democratic Western systems. For this all 18 year old American men and women should be drafted (like the Israelis do) for an effort that will take many years. Either deal with Islam, or Islam will deal with you.

CURRENT EVENTS AND ANALYSIS

War Against Terror vs. War Against Islam

We've been hearing many leaders of Western countries speaking about the nature of this war against terror.

In every war it is vital to target the right enemy. What or who is the enemy in this war? Is it Bin Laden and his organization El-Qaida? Is it the Taliban regime? Is it all the Islamic terrorist organizations? It just goes on and on, but in the end you always get to the same answer - all the above are merely symptoms.

When treating a disease, pain relievers are just a way to make it less painful but the sickness is still there and if not treated well, it'll just become worse. No doubt, the sickness is the ideology behind these acts of terror. It's simply Islam.

It looks like the US was able to attack the main Taliban and El-Qaida installations.

The leaders of the two factions are hiding in caves and giving orders to their forces. They are waiting for the US and its allies to start the ground attack. It is then that the Taliban can and will show their abilities. They have done so in the 1980's during Afghanistan's occupation by Soviet forces.

When the ground attack will start, the West is in for a surprise. There have been many reports about civilians from Pakistan who are crossing the border in search of Taliban and Bin Laden forces. No, they are not trying to help the US and the Northern Alliance. They are risking their lives in order to join forces with the Taliban in "the holy war against the Crusader invasion."

Bin Laden has recently sent a letter to Pakistan through the "El Jazira" news agency warning the Pakistani regime from the continuation of aid to the attack against them. He used the term "Crusader invasion" and so has his fellow terrorists. So the cross is the enemy, not the US as a state or the West as a civilization, but Christianity as a whole.

If the Enemy targets your religion as the enemy, what is the right response? Attacking the terrorist cells all over the world is just a pain reliever. In doing so we must remember what the disease is. So when the time comes, we will be prepared to deal with the outcome of confronting the right enemy.

PRIVATE INVESTIGATION

Saddam Hussein and the Oklahoma City Bombing

It is now over six years since the Oklahoma City bombing of April 19th, 1995. At the time, I was in Tulsa, Oklahoma, only a hundred miles away. As fate would have it, my Christian friends arranged for me to speak on CBS News Channel 6 during the evening live broadcast. I was asked whether or not the bombing had Islamic fingerprints. I answered, "Absolutely yes!" When they asked me why, I told them.

"Do you remember Beirut 1983, when Islamic militants blew up the barracks of the US Marines killing 243 Marines? Do you remember just a few years later, when the same terrorists blew up the Israeli barracks in South Lebanon killing hundreds of Israeli soldiers? And what about the blowing up of the Israeli embassy in Buenos Aires, Argentina, in 1992? What about the bombing of the World Trade Center in New York City by Sheikh Omar Abdul Rahman in 1993? What about the bombing of the AMIA Jewish center in Buenos Aires in the summer of 1994?

"These were all Islamic car-bombs. According to the PBS anti-terrorism video tape of Steven Emerson, 'Jihad in America,' aired on US television in November 1994, the Moslems have promised more such terrorism in the future."

By now, my interviewers in Tulsa, Oklahoma, CBS TV were visibly sweating and were trying to find a way to end the interview. All of this was based on general information with nothing yet in the way of specific information regarding the bombing at the Murrah

Federal Building in Oklahoma City.

But within a very short time, my Christian hosts were feeding me with firsthand, incontrovertible information.

First, a local CBS affiliate in McPherson, Kansas, just across the border from Oklahoma, filed a report that three Moslem men bought a ton and a quarter of ammonium nitrate fertilizer, for which they paid cash. (This is something unusual for American farmers, who pay on credit or by check.) They asked the merchant to package the fertilizer in 80-100 lb. reinforced bags (which would increase the concussion effect in the event of a bomb) instead of receiving the fertilizer in bulk, something that would make more sense if they were farmers.

Secondly, the media spoke of Timothy McVeigh renting three Ryder vans.

Thirdly, Israeli newspapers reported immediately about the bombing that one of the vans made a clean getaway and was left abandoned at Dallas-Ft.Worth Airport.

Fourthly, the US had received warnings from the Middle East prior to the bombing.

Fifthly, CNN, a few months after the blast, issued a Public Service Announcement on behalf of the FBI seeking the assistance of any witnesses who might have been at the scene of McVeigh's arrest by the Oklahoma Highway Patrol, because the third van with the three Middle Easterners was right behind McVeigh's van, but fled the scene the moment they saw McVeigh being handcuffed. They then made it to Dallas-Ft.Worth Airport.

Now, all the above appeared on page 265 of my book *Is Fanatic Islam a Global Threat?* Yet many people refused to accept my findings because of political correctness or simply because of the attitude that if the mainline media said nothing about my evidence or other people's information, then this was just another conspiracy theory.

A few days after the April 19th, 1995, attack in Oklahoma City, I also met with Oklahoma State Representative Charles Key, who showed me an album with the pictures of the Middle Eastern men seen with McVeigh. Charles Key was also reviled by the "agenda" and his reputation tarnished.

This was six years before the "earthquake." Then on March 20th, 2001, Jana Davis, an investigative reporter for NBC Oklahoma City affiliate KFOR, went on Fox News "O'Reilly Factor" program with the following information:

1. A Middle Eastern terrorist group was living and working in the heart of Oklahoma City, just a few miles from the Murrah Federal Building.

2. A former member of Saddam Hussein's Republican Guard was identified with McVeigh on the day of the bombing, prior to the bombing, outside of the Murrah Federal Building in the Ryder truck on the truck that was later identified as a possible getaway vehicle.

3. On the day of the bombing, a Republican Guard from Iraq accompanied McVeigh and Nichols to the Murrah building.

4. Davis has 24 sworn witness affidavits that tie 7 to 8 Arab men to various stages of the bombing plot. She says she had hundreds of documents. The evidence does incriminate McVeigh and Nichols but shows that the bombing was masterminded and funded by Usama bin Laden. The Oklahoma City bombing was, in her opinion, a foreign conspiracy.

5. In addition, there were witnesses that Ramzi Yousef's terrorist group had connections with Nichols, who visited the Philippines on a number of occasions. (By the way, Ramzi Yousef built the bomb used in the NYC twin trade tower attack in February 1993. According to Washington, DC, investigator Dr. Laurie Mylroie, evidence from Sheikh Omar Abdul Rahman's trial led to Saddam Hussein and Iraq.)

When Jana Davis turned to the FBI in September 1997, the FBI outrightly refused to take the information. The US media claims that this was an oversight. But according to Dr. Laurie Mylroie, there is a federal gag order on her that she cannot come out publicly saying that Oklahoma City was a Saddam Hussein Iraqi state terrorism attack.

So my belief is that, contrary to the mainline American media, this was not an oversight, but a conscientious agenda to ignore the evidence and place all the blame on "Christian Militia-man" Timothy McVeigh, who said (according to the media) that he acted all alone. I find it ludicrous, therefore, that now, all of a sudden, there is a co-conspirator, Terry Nichols. Either the media was lying that McVeigh was alone, and/or it is lying now when they say Nichols was a co-conspirator. Either a woman is pregnant or she isn't. There are no percentages here. How can the American people be so gullible to swallow that McVeigh was all alone, and then he wasn't all alone?

What I can't understand is that to this very day, no one is asking the FBI what was in those thousands of documents. What were the circumstances surrounding the resignation of Louis Freeh of the FBI soon after Jana Davis's revelations?

In April 2001, I was driving across the American Midwest. I called a Christian TV host with connections to Oklahoma City. I asked him, "Why don't we blow the lid off this can of worms? Isn't it treason that the American people have been lied to?"

He answered, "Leave it. I know several witnesses, patriotic Americans, who came forward with information immediately after the bombing, about the Islamic aspects of the bombing, and they are all dead now." He was trembling.

On April 21st, 2001, I did a radio show from Dallas, TX, over the phone with Keith Gadschalk in Bloomington, Illinois. He told me about a gentleman he had interviewed previously by the name of Gagin. Gagin, according to Gadschalk, was offered $250,000 by two Iraqis named Omar and Ahmed to blow up the Murrah Federal Building. He even flew to Las Vegas to meet them. They asked him to reconnoiter the Murrah Federal Building. When the FBI refused to offer him immunity, Gagin discontinued meeting these two Iraqis.

I have been talking myself blue in the face in churches and synagogues, radio and TV for the last six years. I now stand vindicated. What about TWA800? Does anyone really believe it came down as the result of a fuel injection explosion? I write about this on page 266 of *Is Fanatic Islam a Global Threat?* Why the cover-up here as well? Maybe if you cover up and ignore terrorist attacks, they will go away. But the attacks on September 11th, 2001, were just too colossal to cover up. Maybe if the truth had not been covered up in Oklahoma City and TWA800, then maybe, just maybe, the September 11th attacks could have been avoided if the Americans weren't so lulled to sleep by their media and by their leadership.

MILITARY INTELLIGENCE INFORMATION

What's Next?

President Bush has declared war against terrorism. His first step has been to attack Bin Laden and his terrorist organization, El Qaida, and to attack the Taliban who support Bin Laden's infrastructure. Reports show good progress and the second phase of ground attack is close.

One asks what next does President Bush plan? Who or what is the next target?

Before the attack on Afghanistan, the United States tried to establish a coalition with Muslim states such as Egypt and Saudi Arabia — countries that receive financial and military support, a natural move in organizing a base of operation close to Afghanistan. But many eyebrows were raised when the United States ignored Israel's wish to join the coalition and instead turned to Iran... a country known for its "peaceful and loving nature" and "strong opposition to terrorism." It sounds like a bad joke.

Just a reminder: according to the official reports of the State Department dating from 1979 on, Iran has had an active role in many terrorist activities. Starting in 1984, Iran appears in the State Department's list of countries that support terrorism. It is the Ayatolla Ahmad Jenati, one of Khomeini's comrades, who said in 1992: "The Americans argue all the time that Iran poses a threat. We are happy to know that we pose a threat to our enemy. We should not be afraid of declaring our intentions." Jenati also said that Iran is maneuvering agents all over the world to prepare for "World War III between Islam and the West" and that Islamic leaders all over the world have taken it upon themselves to make the 21st century "The Century of Islam."

Iran Threatened and Carried Out:

April 18, 1983 — A suicide bombing at the US embassy in Beirut; 63 Americans died.

October 23, 1983 — A double-suicide bombing using two truckloads of explosives driven into the dormitories of US marines stationed close to the Beirut Intl. Airport, and a French paratrooper base a mile away; 240 US marines and 58 French paratroopers were killed.

March 17, 1992 — A car explosion into the walls of the Israeli embassy in Buenos Aires killing nine.

July 18, 1994 — An explosion causing the collapse of a seven-story building in Buenos Aires and killing 86 people.

In all of the above instances, Western intelligence agencies found a direct link to Iran's government and security forces.

Although there has been a decrease in Iranian terrorism, intelligence reports say that there are dormant terrorist cells all over the Western world waiting for an order from Iran.

Why then has Iran decreased its terrorist acts? More terrorist acts mean bigger chances of Western "interference" to Iran (especially now after the US has shown determination in fighting Bin Laden and the Taliban). This interference might delay other more important goals that Iran is striving to achieve. In the October issue this newsletter spoke of the Iranian nuclear weapon development plan and the smart move Israel did to blow up the Iraqi nuclear plant and by that, stopping Saddam from producing atomic weapons. In two to five years Iran will achieve nuclear capability. Nuclear terrorism will make the anthrax menace look like another bad joke.

Chapter III
DECEMBER 2001 NEWSLETTER

Victor Mordecai's Monthly Message

"A Strong Horse or A Weak Horse?"

Usama bin Laden was quoted on a much anticipated video-tape shown on December 19th, 2001, as saying that the world loves a strong horse always over a weak horse. In Western terminology this is the equivalent to the saying: "The world loves a winner." However, there are differences. Let's look at them.

It seems there is a dichotomy here. The former expression seems to deal with a stronger horse which is capable of murder, rape, larceny, slavery and any other crime in the book. As long as the horse wins the race, however, the horse is simply adored. Examples of this are Saddam Hussein, Usama bin Laden, Yasser Arafat, and Muammar Gaddafi, just to mention a few. These are strong horses. In the Islamic world, to succeed, you must be strong. If you are weak, you will never maintain power.

Kindness is a sign of weakness; cruelty is a sign of strength.

Let's look at what kind of a winner the world loves. A man or leader who builds, creates, strengthens and blesses his people, who is kind to his people, is considered a winner. In the West, a warmonger is considered a loser. One who saves a life saves the world. Whoever takes a life destroys a world. The world loving a winner is a positivist approach. A strong horse is a negativist approach. The strong horse mentality requires massive killing to remain a power. A weak horse in the Middle East falls from power very quickly.

Here are some examples: Former Israeli Prime Minister Ehud Barak offered Yasser Arafat 98.5% of what Arafat was demanding at Camp David in June 2000. Arafat's response was to walk away and in September 2000 start WWIII with his Jerusalem Intifada. The Israeli public supported Barak because Barak was seeking peace, even if compromise hurt. He was not a warmonger but a peace seeker. So in Western thinking, Barak was a winner, a champion. But this is not so in Islamic thinking. For Islam, Barak was a weakling to be despised. The Arabs and Moslems understand a strong horse, not a weak one.

This reminds me of two stories, one a true story and the other a parable. The true story involves an attempted robbery at a "7-11" convenience store in the US in the year 2000. A woman high on drugs entered the store with a sawed off shotgun demanding all the cash in the register. A 21-year-old attendant dutifully cleaned out all the cash from the register, put it in a paper bag and placed it on the counter for the woman to take it and leave. All this was done according to "7-11" corporate policy regarding holdups.

But instead of taking the money, the woman cocked her gun and seemed to get more and more agitated. The young recently married attendant, father of a newborn baby, realized that the woman was so high on drugs that she was not taking the money and leaving but getting more and more nervous. He was afraid he would never again see his little baby or wife. So in a moment of distraction for the woman, he jumped her, wrestled her to the ground and everyone came to disarm and to detain the woman until the police came.

This young attendant was really a hero, because it seemed blood was going to be spilled. Yet he was fired from the "7-11" convenience store for "needlessly endangering the lives of others in the store." In the case of the Palestinian-Israeli conflict, the young man was Israel and the crazy woman was Arafat. Here Ehud Barak offers all the cash in the register, and yet Arafat goes berserk. The woman never wanted the money. Arafat never wanted 98.5% concessions from Barak.

The parable involves a young man and woman who have "shacked up." After a few years, the woman says to her companion, "You know what? Let's just get married. Here are the keys to the house, the car, the bank vault and everything else. Just get a wedding ring!" And then the guy takes off, because it was never his intention in the first place to get married.

Now the peace process between Israel and the Palestinians seems to be dead. Israelis and Palestinians living together, sharing the same land, is like the man and woman living together. A peace agreement signifies something like a marriage agreement between the two. But it was never Arafat's intention to make peace. He ran off and started a war.

There is a saying that the difference between neurotic and psychotic people is that while neurotic people dream about castles in the air, psychotic people live in them. Keeping this in mind, let's look at who wants a Palestinian state and who doesn't. There are three parties to the Mid-East conflict: the US, Israel, and the Palestinians. Now the US wants a Palestinian state because it solves all of America's foreign policy problems (or so they think). Israel wants a Palestinian state because it gets the Palestinians out of Israel's hair (or so they think). The only group that does not want a Palestinian state is the Palestinians! This is because, by definition, such a Palestinian state would have to co-exist in peace alongside a Jewish Israeli state. Since this is contrary to Islam, by definition, the Palestinians will never consent to a "marriage agreement" with Israel, and they don't want the cash in the register. What the Palestinians want is to genocidally kill all the Jews and destroy the Jewish state. In other words, the Palestinians are living in castles in the air. They are psychotic. Islam makes them psychotic. Therefore, there will never, ever be a Palestinian state.

Let's look at Usama bin Laden. He talks in the "smoking gun" video about a strong horse and weak horse. The Islamic role model for all children is Saladin (Salah-ed-Din in Arabic). Saddam Hussein, Usama bin Laden, Hafez al-Assad, Muammar Gaddafi and Hosni Mubarak have all said that Saladin is their role model. Why? Because Saladin defeated the Christian Crusaders with his victory at the battle of the Horns of Hittin in 1293 and ended the 200 year Crusade period. Allah is a god based on the pagan war god al-Ilahi of pre-Mohammedan Mecca and Medina. Ishmael is the war patriarch of Islam. Saladin is the war role model for all Moslems. Saladin is the strong horse. The Christians and Jews are the weak horse.

Similarly, these Islamic leaders and all Islamic children are taught that Islam will defeat Israel, the "modern day crusader state," and of course the US, which backs Israel, and which is considered the greatest of all Christian countries. America is considered the great Christian Satan by the Moslems. Whereas the military is considered the role model in Islamic countries, the military is not considered a role model in the peace-loving Western countries. In the West, it is the successful businessman and/or sportsman who is considered the role model, just another sign of Western decadence in the eyes of Islam.

Democracy, a true symbol of Judeo-Christian Western civilization, has been gaining ground during the latter part of the 20th century. Latin America, which was rampant with military dictatorships until the 1980's, is now entirely democratic with the exception of Cuba. Soviet-Socialist eastern Europe and the former USSR are now increasingly democratic. Only in countries of the Islamic world is democracy an impossibility. The Islamic world is convinced that it will supplant the Judeo-Christian West and on the day of judgment, all Jews and Christians who have not embraced the pagan god Allah and the "greatest of all prophets [what a joke] — Mohammed" will be put to the sword by Jesus Christ the Moslem.

Now, Adolph Hitler was psychotic. He thought he could kill all the Jews. He succeeded in killing a third of all the Jews on the face of the earth. Killing all the Jews is psychotic because anyone who entertains this idea is living in castles in the air, because it is an impossible thing to do.

Islam believes in killing the Saturday people (the Jews) on Saturday and killing the Sunday people (the Christians) on Sunday. So if Adolph Hitler was psychotic in thinking he could kill all the Jews and conquer the whole earth, what should we think about the Moslems who want to kill all the Jews and all the Christians in the world and conquer the whole earth?!!! Super-psychotic. This is the strong horse of Islam.

Usama bin Laden signalled the beginning of the end for Islam on September 11th, 2001. The inexorable conclusions of the Islamic terrorist attacks are that one by one, the "strong horses" of Islam will be toppled and replaced with democratic and peaceful governments — kind to their people. If this goes against Islam, so this satanic, mentally retarded religion will be terminated and replaced by the religion of the God of Abraham, Isaac and Jacob.

Many times, I am asked in churches, "When will there be peace in the Middle East?" My answer: "When the US will have a Christian 'Clint Eastwood' type President who says to the Moslems: 'You want to destroy Israel and the US — the apples of God's eye? Feeling lucky? Make my day!'" When will there be war? When the US President says, "Hey, it's the economy, stupid." That was Bill Clinton's favorite saying. To that the Moslems will answer, "That jerk is in our pocket. We Moslems are the economy. We own him." For the Moslems, Bill Clinton was a weak horse. George W. Bush is the strong horse. We must pray for George W. Bush and pray for him to continue the battle against Islamic terrorism until God's total victory over Satan is achieved.

PRIVATE INVESTIGATION

Islamic Infiltration Into the US Along the Mexican and Canadian Borders

US - Mexican Border

As part of my travels around the US, Canada and Mexico, I have encountered numerous testimonies regarding cases of Islamic infiltration in the US. After many lectures I have given in churches, people would come up to me and would share with me their personal experiences.

My first experience was right after Desert Storm in 1991. I had spoken in Brownsville, Texas, and afterwards the pastor, the elders of the church and their wives took me out to dinner. One of the ladies mentioned that her son was a former senior Green Beret officer stationed in that area. There was, she said, a contingency plan for a terrorist attack in Brownsville, from across the Mexican border. When I asked, "What problem do you have with the Mexicans?" she answered me, "Not with the Mexicans but with the agents of Saddam Hussein."

A few years later, in 1997, after the appearance of the fifth edition of my book *Is Fanatic Islam a Global Threat?* I returned to that same church and thanked them for the "Green Beret" testimony that was in my book. At the reception following my lecture, three people came up to me to apologize for not having been able to come to church years before during my first visit, but that they, too, had had experiences they needed to share with me.

The first was a former cop, who remembered receiving an urgent call for assistance at 4 AM from his sheriff who was calling from Boca Chica, the point where the Rio Grande River (the US-Mexican border) flows into the Gulf of Mexico. This deputy and another officer joined the sheriff and found him aiming his gun at six men seated in the back of an open van as well as at two seated in the front seats.

The six men in the back of the van were wet from the waist

down because they had just waded across the Rio Grande. After handcuffing these men, and removing them from the van, the three police officers' suspicions were aroused by the fact that none of these men spoke Spanish (they were Palestinians), and that the van was sagging very low to the ground.

They started emptying out the van and found AK-47 Kalatschnikov machine guns, cemtex plastique dynamite as well as other weapons. When they called in the Border Patrol, the latter explained that this was "too big" for them to deal with because the Border Patrol deals only with Mexicans coming across looking for work, and not Islamic terrorists. So they called in the ATF from Houston. When the ATF agents arrived, they swooped up the terrorists, the weapons and the van and took them back to Houston.

The next day, these three Brownsville cops were filling out their reports. The ATF reappeared, shredded the reports and told them to forget about the affair, that it "never happened." The former cop told me that this took place in 1982-83 (during Israel's "Operation Peace in the Galilee," commonly known as the Lebanon War) and that indeed he had forgotten about it until I appeared in his church in 1997!

The second testimony was that of a lady from the church who was a State of Texas health inspection official. She related that there had just been a seminar held on South Padre Island by the Texas Department of Health regarding biological and chemical warfare. She and other coworkers were told to look for "anthrax, botulism, bubonic plague as well as 20 other biological maladies."

When she mentioned to her superiors that these had all been eradicated in Texas decades ago, she was told, "Look for it. It is there. Find it. Deal with it." When she answered them asking, "But who would do something like this and why?" her superiors answered her, "It's not our job to tell you who or why. Just look for it and find it." This woman then said to me, "After hearing you in church, I now know who and why!"

By the way, at the back of my book *Fanatic Islam,* I report on a press conference held at the very end of 1997 by then US Secretary of Defense William Cohen. Cohen appeared holding up a

5-pound bag of Domino Sugar and said, "This much anthrax could destroy the world." He added, "At this very moment, 28 US cities are being targeted by" what he euphemistically called "religious and nationalist fanatics, for anthrax, botulism, bubonic plague as well as 20 other maladies." This press conference was never re-aired or replayed.

The third testimony involved a State of Texas house of detention called "Casa Romero" and that 30% of the inmates there, who had been apprehended crossing the Rio Grande, did not speak Spanish. Guess where they were from!

In a recent report appearing on Jo Farah's worldnetdaily.com, there was an interview with Mexico's National Security Adviser, Adolfo Zinser, that Mexico's police and military were coordinating their activities with their American colleagues in apprehending the considerable Islamic terrorist concentrations on their common border. This appeared in July in the Mexican daily *Universal* and in San Diego's *Union Tribune.*

On the Canadian side of the border, there have also been attempts at infiltration of Islamic terrorists. A famous but failed attempt was that of Algerian terrorist Ahmed Ressam, who tried to smuggle in bomb-makings in the trunk of his car. He was apprehended after crossing into the US on a ferryboat from Canada. At first, it was thought his objective was blowing up the Space Needle of Seattle. Later, under interrogation, it was revealed that his target was LAX, Los Angeles International Airport.

I have many more testimonies such as the above. The American borders with Mexico and Canada are very porous and penetrable. Not mentioned in this article is just how easy it has been to infiltrate the US via the major airports with false passports. This was also reported in the 1994 Steven Emerson/PBS anti-terrorist documentary, *Jihad in America.* America now has no choice but to wake up and deal with these Islamic terrorist phenomena.

Islamic Infiltration From Mexico, Part II

As I travel around the US, especially in the southern border areas with Mexico, I encounter reports and testimonies of people who come up to me in the churches, synagogues or TV stations where I appear.

The following is a synopsis of articles by Kevin Buey appearing in two local newspapers of Oct. 7th and 8th, 2001: *Las Cruces Sun-News* out of Las Cruces, NM, and the *Deming Headlight* out of Deming, NM.

A man armed with a knife, his face covered by a black hood, tried to commandeer a King Air twin turbo-prop plane Friday night at Deming Municipal Airport.

His effort was foiled by the pilot, who veered her plane off the runway.

"At this point we consider it an isolated incident and unrelated to anything going on nationally," FBI Special Agent Doug Beldon told the Associated Press, referring to the Sept. 11 terrorist attacks on the Pentagon and the World Trade Center.

He said the pilot and three medical personnel from the University of New Mexico hospital arrived in Deming at 9:40 p.m. to fly a patient from Mimbres Memorial Hospital to UNM Hospital.

While the medical staff went to Mimbres Memorial to collect the patient, the pilot completed paperwork on the plane, and then laid down to rest, Beldon said.

"A man crashed through the back door of the plane," Beldon said, "threatening the pilot with a knife at her neck, and said, 'Let's fly.'"

As the pilot taxied for takeoff, Beldon said, a warning light alerted her that the plane's back door was open. The attacker told her to keep going.

As she did, the plane door swung open, crashing against the plane fuselage and the pilot veered off the runway.

The man held what appeared to be a hand-sized police scanner, Beldon said, and hit the woman in the head three times with the scanner and pushed her out of the plane.

Beldon said the man periodically said "Salama" — a word Beldon said he could neither identify by language nor confirm spelling.

The assailant jumped from the plane, fleeing into the dark.

Beldon said the FBI would like to talk with three boys who spoke Friday night with law enforcement in the aftermath of the aborted hijack attempt.

"A deputy talked with three boys in the vicinity of the World War II hangars," Beldon said Sunday of Friday night's investigation. "They told the deputy they had seen a guy dressed in the manner of the assailant, running in the direction of those hangars.

"Apparently, the deputy pursued in the direction of the sighting and didn't get the boys' names."

In addition to the above newspapers reports, I received here in Alamogordo, New Mexico, other testimonies about "coyotes," Mexican immigrant smugglers, smuggling in groups of up to sixty armed Islamic terrorists at a time into the US from Mexico all along the border between El Paso, Texas, and Nogales, Arizona.

It seems something major is being planned in the way of an Islamic terrorist offensive in the US.

MILITARY INTELLIGENCE

Excerpts From Article in the Israeli Hebrew Daily "Yediot Ahronot" of Dec. 10, 2001

Israeli police are not overly concerned about herbicides or pesticides that were added (this is not the first time) to the triple bomb attack on Ben Yehuda Street on Saturday night, Dec. 1st, 2001, which killed 10 teenagers and injured 182. Emergency personnel noticed a strange smell in the air that turned out to be herbicide-pesticide type chemicals used by the terrorist as part of the bombs.

The police should be more concerned about a bigger problem in which a more developed and sophisticated chemical or biological material may be part of a future car bomb explosion or the suicidal self-exploding terrorist.

Some of those chemicals can be found and bought in any agricultural supply outlet in Israel, in addition to the more dangerous ones bought by the Palestinian Authority.

In theory, there are chemicals, a small quantity of which can cause major damage. The questions raised are: do they have the right equipment and laboratories to produce these materials, and can they defend themselves from those materials before exploding them?

Usually, a bomb is composed not only of explosives, but also of nails and screws, to create more injuries as the nails and screws fly fast hitting and penetrating people's bodies.

Now the fear is that chemical substances will be added to those nails and screws, and when they penetrate the body, they will act as poison, and unfortunately there is not much the doctors can do when that happens.

Another growing fear is the possible contamination of water resources in Israel by those whose intentions are inimical. In a serious malfunction that happened some months ago, more than 1.5 million Israelis were cut off from water supplies for more than 12 hours because of a water contamination (probably sabotage). A lot of shortcomings were discovered, showing just how easy it is to poison Israel's water supplies.

We can all remember the terrorist attack on the subway in Tokyo, Japan, in 1995 when Sarin gas was deployed: 5,500 people were injured and 12 of them died.

In the first attack on the Twin Towers of the World Trade Center in February of 1993, Ramzi Youssef, the builder of the bomb, included cyanide as part of the bomb. Fortunately, most of the cyanide gas was neutralized and consumed by the fire produced by the blast.

We can also remember that immediately after the WTC attacks on September 11th, 2001, crop-dusters were grounded for fear of a biological attack.

Chapter IV
JANUARY 2002 NEWSLETTER

Victor Mordecai's Monthly Message

State Department Arabists Strike Again!

On Thursday, January 3rd, 2002, combined Israeli air, sea and intelligence units intercepted a 4,000 ton gun-running Palestinian ship, the *Karine A,* in the Red Sea about 500 kilometers (300 miles) south of Israel's port of Eilat.

Friday morning, the next day, the ship arrived in Eilat and Israeli security forces began the task of unloading 83 containers holding about 50 tons of weapons supplied by Iran to the Palestinian Autonomy.

These containers were specially designed to be dropped at sea off the Gaza Coast, lie submerged just below the surface and then later be retrieved by smaller fishing boats. A small float was attached to them that would indicate their location to Palestinian fishermen or members of the Palestinian Naval Police.

The contents of the containers included:
122mm Katyusha rockets with a range of 20 km (12 miles)
107mm Katyusha rockets with a range of 8 km (4.8 miles)

80mm and 120mm mortars
Anti-tank rockets (LAW, RPG, and Sagger)
Anti-armor mines
Sniper rifles
AK-47 assault rifles
Scuba and rubber raft equipment
Explosives

It is interesting to note that items 1, 2, 3 and 9 are not defensive but offensive weapons. Item 9: explosives refer to C-4 (Cemtex), one of the most lethal and effective forms of dynamite. It is the kind of dynamite used by Islamic suicide bombers in killing Israeli civilians in bus stations, malls, and discotheques. All the weapons in the *Karine A* are expressly forbidden by the "so-called" Oslo I & Oslo II peace accords and justify the nullification of what remains of the accords.

Last May, the Israeli navy intercepted the Santorini fishing boat, which was filled with large quantities of weapons en route from Lebanon to the Palestinian Authority in Gaza. The catch included Katyusha rockets, SA-7 Strella anti-aircraft missiles, rocket propelled grenades, anti-tank grenades, mortars and shells, mines, Kalashnikov assault rifles and ammunition.

SA-7 Strella anti-aircraft missiles are not exactly what one would call "defensive" missiles. They are, however, capable of bringing down civilian airliners taking off from any of Israel's airports. On page 266 of my book *Is Fanatic Islam a Global Threat?* I explain how such a Strella brought down TWA800 in July of 1996.

Again, all of these smuggled weapons are in direct contravention of the "so-called" peace accords with the Palestinians and represent a *casus belli* (cause for war) with the Palestinian Autonomy. This reminds me of the Japanese Imperial government negotiating peace in Washington, D.C., while the Japanese fleet was steaming towards Pearl Harbor for its day of infamy on December 7th, 1941. Yasser Arafat even had the audacity to offer "hudna," which in Arabic means a wall to wall coalition supporting a cease fire with Israel, when in fact his arms supplies for renewed warfare were just about to arrive on the *Karine A*. It was yet one more act of deception.

On Sunday (three days after the interception of the *Karine A*) CNN, BBC as well as the enemy we love to hate — the US State Department — continued to ignore the entire incident or to say that the gunrunner was actually on its way to Lebanon, and that indeed, this whole affair had nothing to do with the Palestinians. Not even a TV interview with the Palestinian captain of the *Karine A* proving the PA's complicity and direct connection made any difference.

On Tuesday, January 8th, CNN added to the "theater of the absurd" by quoting God's gift to humanity, Saddam Hussein, as describing Israel's preventive security action as an act of "international piracy on the high seas."

It wasn't until Wednesday, January 9th, that the State Department and CNN finally admitted that there was something wrong here with Arafat and the Palestinian Autonomy.

As of Saturday, January 12, 2002, 10 days later, CNN still describes the incident in terms of "Israel claims, PA denies," when everyone understands the truth in spite of CNN. And, of course, Palestinian spokeswoman Hanan Ashrawi repeats the Iraqi canard of "Israeli piracy on the high seas."

But the key to the problem is not what was said, but rather what was omitted. The problem, and we see this from the agenda of CNN and the State Department, is that the Palestinians can do no wrong, and Israel can do no right. General Anthony Zinni's visits to the Middle East have only one purpose: Israel will have to make agreements with the Palestinians, agreements detrimental to Israel, because the world is on the side of the Palestinians. Palestinians will break any agreement they sign. But as the State Department and CNN say: "Don't confuse me with the facts; my mind is made up."

In my last newsletter of December 2001, I explained the difference between a neurotic person and a psychotic person. The former dreams about castles in the air; the latter lives in them. I explained that there are three parties to the Mid-East conflict: the US, Israel and the Palestinians. Two of them want a Palestinian state; the third doesn't. The US, and in particular the State Department, wants a Palestinian state because it believes such a Palestinian state would solve all of America's foreign policy problems. (The truth is that it wouldn't.) The Israelis, at least the leftists and politically correct ones, want a Palestinian state to get the Palestinians "out of our hair." (The truth is that it wouldn't.) The only group that does not want a Palestinian state is the Palestinians, because by definition, such a Palestinian state would have to live in peace alongside a secure State of Israel. Since the Islamic religion will not allow for this, and will assassinate any Arab, Palestinian, or Islamic leader who makes peace with Israel, therefore the conclusion is that a war to the finish is the only option for the Palestinians. The Palestinians are "psychotic" because what they really want is not a Palestinian state but the destruction of the State of Israel and the annihilation of the Jews. This is, in my opinion, equivalent to "living in castles in the air." The Islamic religion calls for killing all the Jews on Saturday and all the Christians on Sunday. If Adolf Hitler was psychotic for dreaming he could kill all the Jews on this Earth, how much more so are the Moslems psychotic for thinking they can kill both the Jews and the Christians. And any Israelis or Americans thinking that "peace negotiations" with psychotics will bring peace are psychotic too! It's like going to an insane asylum and discussing a serious business deal with crazy, psychotic people.

This is the real problem for the American Administration, the State Department, CNN, BBC, the EU, etc. Because these entities are not Jewish, Christian or "Judeo-Christian" but rather "liberals," globalists, and money people, they are not capable of understanding that the war between Israel and the Palestinians is a war of the Judeo-Christian God versus the satanic moon-god, war-god, "Allah," of the Moslems.

If one doesn't believe in God, that's one's personal choice, but for those of us who believe in God, God's word is very clear, and his promises to Israel and the Christians (the true Christians who love Israel and are committed to Israel) are irrevocable. God's word, also, to those who go against God is very clear. "I will bless those who bless you and curse those who curse you" (Genesis 27:29 and Numbers 24:9).

Two weeks before the September 11th Islamic attacks on the World Trade Center in NY, the Pentagon in Washington, DC, as well as the flight which came down in Pennsylvania, Palestinian spokesman Nabil Sha'ath was quoted as saying that he was in possession of a written secret agreement between President George W. Bush and the Saudis, that the US was committed to a total withdrawal of Israel to the indefensible borders of June 5, 1967. This would mean, God forbid, that if implemented, this forced withdrawal by Israel would lead to Israel's destruction. Henry Kissinger described the 1967 borders as "Auschwitz Extermination Camp" borders. Two weeks after this secret Bush-Saudi-Palestinian agreement was revealed by Nabil Sha'ath, the Satan-god Allah and his followers carried out the attacks of September 11th, 2001. Call it God's judgment on America or God's returning President George W. Bush to God's intended path. No matter what the US does to placate Satan-Allah and the Moslems, America will still be the ultimate target, the great Christian Satan in the eyes of Islam. Without the destruction of America, Islam cannot conquer the rest of the world and kill all the Jews and Christians.

Two weeks after 9.11, Israeli Prime Minister Ariel Sharon made a speech warning the US that Israel was not Czechoslovakia of 1938 and that Israel would not be sacrificed by its liberal, Western, "enlightened" allies for temporary convenience, as Czechoslovakia was by then British Prime Minister Neville Chamberlain, who thought that by handing over the Sudetenland to the Germans, peace could be "bought" at the expense of the poor Czechoslovaks. For Israel, the modern day Czechoslovakia, the West Bank, Gaza and the Golan are Israel's version of the Sudetenland. Force Israel to return to the borders of 1967, and Israel will be absolutely indefensible.

In both my books, *Is Fanatic Islam a Global Threat?* and "Christian Revival for Israel's Survival," I share a testimony that changed my life forever. To make the testimony very short, I was invited to speak before an economic forum known as the Dallas

Council on World Affairs, the Dallas branch of the Council on Foreign Relations (CFR). After I spoke, I was told that 6 million Jews were killed in WWII for a barrel of oil. So, too, would Israel (today 5 million Jews) also be sacrificed for a barrel of oil and that Israel and the Jews would not come in the way of oil supplies.

I was told that the only thing that made America great was the barrel of oil. My Christian friends there that night corrected the Dallas Council people, saying: "You call yourselves Christians? What made America great was not the barrel of oil. What made America great was Jesus Christ!"

In conclusion, I would say that America must search its soul. America must decide what is more important, the barrel of oil, or the God of Abraham, Isaac, and Jacob, the Bible and Jesus Christ.

Alexis DeTocqueville wrote in his 1820 book *Democracy in America* that America would one day be the greatest country on earth, because the American people were a good people and that their pulpits were on fire for the Lord. Conversely, he said: "America will lose its preeminence in the world when its pulpits are no longer on fire for the Lord. (Not on fire for oil or petrodollars.)

In Professor Samuel Huntington's book, *The Clash of Civilizations and the Remaking of World Order,* this noted Harvard professor predicts the decline of the US over the coming decades. According to Huntington, Islam is one of the rival systems waiting in the wings to take the place of the declining, decrepit America. America must choose, now, whether it continues the decline or stops the decline by returning to God's word, the Bible.

My belief is that America's supporting Arafat and Islam means the beginning of the end for America. Supporting Israel blatantly in the face of the Arab-Islamic petrodollar paymasters may be a difficult option for a cash-strapped America, but it will keep President George W. Bush and America on God's chosen path to continue being the greatest country on earth.

CURRENT EVENTS AND ANALYSIS

This Is What Islam Does to People

There are a number of names that have recently come up, and they attracted my attention:

> Johnny Walker Lindh (Suleyman Al-Lindh - Taliban fighter)
>> Richard C. Reid (Abdel Rahim or Tariq Raja, the shoe bomber)
>
> Charles Bishop (Bishara - young 15-year-old pilot who crashed his plane into skyscraper in Tampa in solidarity with Usama bin Laden)

What they all have in common is that these are former Christians who decided to fight alongside the Moslems in a war against the Judeo-Christians. Another common characteristic is that they all have Arabic-Islamic names and finally, at least in the case of the first two names, these converts to Islam came from divorced parents, causing the offspring to be hardship cases, mixed-up, confused kids, who were easy prey for Moslem "talent-scouts."

The following is an article taken from the Associated Press appearing in the *Jerusalem Post* of Thursday, December 27th, 2001.

> The man who allegedly tried to blow up a trans-Atlantic flight with explosives hidden in his shoes was a convert to Islam who attended the same south London mosque as an accused conspirator in the September 11th terrorist attacks, the mosque's leader said.
>
> Abdul Haqq Baker, chairman of the Brixton Mosque, said shoe-bombing suspect Richard C. Reid converted to Islam while serving a jail sentence, and approached the mosque asking to learn the tenets of the religion.
>
> "He was someone out of prison who wanted to learn. There was no indication or suspicion he was linked with terrorist organizations," Baker said.
>
> During an American Airlines flight from Paris to Mi-

ami on Saturday, Reid allegedly tried to touch a lit match to a fuse protruding from one of his shoes. Two flight attendants and several passengers grabbed him and used belts to strap him into his seat, and two doctors sedated him with drugs from an airplane medical kit.

The Boeing 767, carrying 197 people, was diverted to Boston with an escort of two fighter jets. Baker said that for part of 1998, Reid attended the mosque at the same time as Zacarias Moussaoui, a Frenchman charged with conspiracy in connection with the Sept. 11th attacks on New York and Washington. He said it was possible the two men had met.

A small mosque located in a row of Victorian houses, Brixton has a young, multicultural membership that includes a large number of converts.

Baker said at the mosque Moussaoui "made his more radical beliefs known and as a result, in the end, his beliefs were not welcome."

Reid, on the other hand, "didn't come to propagate his beliefs, he would be asking questions and probing." Investigators are still attempting to confirm the suspect's identity, but *London's Times* newspaper and a French police official both have identified Reid as a British petty criminal with an English mother and a Jamaican father.

Richard C. Reid is the name listed on a British passport issued December 7th by the British embassy in Belgium, but after the man's arrest Saturday French officials initially said they thought he was from Sri Lanka and named Tariq Raja.

US investigators said they thought his mother was Jamaican.

The *Times* said Reid was born in Bromley, southeast London, in 1973 to an English mother and a Jamaican father and had served several jail sentences for street crimes such as mugging.

Baker said Reid — who also used the name Abdel Rahim — was initially a normal, street-wise London youth, but developed extreme views. He said the Brixton Mosque attracted some "extreme elements" which targeted enthusiastic converts like Reid.

"I would say he was very, very impressionable," Baker said.

"If they have got the likes of Rahim, there are a lot more and we are very concerned about that," he added.

Baker said he doubted Reid could have devised the shoe-bombing plot on his own.

"I definitely believe there are individuals behind him and that he was a test and they were watching to see if he would succeed," Baker said.

The following are excerpts from an article written by Douglas Davis in the *Jerusalem Post* of January 4th, 2002:

...Terrorism in the 21st century is a growth industry, a well-organized globalized business, constructed on the basis of small, dynamic, highly mobile, discreet cells which, by their nature, are almost impossible to penetrate. They are formed for specific operations and then quickly dismantled.

The new terrorist "executive" slips easily across national boundaries and hops between continents to forge an alliance-of-convenience with disparate other groups. He is often highly intelligent, well educated, multilingual and sophisticated, at home in a variety of cultures.

In other circumstances, he might have been a smart-suited investment banker. As a servant of radical Islam, however, he is disinterested in achieving political reform. On the contrary, he is uncompromisingly committed to the total destruction of what he perceives to be the corrupt, decadent, Godless West.

That does not, of course, describe Reid; rather, he is counted among a far larger cast of "useful idiots" to the cause.

...Reid was simply regarded as a "mule"... a man in search of a cause who is ultimately prepared to be the uncomplaining carrier of a suicide bomb.

...After dropping out of school still virtually illiterate at age 16, Reid drifted into crime — shoplifting and petty theft — before graduating to street mugging. Within months, he was sent to a prison for young offenders after the vicious mugging of an elderly pensioner.

The alienated, friendless, shiftless youth was red meat for the Muslim chaplain who approached him there, and by the time Reid emerged from jail in 1996, he had transformed into Abdel Rahim, a devout Muslim.

...The Brixton mosque offered an introduction to another regular worshiper: Zacarias Moussaoui was a French national who had been born in North Africa and moved to London some eight years previously.

Some intelligence sources are convinced that Moussaoui was using the mosque as a recruiting base for al-Qaeda; that he had used it to recruit Reid and draw him into the shadowy heart of Islamic terror.

They believe that between 1998 and 2001, the two men attended the same training camp at Khalden in Afghanistan, the principal base for al-Qaeda's foreign recruits, who were known as "tourist terrorists." And, say the sources, there are records of phone calls between them.

...There is also a strong likelihood of Palestinian, particularly Hamas, involvement.

It does not necessarily follow that Reid's act was a joint venture by al-Qaeda and Hamas; rather, he says, it could be an example of an arrangement that the intelligence community describes as "subcontracting" or "franchising."

...Reid received training in Pakistan and Afghanistan during extended visits there between 1998 and 2001; ...Reid visited Israel and the Gaza Strip last July; and the TATP (triacetone triperoxide) explosive embedded in Reid's trainers is the signature brand of Hamas, whose master bomb-makers developed it in Gaza for use in suicide attacks.

To the Palestinians, the explosive is known as "the Mother of Satan," so called because of its two characteristics (in addition to its lethality): it is fairly easy to make and it is highly unstable.

Some 40 Palestinians are estimated to have been killed when the explosive detonated spontaneously and prematurely while being handled.

Despite this risk, TATP is used almost exclusively by Palestinian terrorists, recalling that it was the explosive of choice for the Palestinian car-bombers who devastated the Israeli Embassy and damaged a building housing several Jewish community organizations during a 12-hour reign of terror in London eight years ago.

Two Palestinians — Samar Alami, a chemical engineer who had studied at London University's Imperial College, and her accomplice, Jawad Botmeh, who had studied engineering at Leicester University — are currently serving 20-year terms for their role in the attacks. Both were found in possession of TATP.

What is really so alarming is that hundreds, possibly thousands, of young British Muslims have received some form of military training abroad from Islamic militants.

He divides them into two groups: The first are those who travel abroad for their "gap year" — just as many Jewish youngsters travel to Israel — in order to deepen their religious knowledge in Islamic countries. Many young Muslims who participate in such programs, however, discover that an element of military training is built into their studies.

The second, far smaller, group is exemplified by Reid: vulnerable individuals who are recruited at mosques specifically for training in hard-core military skills and suicide attacks.

Some are sent on to fight in Afghanistan, Bosnia, Chechnya, Kashmir and other Muslim battlefields.

Others return to Britain, where they slip back into their

old lives as "sleepers," awaiting the call to action.

Such is now the stuff of nightmares for political and security officials in Britain.

In 2000, the government moved to outlaw a score of organizations, many of them Islamic extremists. Last month, now recognizing the full extent of the country's vulnerability, it rushed through sweeping anti-terrorism legislation which allows the police to detain foreign nationals without trial if they are suspected of involvement in international terrorism. Eight suspects were immediately arrested. Their identities, nationalities, affiliations and offending acts remain secret.

And after the Reid debacle, the Prison Service announced that a clutch of Muslim chaplains were being suspended, pending an inquiry into what are considered to be "inappropriate remarks" they have made since September 11th.

One Saudi dissident in London, Dr. Sa'ad al-Fagih, who is regarded as close to al-Qaeda and runs the benign-sounding Movement for Islamic Reform, says fundamentalist Saudi sources are warning of an imminent "second wave" of attacks... "even bigger than the World Trade Center."

Some intelligence sources believe that despite the US destruction of al-Qaeda bases in Afghanistan, the movement remains essentially intact and that "sleepers" such as Reid remain ready to be mobilized at any moment for the sake of jihad (holy war) against the West.

"These people are dedicated," says al-Fagih. "It is not just 10 people, or 20. It is hundreds, or thousands, and they are in the pipeline."

Muslim Schools in Britain Are Turning Youngsters Into Terrorists

The following is the translation of an article in Hebrew in the Israeli daily *Yediot Ahronot* of Friday, December 28th, 2001, by its London correspondent Ilan Nachshon.

Three hundred Muslim schools in Britain are schools for terrorism. Extremist Muslim organizations are free to act unhindered in the after school hours, and entice youngsters, from an early age, to join the holy war against the West — using Bin Laden's methods.

This is according to Hajj Abdel Baker (35), a Muslim heading a community mosque in Britain. Richard Reid, the "shoe bomber" who tried to blow up an American Airlines passenger flight, prayed in Baker's mosque in Brixton, south London.

Baker has recently received death threats after having revealed that Reid had prayed in his mosque, and that he had expelled Reid after the latter spoke bluntly expressing extremist views.

Baker and Dr. Zaki Badawi, director of an Islamic college in Ealing, west London, have been warning for years about this increasing worsening problem of extremist Muslims in Britain. They claim to have turned to the British Ministry of Interior as well as to the Police to warn about the hostile activities of such bodies as the Al-Qaeda and Taliban, but nothing was done about it.

"There are more than 1,000 extremist Moslems in Britain, who openly support the use of suicide terrorists against innocent people, such as happened in the World Trade Center in NY. At least 100 of them are ready to be suicide terrorists themselves," Baler said.

PRIVATE INVESTIGATION

Islam Replaces Christianity in Bethlehem and Nazareth

Islamic Persecution of Christians in the Palestinian Areas

The following is a translation of an excerpt of an article by Hanan Schlein in Israeli Hebrew daily newspaper *Ma'ariv* of Friday, December 28th, 2001.

CHRISTIAN RESIDENTS IN THE BETHLEHEM AREA COMPLAIN OF VIOLENCE DIRECTED AT THEM BY YOUNG MOSLEMS.

ARMED MEMBERS OF THE TANZIM RELEASED BY FORCE A SUSPECTED RAPIST OF A YOUNG CHRISTIAN WOMAN

TWO YOUNG CHRISTIAN WOMEN FROM BEIT JALA WERE MURDERED BY MEMBERS OF THE FATAH SPONSORED TANZIM

ONLY A THREAT TO PA CHAIRMAN ARAFAT BY THE CATHOLIC PATRIARCH MICHEL SABBAH MADE ARAFAT ACT AGAINST MOSLEM ATTACKS ON THE CHRISTIAN POPULATION

A young Christian woman from the Bethlehem area was brutally raped in her home a few months ago by a young Muslim Tanzim activist. When relatives complained, the rapist was arrested but then released within a short time due to pressures exerted by the rapist's brother and other armed members of the Tanzim, who appeared at the police station. This is but just one story regarding numerous acts of violence against the area's Christian population, whose instigators are Moslems, many of whom are members of the Palestinian Autonomy's security apparatus.

These incidents verify the claim of Minister Dan Naveh the day before yesterday in the Knesset that Arafat's men were involved in violent actions against Christians. His speech stirred up a major whirlwind in the plenum, when Arab MK's called Naveh a racist and an inciter against Arafat and the Palestinian Autonomy.

However, *Ma'ariv's* investigation reveals that only as a result of the determined intervention of Jerusalem's Latin (Catholic) Patriarch Michel Sabbah did Arafat issue unequivocal instructions to his men to prevent the activities of criminal Moslem groups against the Christian population. This was as a result of the ineffectualness of the Palestinian security forces in dealing with Moslem criminals. Patriarch

Sabbah notified Arafat that if the attacks on the Christians did not cease immediately, he, Sabbah, would move his office from the Old City of Jerusalem to Beit Sahur, as a sign of solidarity with the Christians. It was this threat that led to the intervention of the Palestinian Authority's chairman.

Bethlehem area residents are not forthcoming in talking about the phenomenon. The Christians are afraid, the Moslems uncomfortable because of the activity of criminal elements against the Christian population. There is a report of two young Christian women in Beit Jala who were murdered by members of the Fatah Tanzim. A Palestinian source told us that because the Christian population has no political backing in the area, young Moslems are able to attack them unhindered. "It is clear to everyone that attacking Moslems (girls) would lead to revenge reprisals of a tribe or family. But Christians are at the mercy of the Palestinian Authority, which is mostly Moslem anyway — and this is what the attacking Moslem youth are counting on," a Palestinian source said.

There was also another example of young Moslem attacks on the Christian population by activists known as the "Shabiba" of the Fatah toward a Christian couple that got married at the beginning of the intifada (uprising). Fatah activists gave instructions to "tone down" glittering celebrations. The Christian couple decided anyway to go ahead and to hold the wedding in a wedding hall not far from Rachel's Tomb (near Israeli army positions). Shabiba activists of the Fatah arrived at the wedding hall and demanded to stop the festivities. The family refused, which led the activists to start shooting at Israeli army positions nearby at Rachel's Tomb. The soldiers returned fire, thus ending the wedding party.

Translation of excerpt of article by Uri Dan in *Makor Rishon*
weekly Jan. 4th, 2002

"Christian Exodus"

"The immigration of Christian Palestinians from
Palestinian Autonomy areas testifies to the audacious pretensions of Yasser Arafat, who tried to attend the Midnight Mass
of Christmas posing as 'defender of the Christians.'"

The official figures appearing in official Israeli reports
testify perhaps more than anything else to the true mood of
Arab Christians living among the Palestinians in the West
Bank. According to the numbers, between October 2000 (the
beginning of Arafat's terror offensive) and November 2001,
2,700 Palestinian Christians emigrated abroad from the West
Bank. Of these, 1,640 left the Bethlehem area and about 880
left Ramallah. Some 10,000 Christians have left for abroad
since Arafat gained control of Judea, Samaria and Gaza.

These numbers speak for themselves. They testify to
just how great the pretensions of Arafat were when he tried
to attend the Christmas midnight mass in Bethlehem posing
as "defender of the Christians."

The Christian exodus from the Palestinian Authority
areas takes on a special significance taking into account that
the Arab Christian population in Judea, Samaria and Gaza
today totals 61,000, or 2% of the Palestinians, who total 3
million.

The Bethlehem, Beit Jala, Beit Sahur areas used to
be considered a Christian "bastion" but today contain only
30,000 compared to 120,000 Moslems.

In spite of the fact that Arafat and the Palestinian Authority highly regard the Christians as a tool for mobilizing
the support of Christian Western countries regarding PLO
claims, the Christian population actually encounters a hostile
relationship with the Palestinian Moslems.

According to information from Israeli sources, the

Moslems desecrate Christian holy places, damage property, extort businessmen, and even dishonor Christian women. Official reports from Israeli government sources include shocking stories. Amongst them is a report that Tanzim activists often harass young Christian females when they go for entertainment in Ramallah — and no one does anything to stop it. According to another report, the head of the Tanzim in the Al-Amara refugee camp in Ramallah, Nasser Abu-Hamid, collected five thousand shekels in order to release from arbitrary detention a Christian Palestinian who had been kidnapped. Even the Palestinian Authority itself refused to provide protection for an Arak distillery owned by Christians in Ramallah, which has been repeatedly attacked by Islamic activists.

Many months before Usama bin Laden declared war against the "Christians and Jews," Islamic imams were inciting in the "territories" against their Christian brothers and sisters. Dr. Ahmed Abu Halbieh, whose incitements were broadcast live on Palestinian TV, exhorted against the Christians already in October 2000. Abu Halbieh, former rector of the Islamic University in Gaza, preached a sermon in the Halil el-Wazir Mosque, and said that the Christians in the "territories" were linked to the British and the US, and together with the Jews were collaborators in the struggle against and the hatred for the Moslems. He therefore called upon Moslems to struggle against these two religions. The very same evening, thousands of Hamas activists went down to the seashore area of Gaza and destroyed and burned stores owned by Christians where alcoholic beverages were being sold, claiming that alcoholic beverages were "against morality."

Then, in February 2001, the Christian cemetery in Beit Jala was desecrated by Moslems. Arafat's police did nothing to detain those responsible for the crime in spite of their identities being known to everyone. When the Christian residents of Beit Jala appealed for international Christian assistance, with the Vatican at the top of the list, and complained that the Palestinian Moslems were intentionally using Christian homes from which to shoot at the Jewish neighborhood of Gilo, Christian solidarity disappeared as if it never existed. The Christian churches did not dare to really pressure the Palestinian Authority to stop the shooting. Even the threat of the Catholic Patriarch, Michel Sabbah, to move his offices to Beit Sahour if the Tanzim continued shooting from Beit Jala, thus endangering the lives of the Christians of that town, was unsuccessful. Only when Israeli tanks returned again to the Bethlehem area did the shooting stop. This did not hinder Patriarch Sabbah from rushing to bless Arafat in Ramallah on Christmas Eve after the Israeli government prevented Arafat from going to Bethlehem.

Attacks on the Christian population were not limited only to shooting by Tanzim activists from Christian areas. The Moslems, especially in the Bethlehem and Beit Jala area, who were furious at the lack of involvement by the Christians in the struggle, accused them of collaborating with Israel. Many of the Moslems raised the question as to why there are no dead Christians in this war. (The first Christians died only after the entry of the IDF into Bethlehem in October 2001.) The Tanzim began handing out leaflets in the Bethlehem area against Christian leaders and at the head of the list was Hannah Nasser, mayor of Bethlehem and his associates in Bethlehem, Beit Jala and Beit Sahour, accusing them of collaboration with Israel.

During the last few months, two Christian community leaders were shot and wounded by Tanzim activists, and at least three young Christian women were accused of prostitution, and were murdered. It turns out that Tanzim terrorists had had sex with them, murdered them, and afterwards made up excuses for the crime, that it was the immoral behavior of the Christian women that necessarily turned them into collaborators with Israel.

Acts of persecution against Christians by Arafat's

emissaries were revealed in the Knesset by Minister Dan Naveh, and in response Ahmed Tibi called him an inciter, provocateur and "Danny Geobbels."

The shocking testimonies regarding these crimes and others by members of the Palestinian Authority against the shrinking Christian community are known to Israel, but "official Israel" remains silent, as fearing getting into a Palestinian Christian-Muslim controversy.

[Victor Mordecai: In my first book, *Is Fanatic Islam a Global Threat?* I carried out private investigation work to uncover an article from the Catholic magazine *Terra Santa* which proved in 1991 that the Christian population of Bethlehem was shrinking due to a plan backed by Iraqi petrodollars to force the Christians to sell out their homes, lands and businesses and to emigrate, thus decimating the Christian community there. In my second book, *Christian Revival for Israel's Survival,* I reveal how the same is now happening in Nazareth. I believe that very soon there will be a major confrontation regarding the building of a mosque next to the Church of the Annunciation in Nazareth. This could explode the whole region into ethnic violence. Israel's decision this week to stop construction of the mosque is the right decision because Nazareth is holy to the Christians and not the Moslems. The Moslems have no business building a mosque so close to the church. But again, this could lead to major violence between Islam and Judeo-Christianity, maybe even a war.]

MILITARY INTELLIGENCE

Arafat Prefers Guns Over Bread and Butter for His People

Financial Realities of the Palestinian Autonomy

In a military intelligence briefing held in November 1993 as part of an IDF Spokesman's Course, we participants were privy to a lecture regarding the future economy of the Palestinian Autonomy.

We were told that the failure or success of the Palestinian Authority was dependent upon it providing the bread and butter the Palestinians need to survive. Yasser Arafat has received billions of dollars in aid from the US, the EU, Japan, and many other countries including Arab and Islamic. The rhetorical question was asked: What would Arafat do with these monies? Would the monies go to the people and in particular to the businessmen on whose shoulders the Palestinian economy would be based?

The answers we received were very simple. The monies received from the world were to be controlled in a very tight-fisted manner by Arafat and his closest associates. Not only would Palestinian businessmen not receive monies (upon which a Palestinian economic infrastructure would be based) but they would be stymied and hindered. In Arafat's view, money is power, and the financial success of the businessmen would create a direct threat to Arafat should the businessmen succeed. Laissez faire is considered by Arafat to be a curse because it would create competition. Everyone must be broke and hungry in order to remain totally subservient to him and his Palestinian Autonomy hierarchy. It was estimated at that time in 1993 that Arafat was personally worth over $3.5 billion.

In spite of all of this, on the eve of the Intifada Al Quds uprising that began in September 2000, Palestinian unemployment was down to the levels in Israel among the Jews — somewhere under 10% unemployment. The Palestinian economy was flowering because of massive investments from ex-patriot Palestinians coming home. There was optimism and a real boom. Then came the bust.

Yasser Arafat decided to reject the more than generous offers made by then Israeli Prime Minister Ehud Barak at Camp David II in June 2000. Instead of accepting the 98.5% concessions that Barak offered, Arafat opted for war. By destroying the newly nascent Palestinian economy, Arafat thought he accomplished four things:

He destroyed the financial power of the businessmen, a threat to him. He made the Palestinians in the street all the more dependent on him. Arafat could blame the misery, poverty and desperation of the Palestinians on the Israelis. Good for PR. Arafat would make life so intolerable for the Palestinians that they would be malleable and ready for a military confrontation with Israel bordering on mass suicide. What did they have to lose? And of course, Israel would be blamed for everything. Arafat thinks like a terrorist, not a businessman.

In light of the above military intelligence, the following two articles from the *Jerusalem Post* of Friday, December 28th, 2001, and January 1st, 2002, are most enlightening:

Palestinian Umemployment in Gaza 78.8%

Seventy-eight percent of Palestinians in the Gaza Strip are unemployed, according to a report published yesterday by the Palestinian Labor Ministry. It said the number of unemployed reached 597,000, including more than 100,000 who worked in Israel before the current conflict began 15 months ago. The ministry blamed Israel's closure policy for the high unemployment figures.

[Victor Mordecai comments: From unemployment of less than 10% in September 2000 we now find 78.8% unemployment thanks to Yasser Arafat's policies.]

Positive Prospects for Palestinian Stock Exchange

Despite a dramatic drop-off in nearly all indicators over the past year, economists remained optimistic about the future of the Palestine Securities Exchange (PSE) in Nablus, which has recently announced its decision to increase trading hours.

"The stock exchange's troubles are mostly due to the poor economic situation," Dr. Roby Nathanson, an economist and chairman of the Israeli Institute for Economic and Social Research told the *Jerusalem Post,* "but the fact that its overall market cap is almost $1 billion is encouraging, considering that the whole economy (in national income) of the Palestinian-controlled areas is only about $5b."

According to data provided by the PSE, trading volume for the first 11 months of the year plummeted 76 percent to $36.9 million from the $172.2m. in the same period last year. The stock exchange's total market capitalization has lost 7% of its value over the past year, totaling $742.6m. at the end of November, compared to $800.9m. in November 2000. The benchmark Al-Quds Index, which is a weighted average of the market capitalization of 10 companies, each representative of an economic sector traded on the exchange, has dropped 8% over the period.

Dr. Hasam Yasim, who recently replaced Naim al-Khoshashi as the PSE's general manager, was unavailable for comment.

Nathanson was particularly encouraged by the symbolic value of the PSE. "When the Palestinians first received autonomy years ago, there was a lot of concern as to what kind of economy they would have. People were worried that it might be a completely centralized, command economy," he said. "But, the very existence of the stock exchange demonstrates the Palestinian Authority's commitment to a market economy, which is a very positive sign."

Commenting on the PSE's low turnover figures, Nathanson said, "It's a modest start. I believe that if the cease-fire continues [Victor Mordecai: What ceasefire?] and there are advances in the peace process, we'll see the exchange recover somewhat and its market cap rise. The important thing, though, is the Palestinian Authority's commitment to provide the necessary infrastructure for the exchange to function properly."

The PSE, which has increased trading from three to four days a week, continues to be dominated by two companies: the Palestine Telecommunications Co. (Paltel), which has a market capitalization of $6.9m., with shares traded for $3.59 each; and the Palestine Development & Investment

Co. (Padico), which operates the joint Israeli-Palestinian industrial zone at Carni, had a market cap of $2m., with shares traded at $1.09 each, at the end of November. Other companies with active shares on the exchange include the Jerusalem Cigarette Co. (market cap: $23.2m), the Palestine Real Estate Investment Company ($19.9m.) and Al-Quds Bank for Development & Investment ($19m.).

[Victor Mordecai comments: Remember, in 1993, Yasser Arafat was worth $3.5 billion. The numbers above are ridiculously low and do not represent a threat to Arafat's control. He will not allow it to be a threat. For the Palestinian economy to develop Arafat must be removed and businessmen must take his place.]

Chapter V
FEBRUARY 2002 NEWSLETTER

Victor Mordecai's Monthly Message

As the world enters the month of February 2002, we see certain worrying, though totally expected signs of escalation coming from the Palestinian-Arab-Islamic axis forces against Israel, the US and the West.

My work involves travels away from Israel almost eight months out of every year, mostly in the US, but also in Canada, Mexico and Europe. It is usually at a proportion of two months away and then one month at home. This cycle with the jet lag involved is therefore repeated every three months.

It is during these last weeks in Israel that I published my January newsletter #4 and, God willing on February 1st, the February newsletter #5. Since I will be in the US hopefully next week, I have made efforts to do most of the research for the March newsletter, because frankly, on the road in the US, it is difficult to do the in depth research and be tied in with the intelligence sources here in Israel, if I am driving and preaching, driving and preaching in America. I come home from every trip on the verge of physical and emotional breakdown.

When my sons, my wife and I decided to embark on the newsletter, we were looking at this as another product added to a

growing line of materials such as my two books, audio and videotapes, CD's and DVD's of the message. We have never been a
tax- exempt non-profit organization but rather a ministry in which
a publishable message was at the center. And indeed we pay taxes
on our profitable income as any successful and law-abiding author
must do. So it was decided to offer this newsletter for the price of
a $60 subscription per annum as merely another in a chain of suc-
cessful products to the news hungry and savvy public.

But this morning, I feel God has put it in my heart that though
the newsletter will continue as long as God wills it, and for those
of you who have been so kind as to take out the $60 subscription,
future newsletters will remain free downloads from the computer
and for those who have paid, are paying or will pay for a subscription, the hard copy of the newsletter will be mailed to you as
promised. It is now at the printers and in a few days will be in the
mail to all who have paid.

I feel that the message cannot be limited to a few dozen,
hundred or thousand subscriptions. I feel God has invested me in
this ministry to get the message out for free to millions of people
through the Internet. That's what the Internet is all about. If millions
of people don't get the message, I have failed. Of course, financial
contributions are appreciated and needed, but the newsletter, at least
online, will remain free. For hardcopy, a donation will be appreciated. If anyone who has sent in a subscription feels slighted, I will
return the $60 subscription fee. Otherwise, this will be considered
as a much-needed donation.

One of the reasons for this change in policy is because I am
not expecting to create a magazine like *Israel Today,* with which I
am proud to be associated and for whom I write a monthly column.
Secondly, I have plans to write other books, and this might not be
possible if I am tied down to a financial commitment of issuing a
newsletter.

Finally, realities of the Middle East are too unpredictable
time-wise, and working alone, I do not feel it right to commit to
a project that requires an editorial team and staff, which I do not
have. Another project also which I feel is part of God's plan is the

creation some time in the future of a "Bible Zionist Party" to run for the Knesset. This would be comprised of Jews and Christians who have served in the IDF, pay taxes and vote. Such a project might prevent me from being able to continue issuing this newsletter. I hope I have not offended anyone. I apologize if I have. I am trying to listen to what I think God is telling me to do. As long as I am able to, I will continue to issue this newsletter on a monthly basis, but I must not be bound only to this, and must keep myself open to other projects that may take precedence over the newsletter at some time in the future.

CURRENT EVENTS AND ANALYSIS

On January 29th & 30th, 2002, there were two occurrences which I believe are pointing to the beginning of the end of the current "peace process" delusion that we have all been living under since Oslo I and II began in 1992.

The first was a series of statements by King Abdullah II of Jordan. The second was a series of statements by Egyptian President Hosni Mubarak during a meeting with Israeli Defense Minister Benjamin Ben Eliezer at the Sinai resort town of Sharm el-Sheikh.

The following is an article from AP appearing on page 2 of the English language Israeli daily *The Jerusalem Post* of January 30th, 2002.

AMMAN (AP) — "While the world focuses on combating terrorism, Israel is undermining the Palestinian leadership and trying to blow up Mid-East peacemaking," Jordanian King Abdullah II said yesterday. On the eve of his US visit, Abdullah said high on his agenda of White House talks for Friday will be the "complex situation that the Palestinian issue has arrived at."

"Israel has taken advantage of the preoccupation of the United States and the world community in combating terrorism to implement its agenda in an effort to liquidate the peace process and strike at the Palestine National Authority," Abdullah told the official Petra news agency. Abdullah is expected to arrive in New York today, the day he turns 40.

Victor Mordecai's analysis: King Abdullah, like his father, is very smooth and very erudite. He is the darling, today, of the United States war against terrorism. Jordan, Turkey, Oman, and Kuwait, just to mention the main ones, are states supporting the war against terrorism. This is after the mistaken choice of Abdullah's father, King Hussein, to support Saddam Hussein during the Gulf War.

However, King Abdullah II is either very mistaken in what he says above or is deceiving the world. The present escalation with Arafat and the PLO is because Arafat decided to start an Intifada or rebellion in September 2000, after Israeli Prime Minister Ehud Barak offered Arafat a 98.5% capitulation (not compromise) of the demands Arafat was making. Arafat's problem was: He did not want peace. He wanted war. Ehud Barak's offer was so generous that it infuriated Arafat because it made him look bad in the world. Arafat's solution: start a war. And ever since, Arafat has led his people, the Palestinians, and the Israelis, the Arabs, the Moslems, and the whole world down a steep precipice that can only lead to war, as long as Arafat is in the picture.

Yet King Abdullah II places the blame on Israel in the above article. By doing so, King Abdullah II has shown that he has not learned anything from the many mistakes his father King Hussein, the Arab world and the Islamic world have committed which have provided their peoples never-ending "nakba," the Arabic word for disaster. It is clear, therefore, and very unfortunately, that if and when a war breaks out between Israel and its Arab neighbors, Jordan's position and bitter end are very clear.

The second occurrence was a statement by Egyptian President Hosni Mubarak in Sharm el-Sheikh on January 30th, 2002, that Israel should not allow Jews onto the Temple Mount because this would be a sign against the Arabs.

The fact is that until September 2000, Jews and Christians were allowed on the Temple Mount. Some people, for political reasons, blame Israeli Prime Minister Ariel Sharon's visit to the Temple Mount for the riots that broke out there, and ever since Jews and Christians have been prevented from ascending the Temple Mount. The simple facts show that the "intifada" had already started 10 days before. Even the Palestinian leadership admitted that Sharon's visit was merely an excuse for something that had already started 10 days before.

But today, the Moslems threaten that by restoring the status quo ante of Jews and Christians being able to ascend the Temple Mount, this would lead to war and bloodshed; the Moslems are basically denying free access to the holy places or more so, the holiest of places to the Jews. And this is in Jerusalem, which is supposedly under Israeli sovereignty. But Hosni Mubarak warns us what will happen if Jews and Christians are allowed onto the Temple Mount: World War III.

In my book *Christian Revival for Israel's Survival,* I talk already in 1999 of the erroneous decisions by both Likud and Labor governments in Israel to allow the Moslems to build a mosque in Nazareth, and especially next to the Church of the Annunciation — a place where they have no business building a mosque!

Now, the Israeli government of unity, including both Likud and Labor parties, has come to its senses and will probably not allow the mosque to be built. What is the Moslem response: Blood will be spilt — World War III.

The issues of the Temple Mount in Jerusalem and the mosque vs. church in Nazareth are irreconcilable issues. There will be a Judeo-Christian victory over Islam in both places. Draw your own conclusions.

My dear readers, I now want to tell you a little story about a right wing celebrity-journalist picking on a left-wing "liberal" journalist instead of the usual vice versa.

I was participating in the International Christian Embassy of Jerusalem Feast of Tabernacles in the fall of 2000. As I was standing at my book table talking to people, I noticed Charles Senott of the *Boston Globe* standing at my table listening to my conversation. I had been talking about my service in the IDF Spokesman's office as a reservist officer for 12 years. (This is in addition to my service in artillery reserves for 16 years.)

When the conversation had ended and the people had left, Charles Senott, with whom I had spoken on different occasions in past years, asked me, "So what do you think of your Christians now?" I asked him, "What do you mean by that?" He answered, "Well, what do you think about destroying the mosques on the Temple Mount as some Christians are saying?"

I answered him then: "It is not politically correct to destroy the mosques on the Temple Mount. This is in God's hands. If anybody even touches the mosques, it will spark off World War III. However, if WWIII breaks out anyway, and the Moslems attack us as they have promised to do anyway, then yeah, take 'em out."

His face turned red. He exclaimed, "How did you ever become an Israeli Army spokesman? I am going to speak to your commanders and have you thrown out."

(Interesting that a "journalist" from the US also gets involved in meddling in another country's affairs.) Fortunately or unfortunately, I had already been retired with honors from the IDF spokesman two months before, after giving Israel 30 years of military reserves and compulsory duty.

But the point I wanted to make is that the Moslems have no doubt that they are going to win. They have no doubt that the whole world is with them, that Israel is always wrong, and they are always right.

I won't forget two quotes that are on page 89 of my book *Is Fanatic Islam a Global Threat?*

**"The War with Israel is a certainty,
and we are ready."**

(Former Egyptian Minister of War Amin el Hu-
waidi, January 29, 1995, in Egyptian weekly *Rous
el Yusef*)

**"In spite of the fact that Israel has atomic weap-
ons, Egypt will know how to cut off the arm of
the enemy when the time comes."**

(Present Egyptian Minister of War Field Marshall
Mohammed Hussein Tantawi, **ibid**.)

I won't forget that the above was said at the height of the
"peace process." Our then prime minister, Yitzhak Rabin, who had
made peace with Jordan, who was negotiating with the Palestinians
over Oslo I and II and who was trying to make peace with Syria,
was still very much alive. How could the Egyptians say such things
when Rabin was still alive? It was because their intentions toward
Israel were and remain warlike.

I would indeed be very surprised if a major war did not
break out in the Middle East very soon. Arafat's entire strategy is
to draw in all the Arab and Islamic nations into a cataclysmic war
with Israel and the West. And he will succeed. King Abdullah II
is sucked in and so is Egyptian President Hosni Mubarak. And the
Arab and Islamic nations will undergo (God forbid) a holocaust
like it has never known in history.

The Jews and the Christians (in my opinion) are the apple
of God's eye. That's what it says in the Bible. Anyone who tries
to pluck out the apple of God's eye will get both his eyes plucked
out. Destroying the mosques is not what I want. But if the Moslems
believe and preach that "We kill the Jews on Saturday, and we kill
the Christians on Sunday," then guess who gets killed. Then the
mosques will go and Allah, Satan, will go. The Moslems will have
only themselves to blame. Just as Pharoah's hardened heart gave

God no choice but to bring upon the Egyptian people of that time 10 plagues and the destruction of Pharoah's charioteers in the Red Sea, so, too, do the hardened hearts of the Moslems bring upon them calamity after calamity.

As British Prime Minister Tony Blair has said, "The victory will be ours, not theirs." Sorry about the mosques, Charles Senott!

C. PRIVATE INVESTIGATION

In the summer of 1999, I had the occasion to visit Edmonton, Canada. I speak of the special information I received there about Islamic terrorism in Canada. This is available in my first newsletter of October 2001.

In light of the above, I found the following article from the *Wall Street Journal* reprinted in the *Jerusalem Post* of December 28th, 2001, revealing.

"New World Intrudes on Cloister That Is Canada's Muslim Schools"

By Mark Heinzl and Elena Cherney

Toronto — To devout Muslims in North America seeking an environment for their children free of alarming Western influences, Islamic schools can be a godsend. But since the Um al-Qura elementary school here lost its principal this summer to Canadian authorities who call him a terrorist, that orderly, reverent world has been unsettled.

Majmoud Jaballah, the 39-year-old Egyptian who co-founded and led the school, was arrested in August. The Canadian Security Intelligence Service alleges in court documents that he is "a member of the Egyptian Islamic terrorist organization of al Jihad," which is "closely linked to Usama bin Laden's group al Qaeda."

Through his lawyer, Mr. Jaballah has denied any connection with terrorist activities. He is in solitary confinement while Canadian authorities seek to deport him.

Since the September 11th terrorist attacks on the US, for which Washington blames Mr. Bin Laden, concern about extremist elements within the Toronto Muslim community is "all people are talking about," says Tarek Fatah, who hosts a weekly community-television program called "Muslim Chronicle." About two-thirds of Canada's 600,000 Muslims live in the Toronto area.

At Um al Qura, it's a different story. A woman in full veil, who says she is the principal but declines to give her name, refers questions to Mr. Jaballah's lawyer, who didn't return phone calls seeking comment.

[Victor Mordecai comments: My information from Edmonton in 1999 was that the Moslems in Canada are planning very carefully to document where the Jews are and where the Christians are who oppose Islam. The information they reveal will be sent back to Egypt to the Islamic leadership. At the appropriate time, orders will be given from Egypt to the activists in Canada, the US, and Europe, etc., to massacre all Jews and Christians who oppose the Islamic agenda. Never forget the Islamic teaching: "On Saturday we kill the Jews. On Sunday we kill the Christians." Pretty psychotic it seems, no? Let us pray for the Moslems that they may be delivered of their satanic deceptions and beliefs before it is too late. Amen.]

MILITARY INTELLIGENCE

The European Afghanistan

The following is a translation of excerpts of an investigative report by Ronen Bergman in the weekend magazine of the Israeli daily *Yediot Ahronot* appearing on December 21st, 2001.

Open borders, organized crime and a supportive population are turning Bosnia into a base of Islamic terrorist activity.

The destruction of the Al'Qaeda in Afghanistan hasn't solved the problem of extremist Islamic terror cells scattered throughout the world. The Balkans have turned into a Garden of Eden for Moslem terrorists thanks to Saudi funding. Thousands of volunteers from Arab countries who came to help in the civil war have established themselves in Bosnia, and today they are the biggest ticking time bomb in Europe. Special American and British forces have arrived in Sarajevo to fight terrorism. Their success, for the meanwhile, has been most limited.

This past Wednesday (Dec.19th, 2001), a senior member of Israeli intelligence arrived at the office of Munir Alibabich, chief of intelligence services of Bosnia-Herzegovina. He came to receive a comprehensive briefing about Usama bin Laden inspired extremist Islamic terrorism in Bosnia. The briefing also included a survey of countermeasures taken by the Bosnians with the assistance and under the pressure of the Americans and Alibabich's predictions regarding the coming months.

As in most of the meetings he has held recently, Alibabich lectured to the Israelis about the special problems of Bosnia, and what is turning it into a magnet for terrorists. This time, also, he spoke of the need for urgent assistance from the West.

Israel has a limited interest in the goings-on in Bosnia. Israeli intelligence, and especially the Mossad, like their colleagues in the CIA, do not intend to wage a global campaign against terrorism and are focusing the little resources available to what might be considered a danger to Israel, and to Israeli or Jewish facilities abroad. The Israeli guest agreed with his host about cooperation between the two countries in the war against terrorism by means of information exchange on subjects of mutual interest. Before the Israeli guest left, Alibabich updated him about information that was revealed about massive Saudi support for the Islamic terror networks in Bosnia. This information was uncovered in investigations following a raid on the Hollywood Hotel.

On September 17th, 2001, the US and Britain shut down their embassies in Sarajevo for three days in response to "a tangible threat" of a possible terrorist attack. The information regarding this attack came from intercepted email communications and telephone calls between suspects who were possibly members of the "Al-Qaeda" organization in Europe and Asia. The threads all lead investigators to locations in Bosnia. Surveillance by the CIA in Sarajevo and other places in the country provided information after which rapid action was decided upon.

Some of the telephone calls were made from room 215 of the Hollywood Hotel located in Ilizha, a northern neighborhood of Sarajevo. A visitor to the hotel encounters a wall of silence. Signs of fear are still visible on the face of N., who was that day the receptionist in the small and dim lobby. "They warned me not to say a thing," says N. "They said they would detain me and take me for interrogation."

On the 25th of September, at 3 AM, a unit of the heavily armed British SAS forces, dressed in black and wearing stocking masks, charged into the lobby. They surprised N., who was half asleep in the lobby. One of them stayed with her; the remainder went upstairs and took out of the room two handcuffed detainees. One of them was Abdel Halim Kaffagiyeh, an Egyptian, and the other, Jihad Ahmed el-Gamala, a Jordanian. The operation was carried out without informing the Bosnian authorities.

The next morning, hundreds of soldiers, part of the 20,000-man international peacekeeping force known as SFOR, surrounded the offices of the "Saudi High Committee for Welfare" in Sarajevo. They shot open the locked doors and broke in. Big trucks were loaded up with the contents of the offices: computers, documents, lists, pictures, videotapes and $200,000 in cash that was found in one of the safes. Two Bosnians who aroused suspicion not far away were detained. It later turned out that they were part of the Saudi "Welfare

Committee."

The next day, a force of 1,000 soldiers occupied the Visoko airport, northwest of Sarajevo. According to the information the CIA had received, there were crop-dusters fitted out with very dangerous biological agents instead of pesticides. These chemical agents were intended for spraying the SFOR headquarters.

The raid was inconclusive. Captain Derrell Morel of the peacekeeping force says that: "We did find weapons, including pistols, hand-grenades and rifles. We did not find biological weapons, but we did find two chemical-proof protective suits. Samples were taken from the site, but the subject is still entirely under investigation."

Investigation of the detainees together with the intelligence file that arrived from the CIA opened up a new world to the special anti-terrorism team that was set up in Bosnia.

Zeldko Miltic, coordinator of the combined team, comprised of Americans and British, and who also serves as personal assistant to the prime minister of Bosnia, opens a big safe in his offices and takes out a thick file. "One of the subjects that bothered us the most," Miltic says, "were the documents we found at the Saudi 'Welfare Committee.' It has become clear that Saudi sources sent over $800 million since the end of the war. We have succeeded in understanding what happened to $700 million. According to the material confiscated, we fear that the rest of the money went to purposes related to terrorism."

Elements in the secret service AID add that a careful check of the lists of the Saudi Welfare Committee points to links between the supposedly humanitarian organization and active terrorist elements, some of whom are Ben Laden people in Bosnia. Similarly, a million dollars originally intended for the setting up of an Islamic TV station in Bosnia was not used for that purpose.

At the same time, Serbian citizenship was revoked in the cases of 94 men, and of 150 women and children who were with them. Miltic says that the list of suspects includes about 3,000 names of Bosnians or of those who stayed in Bosnia at some time.

There are five Islamic "charity" organizations being investigated by the Bosnians. Among them are "The Saudi High Welfare Committee," which is being run by Prince Salman, who is also governor of Riyadh (Saudi Arabia) and the Islamic Aid Agency. Another key group is the "Active Islamic Youth," created in 1996 by a group of veterans of the Mujahideen unit of the Bosnian army.

The CIA is also suspicious of the local Red Crescent (the Islamic equivalent of the Red Cross) representatives in Albania, the "Coordinating Committee of Islamic Unions," the "World Islamic Council," and the "Koran Fund." The local police have issued search warrants and demanded full lists of the leaders of these organizations, their activities, countries of origin, and the specific purpose of each organization. The Bank of Albania has given instructions to investigate the private banks in that country.

Spies and Beautiful Women

Immediately after the events of September 11th, 2001, the CIA defined the Balkans as the most problematic area in the world after Afghanistan. A British official said this week that there are three types of creatures prevalent in Sarajevo: "cats, pretty women and spies."

Since the attacks on NY and Washington, Sarajevo has filled up with all kinds of undercover agents. All heads are up and ears listening. Even an Israeli journalist in Sarajevo becomes a target: He is followed and all the other embassies are soon warned he is on his way.

What makes the Balkans in general and Bosnia in particular so attractive? Inexperienced governments, a lack of public security, very loose law enforcement, economic backwardness, administrative corruption and organized crime create an environment in which international terrorist networks can hide manpower and money.

The importance of the Balkans as a central arena in the international war on terrorism increases especially now, after the "Al Qaeda" organization has been all but eliminated. True, Bin Laden has not been apprehended, but he has fled for his life, taking with him the ability now very limited, if at all, to initiate or direct terrorist cells. In spite of this, the danger is clear and immediate, due to the fact that Bin Laden was never the commander of international Islamic terrorism. His departure in essence from the arena changes things somewhat but does not signal the end of the story, not at all.

The CIA tried in 1999 to map out international Islamic terrorism: who supports it, who is supported, who is the commander and who are the soldiers in the field. But very soon, they despaired. It turns out that this business is much more complicated. The journalist Asaad Hachemovich, Bosnian expert on Mujahideen affairs, said that using the term "Al Qaeda" as the title of a movement active in what was formerly Yugoslavia is a mistake: "They never gave themselves a name. At most, they described themselves as soldiers of Islam or Mujahideen. They saw themselves as part of the global Islamic movement, and not as belonging to Bin Laden or Al Qaeda."

According to indictments submitted against the perpetrators of the attacks on the US embassies in Africa in 1998, the "Al Qaeda" organization serves as an umbrella for a long list of organizations which are in contact with it and receiving assistance from it. However, in spite of a picture of similar aims and overlapping methods of operation, it is simply incorrect that there is a terrorist council meeting somewhere in Kandahar, with Bin Laden at its head, issuing orders to all the Islamic fundamentalists in the world.

During the last three months, US and British aircraft have bombed only six Al Qaeda training camps, in which it was thought terrorists from the world over were training. A source in the British Defense Ministry told *Yediot Ahronot* that most of the camps, spread out over huge areas, were completely abandoned. According to the intelligence information accumulated by the West during the last few years, about 30,000 people have been trained over the last decade in these camps. Most did not remain in Afghanistan. Rather, they were scattered throughout the world and today represent a well-trained network of terrorists, experienced and thoroughly motivated.

It is easily possible to identify the roots of the problem of the Balkans as a base for Islamic terrorism going back to the early 1990's. Daniel Kursky, a Jew from Denmark, a graduate of the Center for International Relations at Cambridge University, is a researcher for a non-governmental organization called "The International Crisis Regions Group." Kursky recently completed his writing of a comprehensive report of terrorism in the Balkans: "It is not easy for the world in general and US in particular to be reminded today of the circumstances under which the Republic of Bosnia and Herzegovina became dependent on Arab generosity and Iranian arms during the war. Put aside the causes of it welcoming 3,000 Moslem volunteers into its army, for lack of another savior."

The experience of ethnic cleansing by the former Yugoslavia against Moslems, the civil war, Milosevic's intervention in the struggle and the indifference of the West caused many in the Arab world to volunteer in favor of the Muslim minority. To this day, the exact number of volunteers is unknown. Alija Izetbegovich, prime minister and leader of the Moslem majority, expressly welcomed these volunteers who came to Bosnia during the war years from all over the Middle East, and even from Europe and Asia. Estimates vary from 1,000 to 3,000 trained and motivated fighters. At first, they fought as part of unorganized militias, but very soon, they were grouped together in a special unit formed for them, "Mujahid Brigade." Izetbegovich declared himself honorary commander of the brigade.

The foreign fighters made a considerable military and moral contribution to the Bosnian army. They were trained, disciplined and succeeded in breathing a spirit of enthusiasm into the local soldiers. They established different training programs for the Bosnian soldiers, which included, in addition to the fighting lessons, a lot of religious indoctrination. In Miltic's safe is a video of pictures of Mujahideen training camps. The pictures highly resemble pictures of Bin Laden training camps. Battles are also documented, abuse of Serbian prisoners, and a segment is dedicated to the "martyrs," including photos of them while they were still alive, and a detailed documentation of their bodies.

1994 was critical for expanding Bin Laden's branch in the Balkans. The crimes of genocide and ethnic cleansing against Bosnian Moslems "caused rage in the Islamic world in 1994," according to lawyer David Ronca, the attorney who represented some of the defendants accused in the bombings of the US embassies in Tanzania and Kenya. Bin Laden wrote an article that year saying, inter alia: "The world is a witness to all of this, and not only does it not respond to these evil events, it even prevents these helpless people from obtaining the weapons needed for them to defend themselves. This is all a public conspiracy between the US and its allies defended by the infidel UN."

Asaad Hachemovich wrote in the liberal weekly *Danny,* considered today by journalists to be the leading weekly in Bosnia, at least in regards to coverage of the Mujahideen. From a modest apartment in the Zenitsa neighborhood, he wages a lengthy struggle for years to expose the truth about the extremist Islamic movements in Bosnia. "It might be that from Israel's perspective, all the Mujahideen are cut from the same cloth. Undoubtedly they all spoke brazenly about the need to destroy Israel. But from my perspective, there were differences among them, and not all were subservient to Bin Laden."

Very rapidly, these Mujahideen warriors became the front line troops of the Bosnian army. They also amazed the locals with their originality and ability to penetrate enemy territory. In order to free 13 Mujahideen warriors captured by the Croatian army, Mujahideen commander Mohammed Abu Mali sent his men to abduct one of the commanders of the Croatian army. The team professionally eliminated his bodyguards and abducted the commander. Hachemovich: "With all due respect, it was clear to me from the beginning that these men did not value human life. They were cruel and dangerous."

The Mujahideen high command operated out of the neighborhood of Zenitsa, but the Mujahideen were active throughout the country. They succeeded in breaking out of the blockade imposed on Sarajevo, but the local forces did not take advantage of this success. Photographers always accompanied the special operations of the "Al Mujahid" Brigade. These photographers, mostly Germans, had converted to Islam and sought to participate in the battles. At the end of the battle for Vuzucha in May 1995, the Mujahideen carried out a long series of horrific outrages against the local Serbian population. The three Bosnian commanders of this unit are presently being tried by the international war crimes tribunal in The Hague for crimes against humanity.

Saudi Arabia, Iran and Libya were among those who responded favorably to Izetbegovich for financial assistance, and they also assisted in circumventing the embargo that prevented Bosnia from arming itself legally. Providing the funds and closing the deals for purchasing weapons centered in Bosnia's embassy in Vienna. Much private connections, commitments and capital was involved in this process. Sources at the American embassy in Sarajevo and in the intelligence unit of the international peacekeeping force say that these connections led to the leaders of Izetbegovich's former and present party's leaders, and it is they who prevent the carrying out of a comprehensive investigation of all the deals that were struck to defend Bosnia.

About a month and a half ago, in an article published here, Pentagon chief strategist Richard Perle said: "The Saudis sent billions of dollars to set up schools and seminaries throughout the world in which they systematically taught against the US and the West. This actual transfer of funds should be interpreted, just as in the case of transferring funds to the Taliban, as a hostile move against the US and it should be treated as such. We thought they (the Saudis) were friends, that they felt gratitude for our saving them during the Gulf war, but we were wrong."

Today it is possible to reveal that Perle based his answer, inter alia, on information linking a number of Saudi organizations, governmental or semi-governmental, to terrorism activists in organizations such as "Al Qaeda" and "Islamic Jihad." A large part of this information refers to the Balkans.

Miltic squeezes his fingers to create the impression of a very narrow crack in order to emphasize what was really the humanitarian part of the overall activity of some of the organizations presently under investigation: "Our main problem is that the staffs of most of these organizations are not even in Bosnia and our ability to act against them or to receive information about them is very limited."

The history of the supposedly humanitarian Islamic organizations, which serve today as a pipeline for transferring monies, is linked to the breakup of the eastern bloc in general and Yugoslavia in particular. After the collapse of the one-party atheistic state in 1991, delegations from all over the Moslem world started to arrive in the Balkans. With Islamic assistance, they began the work of renovating and rebuilding destroyed mosques, in which classrooms were built for Arabic language courses for children. In many instances, the Moslem assistance was more efficient than that provided by the West. Islam became a worthy alternative for many.

In Albania, for example, under difficult and crime rich

conditions of this interim period, Moslem leaders claimed that the state must weigh adopting Islamic laws if it is unable to restore law and order.

In the winter of 1992, international aid began to stream into the region. The Islamic assistance agency filled an important role in distributing medical equipment alongside Christian charity organizations. Contrary to the other religious organizations, the Islamic representatives were determined to create a spiritual and cultural basis in the region. In October 1992, representatives of the Islamic Development Bank visited Albania and Bosnia. The bank delegation proposed investing into all the different segments of the economy, to promote export and to provide credit.

The influence of this involvement is clearly visible. Today, there are many more religious Moslems in Bosnia than there were in 1992. Historic mosques were transformed from museums into places of ritual. New and glittering mosques — built in the style of the Persian Gulf, like for example, the new Saudi mosque resembling a space station — and Islamic study centers, funded usually by Saudi princes, sprouted up one after another in Sarajevo as well as in other cities. Anyone strolling in the streets of Sarajevo or Zenitsa, can see today, alongside girls dressed in shorts, not a few women clad in traditional Islamic garb. Rarely does one find pork served in restaurants.

The French Connection

According to intelligence information and Serbian government leaks, Usama Bin Laden, like his deputy Zawaheiri, possesses Bosnian passports. The Bosnian government denies this completely. In any event, the Bosnians cannot deny that by the most legal means, they have provided asylum, patronage, and honorary citizenship to those who represent today one of the most dangerous cadres of international terrorism.

The Dayton Accords of November 1995, which ended the war in Bosnia, turned the country into a kind of federation comprised of Bosnia-Herzegovina with a 2/3 Moslem majority and the Serbska Republic with a Serbian majority. These two units, still drenched in the horrors of war, maintain tense relations and operate under the patronage of the international peacekeeping force.

The issue of disarming the Mujahideen and expelling them from the country has become a stumbling block in regards to Bosnia-US relations. The Bosnians did indeed rapidly disarm the military unit, but have done almost nothing, up until September 11th, to expel them from the country.

From the Bosnian government's perspective, the expulsion of the Mujahideen would quickly become a political scandal. Firstly, because under the protection of Bosnian law, anyone who participated in civil war battles became entitled, automatically, together with his wife and children to Bosnian citizenship. Secondly, because many Bosnian citizens, especially in villages and mountainous areas, feel a deep gratitude to those who came from far away to save them from Serbian ethnic terrorism. All together, the "Democratic Action Party" of Alija Izetbegovich granted Bosnian passports to 12,000 in this manner.

The political adviser at the US embassy in Sarajevo says that the matter of passports very much bothers the US administration: "It must be understood, also, that there isn't actually just one type of Bosnian passport. Because of the war, from 1991 until today, there are 3-4 different types of passports, and only last year was one of them issued with the intention of replacing all the rest. But the old ones remain valid and it is very hard to control this."

In addition to this, a large portion of the Moslem volunteers remained in Bosnia and have meanwhile married local girls. Some of the Mujahideen have indeed settled, become established, married, had children and opened small businesses. For another part, the end of the war served merely as a signal to open the next front — extremist Islam against the West.

Imad al-Masri, one of the senior leaders of the "Al Mujahid" unit in the Bosnian army, wrote about the Dayton Accords: "The real aim of this peace is to stop the conquests and victories of the Moslems, and to extinguish the light of Islamic awakening." Al Masri was detained in Bosnia on July 18th, 2001, due to an Egyptian arrest warrant for having been involved in the murders of tourists in Egypt. His real name is el-Husseini Hilmi Arman Ahmed.

About 1,000 Mujahideen remained in Bosnia after the war. They settled in the cities, villages, and even have established for themselves new villages of their own, and have enlisted hundreds of locals, and are building a regime that does not recognize the laws of Bosnia except for those of the "Sharia" or Islamic law. Thus, for example, in the village of Buchina, the Mujahideen have settled in houses of Christians who were expelled from their homes and they have established a strict religious regime, making the villages resemble Taliban villages more than those of Europe in the 21st century. When the government threatened to deport some of the volunteers, the response was anonymous threats of a wave of terrorism and some attacks against government facilities.

The government and secret service were threatened in April 2001 when Bosnian policemen detained Karim Said Atmani, alias Said Hujich. Hujich-Atmani was detained based on an international Interpol arrest warrant in August 2000. His story is an example of the international indifference that typified the treatment of terrorism that knew no borders until September 11th, 2001.

Atmani was tried in absentia in Paris and sentenced to five years imprisonment for trading in forged passports and providing assistance to Moslem terrorists in Canada, Europe and Turkey. After the deportation, the interior ministry confirmed the detention of more former members of the "Al Mujahid" unit, due to arrest warrants from France, Egypt and Croatia, where they were wanted for different acts of terrorism.

During his detention, Hujich-Atmani held Bosnian citizenship given to him after he arrived in the country and married a local woman by fictitious marriage. The CIA provided the Bosnian intelligence services information that Atmani was an expert in counterfeiting documents, working primarily for the "Islamic Salvation Front," an extremist underground movement in Algeria. The Americans and the Canadians also have a few unresolved issues with Atmani.

Atmani was convicted in Paris together with another accused defendant, Ahmed Resam. Resam was the man who intended to carry out a series of shocking attacks on the eve of the millennium in the US, and was caught with much explosive materiel on the Canadian border. Atmani, so claims the indictment against Resam, was the one who provided him with the forged documents and additional logistical help. The French investigating judge, Jean Louis Brugiere, in charge of the French war on terrorism, appeared as an expert witness in the trial of Resam in Los Angeles. He identified the two as members of the Algerian underground and as having been in close contact with Usama bin Laden.

Brugiere himself arrived to deal with the subject in continuation of the stubborn struggle he waged against what he described as the "Rubiet Gang" — an Algerian underground group, which carried out a series of attacks in France in the 1990's. Many of the gang were senior members in the "Al Mujahid" unit of the Bosnian army or who had received asylum after members of Brugiere's team declared them as being wanted by the law. Sources close to Brugiere this week told *Yediot Ahronot* that French intelligence possessed information regarding at least another six Frenchmen connected to Bin Laden and the Algerian underground and who evidently are in Bosnia. The six are described as "most dangerous."

Long List of Wanted Suspects

Bosnian police detained several dozen suspects over the last few weeks in a few raids by Bosnian police. They represented much of the Middle East. Iran, Iraq, Syria, Pakistan, Afghanistan and Algeria. Some of them were released for lack of evidence. Some were extradited to the countries where they were wanted, like Egypt and Algeria. Some were tried in Bosnia and some are still under investigation. An additional two suspects belonging to an Egyptian Jihad organization were not arrested intentionally, and they are under 24-hour-a-day surveillance.

At least two of the detainees, according to Bosnian intelligence, had a direct link to Usama bin Laden's people. The two, Sayah Bil-Kachem and Saber La'awar, received instructions from two Al-Qaeda superiors in Vienna.

Another proof of links between Bosnia and Bin Laden involve a character by the name of Anwar Sha'aban, one of the central supporters of the Mujahideen, an Italian by citizenship. Sha'aban was a good friend of Sheikh Abu Talal, against whom a death sentence was passed in Egypt in the beginning of the 1990's because of terrorist attacks. Sha'aban was the director of a supposed Islamic charity organization called "the International Islamic Cultural Institute" in Milan, Italy. He fled to Bosnia because of a police investigation against him. Sha'aban was killed when he failed to stop at a roadside checkpoint in 1996. It turns out that he was responsible for sending a group of volunteers from Europe to Bin Laden in Afghanistan.

US intelligence is searching today for another 40 Bosnian passport holders, most of whom have a very high level of military training, who probably joined the Al Qaeda in Afghanistan. If they are not identified among the body bags or in the prisoner camps, they will add considerable concern to the growing list of wanted terrorists of the CIA.

Miltic: "In any event, it is very important to be careful. The networks of extremist Islam are much more developed in Britain or France, and the realities of the last few years, including the evidence of the investigation of the most recent attacks only proves it."

[Victor Mordecai comments: On the very first page in the preface of my book *Is Fanatic Islam a Global Threat?* I relate how Bosnian Prime Minister Alija Izetbegovich wrote his doctoral thesis on how he would cause Bosnia to break away from Yugoslavia and form a Moslem fundamentalist state.]

Chapter VI
MARCH 2002 NEWSLETTER

Victor Mordecai's Monthly Message

This monthly newsletter finds me on the road in the US, and therefore some of the information, garnered in the field during this trip, will be particularly relevant to realities in America, but are still symptomatic of the total war between Islam and the Judeo-Christian West.

In past newsletters, I discussed the backgrounds of the "Taliban from Marin County, California," Johnny Walker Lindh as well as of the "shoe-bomber" Richard C. Reid. It has become clear that many Americans are being duped into becoming Muslims. This is a clear strategy of Islam to get not only blacks, but also whites and Hispanics to convert to Islam and turn them into "ticking time-bombs."

Since Americans are fierce defenders of their individual civil liberties and freedoms, there has been a debate taking place as to whether or not it was "fair" to conduct "profiling" for identifying Islamic terrorists. Of course, in this case, the profiling would focus on Middle East Muslims and perhaps black US Muslims. But what happens when whites or Hispanics convert to Islam? How do you profile them?

In light of this, I want to share an e-mail article I received in August 2001 that was reconfirmed in the *New York Times* in December 2001 about Hispanics converting to Islam. This article discusses the conversion of 15,000 Hispanic Americans to Islam in the US while the *New York Times* article reinforced this amount to 40,000 converts.

My thanks go to Jeremy Saravo, who sent me this article on August 21st, 2001.

New Islamic Movement Seeks Latino Converts

Religion: Leaders estimate there are more than 15,000 Spanish-speaking Muslims in the US. Many say they were confused by Catholicism.

By: Margaret Ramirez — *Times*
Religion Writer

Slipped inside a strip mall across from Exposition Park where the smell of incense mingles with Arabic swirls on the wall, Muhammad Gomez absorbs the message of Allah. Sitting beside him in this storefront Islamic center, Domy Garcia raises her hand and asks why she and other Muslim women are obliged to cover their heads with hijab. Mariam Montalvo takes diligent notes at the Sunday afternoon Islamic lesson with the holy Koran by her side.

Here at the ILM Foundation, a new Islamic movement is being born. Yet it lies far from Mecca, where the faith was founded more than 1,400 years ago. And the language of choice for this group of Islamic followers is not Arabic. These Muslims worship Allah in Spanish.

Montalvo, who immigrated to Los Angeles from Mexico in 1996, left the Catholic faith three months ago, frustrated by what she called contradictions within church teachings and preoccupation with the saints. After research and contemplation, she took the shahada, the simple declaration of faith by which one becomes a Muslim.

"I had a lot of problems with the church. One Bible says one thing, and another Bible says something different. Then there are people who call themselves Catholics and drink and smoke," said Montalvo, 21. "With Islam, it was so pure. I found there were no intermediaries. Everything goes straight to God."

If you were inclined to believe that most Muslims are Arabs, you would be wrong. Over the past 10 years, Islam has become one of the fastest-growing religions, with an estimated 1 billion adherents worldwide and 6 million followers in this nation. About half of the Muslims in the US are African American converts. But in recent years, Islamic teaching has begun gaining acceptance among members of the Latino community. Though precise statistics do not yet exist, Islamic leaders estimate that there are at least 15,000 Latino Muslims across the nation.

Last month, about 30 Southern California converts founded the Latino-Muslim Movement with the intent of educating Spanish-speaking Muslims and spreading Islam to other Latinos. After meeting informally for the past seven years, the group appointed officers and elected to meet at the ILM Foundation once a week.

Scores of Latinos throughout the country — specifically in New York, New Jersey, Chicago and Miami — have fled the church of their birth and embraced Islam as their newfound faith.

In New York, a group of Puerto Rican Muslims opened an Islamic center in the heart of East Harlem called Alianza Islamica, where hundreds of Latinos have converted since 1992. The center, the first of its kind, includes a small mosque where the Friday sermon is heard in Arabic, English and Spanish. Islam has adherents throughout Latin America and the Caribbean as well, with especially strong followings in Argentina, Brazil, Colombia and Panama.

Reymundo Nur, a Panamanian who became Muslim at the age of 12 and studied Islam in Saudi Arabia, helped organize the Los Angeles group. Two years ago, Nur co-founded a national nonprofit organization called Asociacion Latina de Musulmanes en las Americas, which focuses on translating Islamic books and literature into Spanish.

He said one of his group's main projects is translating the Koran into contemporary, conversational Spanish. At least two Spanish translations of the Koran exist, but Nur said they use a more formal Castilian Spanish.

"There have always been Latino Muslims. It's only now that they're coming to the forefront," said Nur, vice president of the Latino-Muslim Movement in Los Angeles. "We have a strong Islamic legacy, and people are rediscovering that part of their heritage. Many learn about it and said, 'Hey, I have more of this in me than I ever realized.'"

Islamic ties to Hispanic culture date back to 711, when the Muslim general Tariq ibn Zayid conquered Spain, and the Christian Visigothic domination of Roderick came to an end. Under Moorish rule, Christians, Jews and Muslims coexisted in Spain. Conversion was encouraged but never forced.

[Victor Mordecai comments: This is false. Forced conversions took place. Jewish philosopher Maimonides had to flee Spain because the Moslems gave the choice of converting to Islam, leaving Spain, or execution. And this is but one of many such examples.]

Because the Arabs did not bring women with them, they took Spanish wives, and within a few generations the Muslim population was more Spanish than Arab.

[Victor Mordecai comments: Moslem women are not allowed to marry out of the Islamic religion, but men are. This is a reason we see so many Moslems coming to America from the Middle East and marrying American Christian women. It is one of the ways to "Islamicize" America.]

For the next 700 years, Al-Andalus, as the Muslims refer to Spain, enjoyed an era of political and cultural splendor, becoming one of the most intellectually advanced countries in medieval Europe. Islamic influence penetrated almost every facet of Spanish life, especially music, architecture and literature.

But gradually, Christian armies advanced. After the fall of the last Moorish stronghold in Granada in 1492, the cross replaced the crescent on Spain's minarets and Muslims were forced to convert to Christianity or be exiled. Many Latino Muslims in Los Angeles see their conversion as a return to their Moorish roots.

Today, Southern California has the third-largest concentration of Muslims in the country, including 58 mosques and Islamic centers in Los Angeles County.

Like Christians and Jews, Muslims are monotheists believing in one God known as Allah. They revere biblical prophets including Noah, Isaac, Abraham and Moses. Jesus is also considered a prophet, but unlike Christians, Muslims do not accept him as the son of God. Muhammad is believed to be the last prophet to whom Allah revealed the Koran.

For former Catholics like Guadalupe Martinez, 26, it is this comprehensive set of beliefs that makes Islam appealing.

"In Islam, there is no separation. You accept the Torah and the Bible," said Martinez, who converted in 1997. "We love Jesus, we dress like Mary. It's like we're putting all the faiths together. It really touched me."

[Victor Mordecai comments: Islam does not accept the Torah and Bible, but replaces them with the Koran. Islam teaches that Allah is an abrogating god and has abrogated the Torah and Bible, as well as his covenants with the Jews and Christians. Also, for Moslems, the Hadith teaches that Jesus Christ comes back a second time as a Moslem and kills all the Jews and Christians who have not converted to Islam and accepted Mohammed as the greatest of all prophets.]

"In Catholicism, there are just so many ways to go. Why am I going to pray to the saints?" she added. "When we find Islam, we don't have to waste energy. It's like if I call the operator to get a number, I waste energy. But with Islam, I have the number. I get connected directly to God."

Along with the formation of more Latino Muslim organizations, conversion stories have begun burning up the Internet.

Ali Al-Mexicano, a 25-year-old Pomona computer technician, created his own World Wide Web page account of how he became Muslim that includes the first time he read the Koran. "It was so clear and written in a simple, understanding way," he said. "It just hit me. This has to be the truth."

Though the Al-Mexicano family accepted his conversion, several other young Latinos who have begun searching outside the traditional confines of Catholicism have found conversion to be a heart-wrenching affair, often tearing families apart.

A 1998 Georgetown University study of people ages 20 to 39 found that 8% of the Latinos had joined another denomination or religion. Of those, at least 65% left for evangelical Protestant groups, Pentecostal churches or Mormonism. A smaller percentage accepted other religions including Islam and Buddhism.

Some relatives see conversion to other faiths as rejecting family and tradition.

Domy Garcia said her family in Mexico was confused and upset by her decision to leave the church. The Buena Park mother converted to Islam two years ago after rejecting the religion she said was forced on her Mexican ancestors. Undeterred by her family's reaction, Garcia said her main concern now is raising her children as Muslims and introducing more Latinos to Islam.

"My family just would not accept it. They said, 'What happened? You've changed so much,'" she recalled. "But it's all right, because on Judgement Day, my family won't be able to help. It will be God."

The Latino-Muslim Movement meets every Sunday afternoon for discussions at the ILM Foundation, a community center managed by Saadiq Saafir, a prominent African American prayer leader, or imam.

About 2 p.m., Elizabeth Chawki, a Native American who is fluent in Spanish, usually begins the sessions, which have focused on women, preparation of food, marriage and Islamic divorce. Despite the perception that all Muslims are Arab, Chawki said, converts see the distinction between religion and ethnicity. "This is about pure religion, not culture. We still eat our tamales and frijoles," said Chawki, referring to some Latino dishes served after the discussions.

Gomez, a native of Nicaragua with no prior religious affiliations, said it was after reading *The Autobiography of Malcolm X* that he began to explore Islam.

Like several other converts, Gomez spoke with resentment about the Catholic Church's involvement in Latin America.

"Viewing Jesus as a prophet and a political leader, and not a God, made more sense to me," he said.

The Latino-Muslim Movement also aims to bring together Muslims regardless of race. At a recent meeting, Saafir reflected on the emerging phenomenon of Latino conversions as similar to the time when African Americans began accepting Islam 50 years ago. In allowing the group to use the Islamic center, Saafir hopes to tear down the barriers that divide blacks and Latinos.

"We all realize that we're Muslim first," Saafir said. "This religion is going to bring us together."

Nur nodded. "Inshallah," he whispered. "God willing."

Victor Mordecai comments: Islam's strategy is to confront the US from within with a Trojan horse comprised of blacks, Hispanics, Native Americans, and yes, even whites like Johnny Walker Lindh. The following is taken from my 1997 book *Is Fanatic Islam a Global Threat?* (pages 230-231):

Gaddafi, Farrakhan Seek to Influence US Election

Dateline, Cairo, January 26th, 1996 News Services

Tripoli, Libya — Libyan dictator Moammar Gaddafi this week pledged $1 billion to influence American minorities in this year's presidential election. (By the way, Clinton won. The Gaddafi-Farrakhan plan worked.)

The pledge was made in the course of a visit to Libya by Nation of Islam leader Louis Farrakhan, according to JANA, the Libyan government news agency.

JANA reported that the two agreed to "mobilize the oppressed minorities" — particularly blacks, Muslims and Native Americans — "to play a significant role in American political life."

"Our confrontation with America used to be like confronting a fortress from outside," JANA quoted Gaddafi as saying. "Today we have found a loophole to enter the fortress and to confront it from within."

According to JANA, Farrakhan replied, "I have met my brother, Col. Moammar Gaddafi, for the sake of unifying Arabs, Muslims, blacks and oppressed communities in America to play a strong, significant role not only in the American elections, but in American foreign policy."

After visiting the ruins of Gaddafi's house, destroyed in an American air raid on Tripoli in 1986, in retaliation for Libya's alleged involvement in a bombing at a German nightclub frequented by US Marines, Farrakhan wrote in the visitor book: "I implore Allah to punish our enemies hundreds of times, just as they did to us and against you," JANA said.

Victor Mordecai adds: I cannot remember the specific date I heard and viewed this, but President Bill Clinton was aired on CNN making a speech about how he was so proud of Congress for approving billions of dollars for "organizations" in the inner cities that were instilling "values" in the youth. Now, for me, this seems to have been "payback" for the above billion dollars Gaddafi gave Farrakhan to influence the elections in favor of Bill Clinton. "Organizations" in the inner cities refers to the black Muslims and "values" refers to Islam.

Finally, I wanted to share a testimony I believe could have only been orchestrated by God Himself.

For years, I have been sharing, as part of my message, a story that took place somewhere around 1986. It involves a 16-year-old Palestinian American high school student. She was dating an American, and her parents forbade her to see him, quoting the Koran Sura V, verse 51: "Believers, Moslems, take not the Jews or Christians for your friends. They are friends with one another. Whoever befriends them will become one of their numbers. Allah does not guide the wrongdoer."

Basically, the girl, who was rambunctious as many 16-year-old boys and girls can be rambunctious, said to her parents: "Come on, Mom and Dad, get real. We are in America now!"

Well, it turns out that was a big mistake. Her mother held her while the father stabbed her to death quoting Sura V, verse 51 of the Koran (above). St. Louis police have this on tape after the young lady dialed 911.

Well, the testimony I want to share is the continuation and completion of the above. I was travelling through the mid-west and arrived in Beloit, Wisconsin. There I spoke before a group of intercessors and leaders of a big charismatic church. That Sunday morning, I was invited to speak before a Spanish language prayer group using the older building as part of that big church.

The pastor, originally from Mexico, heard me speak 3 hours in Spanish and seeing my books were in English, asked about when they would come out in Spanish. I said whenever a courageous Spanish-speaking pastor wanted them to come out. Well, he said to me: "Let's do it." He even had a relative with a printing press in Mexico City who could help with the printing.

To make a long story short, nothing happened over the course of a year. A year later, when I returned to this same church, the pastor invited me to meet with a 30-year-old Hispanic woman who had just gotten a divorce from her Islamic husband.

It turns out that her father was a Palestinian Moslem who married her mother, a Puerto Rican Christian. When the daughter reached puberty, they sent her to "Palestine" on "vacation." She came back from "vacation" with her Palestinian Moslem husband.

They had three children. When the oldest approached puberty, both the grandfather and father pressured the grandmother and mother to convert to Islam. Indeed, according to Islamic law, the mother and three children were Moslems, and this conversion was meant merely as a formality. However, both the grandmother and mother did not want to be Moslems and "reverted" to Christianity. The abuse and violence became intolerable and both the Hispanic grandmother and daughter divorced the grandfather and husband.

This Mexican pastor and the church were providing cover and protection to these Christian women. When I visited them, the daughter revealed to me and to the pastor testimonies that were hair-raising. In addition, the final testimony was about the 16-year-old Palestinian girl in St. Louis killed by her parents for dating a black Christian American. This young woman was the best friend of the murdered 16-year-old when she, too, was 16 years old.

When the Mexican pastor heard this, he asked me: "Did you know this?" I answered: "It's part of my message."

He then said: "We've got to get your message out in Spanish."

First, what would one say are the probabilities of me meeting the best friend of this Palestinian girl who was murdered by her parents? But God set it up.

Secondly, praise God, and God willing, my two books and my video teachings will soon be available in Spanish, which is, by the way, my mother tongue. They will also appear soon in Portuguese,

God willing, in addition to English and German.

Concluding this section, I would like to say I believe God is opening the Spanish and Portuguese speaking worlds now also to my message. This is because Islam is a threat to them as well. This is because there must be an awakening in the Spanish and Portuguese speaking worlds and an alliance between North and South America in dealing with the Islamic threat. Islamic missionary outreach to the Hispanics, Islamic missionary outreach to anyone for that matter, must be immediately stopped by law, and if this is not the case, then by a concerted effort by Jews and Christians to teach Hispanics the truth about Islam. This is the purpose of my books and tapes. This is my monthly message.

CURRENT EVENTS AND ANALYSIS

It is indeed interesting that during the course of my travels in the US and Canada, I come across stories as they are happening and appearing in the local press reports. It is also interesting that many of these reports do not make it to the nationally syndicated press and so the stories remain buried...insignificant. But the following story is astounding and symptomatic of Islamic plans for America as well as the ignorance of Americans in dealing with these Islamic plans.

The following are articles taken from the Memphis, Tennessee, daily *The Commercial Appeal* of Thursday, February 14th and Friday, February 15th, 2002.

FLAMING DEATH NO ACCIDENT, FBI SAYS — GASOLINE FOUND ON CLOTHES OF LICENSE EXAMINER

by Bill Dries (dries@gomemphis.com)

The fiery death of a driver's license examiner at the center of a federal fraud investigation was not an accident, an FBI agent said here Wednesday in federal court.

Federal and state investigators found gasoline on the clothes Katherine Smith was wearing when she died Sunday in a car crash on a stretch of US 72 in Fayette County, FBI agent J. Suzanne Nash told US Magistrate Judge J. Daniel Breen.

Nash also testified that investigators found evidence of some kind of accelerant in the burned-out interior of Smith's car.

Her testimony came during a probable cause and bond hearing for three of Smith's five co-defendants in an alleged scheme to get Tennessee driver's licenses using false information for men with Middle Eastern ties who lived in New York City.

Breen found there was probable cause to charge Mohammed Fares, Mostafa Said Abou-Shahin and Abdelmuhsen Mahmid Hammad. He also denied them bond.

Fares, Hammad and Abou-Shahin, wearing tan prison scrubs and blue wind-breakers, listened to the proceedings through cell phones with an Arabic interpreter on the other end of the line in another city. The courtroom's sound system was piped through the phone line for the interpreter to hear.

After hearing the translation of Breen denying him bond, Fares, 19, set his phone on the table and put his head in his hands.

Smith and her co-defendants, including alleged ringleader Khaled Odtllah and Hammad's cousin, Sakhera Hammad, were charged Feb. 6th with conspiracy to fraudulently obtain Tennessee driver's licenses.

While her five co-defendants have been imprisoned without bond since their Feb. 5 arrest, Smith was released on her own recognizance. She died one day before she was due to appear at a detention hearing before a federal magistrate judge.

"Was this death a result of an accident?" federal prosecutor Tim DiScenza asked Nash, who was the only witness to testify during Wednesday's two-hour hearing.

"No, it was not," Nash replied.

According to Nash, this is what FBI agents and Tennessee Highway Patrol investigators have concluded about the car crash:

Six unnamed witnesses — all related to each other — saw Smith's 1992 Acura Legend veer off US 72 around 12:45 am Sunday. They said the interior of the car was on fire as the car drove across a ditch and hit a utility pole. The fire was arson, Nash said.

"Every single thing inside the car is burnt," she said before noting that the trunk and gas tank were untouched by a blaze so intense that Smith's arms and legs were "burned off."

There was only "slight damage" to the front end of the car from hitting the utility pole, she added.

Nash said gasoline was found on Smith's clothing. She said investigators are still waiting on test results of traces of an unknown accelerant found in the car. A dog trained to sniff out such chemicals detected the accelerant.

Smith died from "inhaling the actual flames," Nash testified. "Her airway system is actually singed."

Attorneys for the three defendants were quick to point out that their clients were all in prison at the time of Smith's death.

"Katherine Smith obviously lived two lives, maybe more," said Karen Cicala, who represented Fares. "She may have had other things going on in her life that may have led to her death."

She also questioned whether Fares is being treated differently because of ties to the Middle East.

Attorney Jake Erwin, representing Hammad, urged Breen to consider only the fraud conspiracy charge.

"You're not saying that Mr. Hammad had anything to do with Katherine Smith's death, are you?" Erwin asked Nash.

"No, not at this time," she replied.

"You're not saying he had anything to do with the World Trade Center attack, are you?" he asked again.

"No, not at this time," she repeated.

DiScenza has said there are "connections" linking two of the accused to the World Trade Center in the days before it was destroyed in the Sept. 11th, 2001, terrorist attacks. Those connections include a visitor's pass to the WTC dated Sept. 5 that belonged to Sakhera Hammad.

DiScenza focused on Smith's death as a factor that Breen should consider in denying bond.

"This court has to consider that Katherine Smith died under very suspicious circumstances, in a manner that was clearly not an accident," DiScenza told Breen. "Coincidence only goes so far."

Bill Dries: 901-529-2643

The following are the six suspects:

Katherine Smith, 49: State employee for 29 years, last nine years in driver's license division. Died in a wreck Sunday, the day before a detention hearing in federal court. On Feb. 5, using forms filled out by her friend Khaled "Kal" Odtllah, she processed four applications. Prosecutor described three of these names as fictitious and "totally untraceable."

Khaled "Kal" Odtllah, 31. Came to the US from Jerusalem 13 years ago. Lived in Shelby County past 2 1/2 years. Owned Phillips 66 gas station until recently. Buys and sells cars, including 1992 Acura bought by Katherine Smith. Formerly lived at 2840 Morning Lake in unincorporated Cordova. Used this address on multiple drivers' license applications.

Sakera "Rocky" Hammad, 24: of New York City, and a naturalized citizen from Jordan, had a visitor's pass for the World Trade Center, dated September 5th, 2001. Said he is a plumber and worked on center's sprinkler system. He arranged transport from New York to Memphis last week for defendants who intended to buy driver's licenses for $1,000 or more apiece.

Abdelmuhsen Mahmid Hammad: age unknown. In the country illegally after overstaying his visa, he was the driver last week for his cousin, Sakhera Hammad. He used a Tennessee driver's license issued in his name last year by Smith.

Mohammed Ali Fares, 19. Born in Venezuela and has Venezuelan passport. Has lived in Lebanon. After walking across the border from Mexico into California, he went to New York. He said he needed license to drive van for clothing company, but the FBI cannot find the firm.

Mostafa Said Abou-Shahin, 26 or 27: Said he is from Egypt and a carpenter. Living in the United States illegally. He said he could not get a driver's license in New York.

Smith Led Low-Impact Life Until Arrest, Fiery End

"Fair" Grades, Work History for Farm Girl

Article by Tom Bailey, Jr., and Richard Locker
(February 15th, 2002)
Baileytom@gomemphis.com
Locker@gomemphis.com

Mystery still shrouds her fiery death, and whether her fate was linked to a scam with violent global implications.

But old acquaintances and state records obtained Thursday by *The Commercial Appeal* shed some light on driver's license examiner Katherine Smith. She died early Sunday when her blazing car ran off US 72 in Fayette County. The wreck, which investigators now say was the result of arson, came the day before Smith was to appear before a federal magistrate judge for a detention hearing. She was

charged last week with helping her five co-defendants —
men with Middle Eastern ties, including three who are in
the country illegally — get Tennessee driver's licenses by
using false information.

The 49-year-old single mother of three adult children,
whose home stands in the shadow of Liberty Bowl Stadium,
grew up the child of sharecroppers in the Feathers Chapel
community north of Oakland in Fayette County, said Fayette
County Schools Supt. Myles Wilson.

His family lived and worked on the same large
farm.

"She was a fair student," Wilson said. "She made some
pretty good grades."

Smith attended the old Wirt Elementary and made Bs
and Cs at Fayette-Ware High, graduating in 1971, Wilson
said.

Later that same year, she landed the first of many
low-level jobs caring for mental health patients. Employers included Arlington Developmental Center, Lakeside
Behavioral Health System, and Memphis Mental Health
Institute (MMHI).

In 1992, after losing her job in a sweep of staff re-
ductions at MMHI, Smith landed work as a driver's license
examiner in Memphis. The job paid $15,480 a year, which
grew to $23,052 by the time of her death.

The boxes checked on her state job-performance
evaluations never dipped below "good," and often included
"superior" and "exceptional."

However, her personnel file reflects several disciplin-
ary actions taken against her over the years.

The most severe, of course, is dated Feb. 5, when she
was placed on administrative leave without pay. She was one
of six people arrested that day on federal charges of conspiring to provide Tennessee driver's licenses fraudulently.

Smith told investigators she and codefendant Khaled
Odtllah were friends who met when she took her car to his

Phillips 66 station, FBI agent J. Suzanne Nash testified Wednesday in a detention hearing for three of the codefendants.

The relationship was nothing more serious than their being friends, Nash added.

Smith was in the process of buying from Odtllah the 1992 Acura Legend in which she died. The car is still registered in Odtllah's name, Nash said.

Smith told the FBI agent that when Odtllah found out she was a driver's license examiner, he asked her if she could help get licenses for his "cousins."

After her arrest, Smith admitted helping Odtllah obtain driver's licenses six or seven times. Previously, the most severe reprimand Smith received in her state personnel field involved an accusation that she altered a document for an excused absence from work in 1990.

Car Fire Set Off Suspicions as Crew Fought It

By Bill Dries (dries@gomemphis.com)

The first firefighters at a fiery car wreck Sunday in Fayette County that killed a Memphis driver's license examiner thought it was suspicious even as they put out the flames.

Investigators began an immediate search for a device that might have triggered the intense fire, said the chief of the Piperton Fire Department.

The fire killed Katherine Smith, the examiner at the center of a federal investigation of an alleged scheme to issue driver's licenses fraudulently to men with Middle Eastern ties.

Piperton Fire Chief Steve Kellett said he, other firefighters and Tennessee Highway Patrol officers immediately thought the fire was suspicious. For one thing, the fire appeared to have started in the rear.

"The thing that was strange about it was how high up in the car it was. Normally, if it's from a gas line, it tends to burn up everything and works from the front to the back," Kellett said Thursday.

His description is consistent with testimony Wednesday by FBI agent J. Suzanne Nash before Magistrate Judge J. Daniel Breen. Nash said a group of six witnesses saw a fire in the back seat of Smith's car as the 1992 Acura Legend veered off a stretch of US 72 shortly before 1 a.m. The car crossed a ditch and landed against a utility pole.

"There was lots of damage for the amount of time it was on fire," Kellett said, noting that the fire also spread to the pole. "We would spray an area that normally would go out, but it would keep catching back. That gives you a feeling that there was something there."

Nash testified Wednesday that Smith's clothing had gasoline on it and that a dog trained to detect the presence of accelerants indicated such substances were in the car.

Samples of those materials are being tested, she said. She also said the fire was set but did not say how or who may have done it.

Kellett said two "bubble spots" on the back of the trunk indicate arson. "Something was pushing the fire. It was focusing it in a direction."

Victor Mordecai comments: First, the US State of Tennessee has become famous or infamous for issuing documentation in the form of driver's licenses to undocumented aliens. Secondly, those who killed Katherine Smith were outside of jail, lending credence to the theory that this gang of license dealers was much larger than the five in jail and were ready to kill for their secrets to disappear in the fiery death of Katherine Smith. Thirdly, Mohammed Ali Fares, the Venezuelan who had lived in Lebanon, walked across the border from Mexico into the US, went to New York, supposedly to become a driver for a garment company that the FBI could not locate. Throughout my two books *Is Fanatic Islam a Global Threat?* and

Christian Revival for Israel's Survival and in past newsletters, I talk of illegal entry or infiltration into the US across porous borders and a law enforcement woefully ignorant of the wily Moslem infiltrators. Another aspect that is increasingly apparent, the "Venezuelan connection" will have to be carefully scrutinized. Military dictator Chavez is working against the US and against Colombia by aiding the FARC rebels and is aligned with the Islamic world and with Castro's Cuba against the US.

C. PRIVATE INVESTIGATION

I began my private investigation regarding the bombing of the Murrah Federal Building in Oklahoma City the day it happened on April 19th, 1995, while I was in Tulsa, Oklahoma (page 265 of my book *Is Fanatic Islam a Global Threat?*). My newsletter of November 2001 adds new information gleaned from Jayna Davis, an investigative reporter, as well as a testimony from a Christian TV talk show host with whom I've been doing shows for over eight years.

Now the *Indianapolis Star* daily newspaper of February 17th, 2002, in an article by Jim Crogan confirms and adds to everything that was in my book as well as in the November newsletter. For example:

> There was an FBI-authorized all-points bulletin issued just minutes after the truck bomb exploded. The alert sent members of the Oklahoma City law enforcement searching for two Middle Eastern-looking men seen speeding away from the blast area in a brown Chevy pickup with tinted windows and a bug shield. The APB was abruptly cancelled several hours later without explanation.

> The week after the bombing, Jayna Davis, a veteran Oklahoma City reporter at KFOR-TV, got a tip, which began her investigation of a local property management company. Dr. Samir Khalil owns Samara Properties, and several employees told Davis they had seen a pickup matching the

APB's description at the office.

Davis discovered that Khalil, a Palestinian expatriate, had pled guilty in 1991 to several counts of insurance fraud and served eight months in a federal prison. Khalil's court papers indicated that the FBI investigated him for alleged connections to the Palestinian Liberation Organization. But Khalil vehemently denied any PLO links. And he's never responded to Jim Crogan's calls for comment.

Former Samara employees also told Davis that six months before the bombing, Khalil hired a group of Iraqi refugees to do painting and construction work. This group had allegedly fled Iraq to escape Saddam Hussein's regime. But a Samara employee told Davis he saw them cheering the terror attack and vowing to die in Saddam's service. Davis then used a surveillance camera to take pictures of these Iraqis. Eventually, she focused on one man, Hussain Alhussaini (also known as Al-Hussaini Hussain), who seemed to match the last FBI profile sketch and description of John Doe No. 2.

Over the next several months, she interviewed witnesses who said they saw McVeigh in the company of Middle Eastern-looking men in the days and hours before the bombing. Using KFOR's photo line-up, they identified that individual as Alhussaini.

Perhaps the most intriguing statements she collected came from a host of staff members at a motel near downtown Oklahoma City. They reported seeing McVeigh with a number of Middle Eastern men at the site in the months preceding the bombing. Using KFOR's photos, those men were identified as Samara employees. Alhussaini was included in that group.

The motel witnesses also said they saw several of the Iraqis moving large barrels around in the back of an old white truck. The barrels, they alleged, emanated a strong smell of diesel fuel, one of the key ingredients used in the Oklahoma City bomb. [Victor Mordecai comments: The other component of the bomb, a ton and a quarter of ammonium nitrate, was purchased in McPherson, Kansas, by three Iraqis. This is on page 265 of my book.]

Davis also discovered that a mysterious, brown Chevy pickup was impounded by the FBI on April 27, 1995. The pickup had been abandoned in an apartment building lot. According to the police report, the truck had been stripped of its license plate, inspection tags and all its vehicle identification numbers. It also was spray-painted yellow, but the original color was listed as brown. One resident at the complex told the FBI the driver was "clean-shaven, with an olive complexion, dark, wavy hair and broad shoulders," in his late 20's or early 30's and of Middle Eastern descent. [According to the *Yediot Ahronot* newspaper of April 20th, the brown Chevy was found abandoned at Dallas-Ft.Worth Airport — p. 265 of my book.]

During the course of her investigation, Davis made contact with Yossef Bodansky, executive director of the 13-year-old Congressional Task Force on Terrorism and Unconventional Warfare. Bodansky told Davis the task force had warned of an impending Islamic-sponsored terrorist attack in America's heartland back in 1995.

On February 27, 1995, the task force had issued its first confidential warning to federal agencies that Islamic terrorists "may soon strike Washington, D.C., specifically the Capitol and the White House." This confidential alert, which he said was quietly distributed to federal intelligence agencies and law enforcement, claimed the attacks were to begin after March 21, 1995.

"Striking inside the US is presently a high priority for Iran," stated the warning. The alert also stated that upcoming terrorist strikes might be directed against "airports, airlines and telephone systems." In light of September 11th, it was a telling note.

On March 3, 1995, the task force issued an update. This "super-sensitive" alert stated there was a "greater like-

lihood the terrorists would strike at the heart of the US."
Bodansky also told Davis that after the truck bombing, he
reviewed intelligence data that confirmed "Oklahoma City
was on the list of potential targets."

Bodansky gave Davis copies of the task force's
original alert and some of his confidential notes detailing the
update and Oklahoma City's target status. His material notes
an independent warning from Israeli intelligence a month
before the bombing. The warning indicated a terrorist attack
was impending and that "lily whites" would be activated.
Lily whites, Bodansky writes, were people without any
background or police records who would not be suspected
members of a terrorist group.

Now, President Bush has labeled Iran, Iraq and North
Korea an "axis of evil." And hyperbole aside, details of
Iran's alleged involvement in terrorism were included in last
summer's US Department of Justice indictment issued in
connection with the Khobar Towers attack in Saudi Arabia.
Moreover, Bodansky told Crogan that Iran and Iraq agreed
to cooperate in terrorist operations against the West. [Vic-
tor Mordecai: On page 258 of my book *Is Fanatic Islam a
Global Threat?* I reveal how Iran and Iraq were cooperating in the counterfeiting of US currency to destroy the US
economy.]

Over the past seven months, Jim Crogan reviewed all
of Davis' documents, including the material she got from
Bodansky. He also conducted his own follow-up interviews
and found no holes in her investigation. As for Davis, she's
tried twice to give her material to the FBI.

Jim Crogan is a free-lance writer and investigative
reporter based in Los Angeles. His work has appeared in
Newsweek, Time, the *Los Angeles Times* and other publica-
tions. His e-mail address is: jc1invrep@worldnet.att.net.

MILITARY INTELLIGENCE INFORMATION

As casualties continue to mount in the Israeli-Palestinian imbroglio, questions are asked about what Israeli Prime Minister Ariel Sharon's next move will be. There are Jews on the right and Jews on the left who, for their own reasons, are critical of Sharon for either doing too much or too little in dealing with Yasser Arafat's violence and madness.

In my opinion, there are three primary concerns facing Sharon.

First, Israel knows that it can shut down the Palestinian Authority within 24 hours and re-impose the Civil Administration after the guns have been confiscated and peace restored. Yet Sharon has opted for a much slower, drawn out standoff with Arafat. An incursion here and pinpoint attack there.

I think this is because what Israel can do with the Palestinians it cannot do with Saddam Hussein or the Ayatollahs' regime in Iran. To deal with the latter two, it is only the US that can, must, and will get the job done of terminating those regimes and liberating the Iraqi and Iranian people from those hateful, despotic regimes.

By an all-out attack against the Palestinians, Israel would be going against its own existential interests by undermining the US efforts in Iran and Iraq. With all the pain in losing over 328 people up to March 8th, 2002, as I write this newsletter, Israel's existence is not threatened by the Palestinian pinpricks. But Israel's existence is threatened by Iran and Iraq, which would not flinch for a moment at using ABC weapons (atomic, biological and chemical). Since it is in Israel's interest to remove Iran and Iraq from the circle of confrontation states facing Israel, Israel therefore will hold its fire so as not to disrupt whatever support, minimal as it may be, the Arabs-Moslems can provide to the US-led efforts in Iran-Iraq. Of course, an all-out attack on the Palestinians would unleash an all-out Islamic war against the US if the US did not "take out" Israel. (This is discussed in both my books *Fanatic Islam* and *Christian Revival for Israel's Survival.* The sixth fleet in the Mediterranean has its orders for this type of a nuclear strike against Israel should it threaten US oil supplies from the Arabs.)

Secondly, in my second book, *Christian Revival for Israel's Survival*, I discuss the plight of Slobodan Milosevic, who is now on trial in The Hague, capital of the Netherlands, for so-called war crimes. Milosevic is only guilty of doing his job: defending Yugoslavia (Serbia), its integrity, sovereignty and people. To do that, Milosevic had to order police and military action against Albanian Kosovar Moslem terrorists aided and abetted from across the border in Albania. Over 2,000 Islamic armed terrorists were killed by Serb forces.

For doing his job, Milosevic is now branded a war criminal by the globalists. CNN says he's the greatest war criminal since WWII. Now of course, Omar Bashir of Sudan has killed over 2 million black Christians. No matter. Saddam Hussein has killed over 2 million Moslems in Iran, Iraq and Kuwait. No matter. The Indonesian Islamic government and military have killed over 300,000 Christians in the last twenty years. No matter. And the list goes on and on of all those who have been killed by Moslems.

But Slobodan Milosevic killed 2,000 armed Islamic terrorists threatening the integrity of his country. For that the "globalists" have turned him into a war criminal.

The lesson is not lost on Israeli Prime Minister Ariel Sharon. For hundreds of years, the Lebanese Christians, Moslems and Druse factions have been slaughtering each other. When a couple of hundred Palestinian Moslems were slaughtered by Christian militiamen in the refugee camp of Sabra and Shatilla in September 1982, it was then Israeli Defense Minister Ariel Sharon who was blamed. Christians were killing Moslems, and a Jew was blamed! Of course, no one mentioned the fact that just previously to this heinous massacre of Moslems, there was an equally heinous murder of Christians at a place known as Tel e-Za'atar. No one mentions that Yasser Arafat was the direct cause of the deaths of 45,000 Palestinians in Jordan in "Black" September of 1970. Yasser Arafat broke over 23 written agreements with King Hussein and was threatening Jordan with total anarchy.

Arafat and the Palestinians were then exiled to Beirut, where Arafat proceeded to do the exact same shenanigans in Lebanon as he did in Jordan. Hundreds of thousands of Lebanese were killed in a civil war sparked by Arafat in 1975 in Lebanon. Is it any wonder that the murderous crimes of Sabra and Shatilla took place? The Lebanese Christians were trying to do what King Hussein of Jordan did in "Black September" of 1970.

But what concerns Prime Minister Ariel Sharon is not whether he is guilty or innocent, because we all know he is innocent. What is of concern is that he or any other Israeli leader can expect the same kind of treatment meted out to Slobodan Milosevic if and when Palestinian casualties (dead) reach 2,000 like in Kosovo. Even Shimon Peres this week warned Sharon of an international war crimes tribunal for this very reason. This is just another reason why Israel is careful to surgically pinpoint and destroy only the terrorists, and to leave the civilian population alone. (The Palestinians target Israeli innocent civilians, children, women and synagogues on Sabbath. That's OK. But when Israel retaliates and takes out the criminal orchestrators of the terrorism, that becomes a war crime in the eyes of the global leaders.)

Thirdly and finally, Israeli Prime Minister Ariel Sharon is the leader of the Israeli nation. He has successfully kept together a national unity coalition including the Labor Party. During a time of war, the nation must be united by a national unity coalition. Just as US President George W. Bush has maintained a surprisingly high popularity rating of close to 90%, so, too, has Israeli Prime Minister Ariel Sharon.

With all the pain that the families of the 328 dead Israelis have suffered, it must be remembered that in the same period of time of about 18 months, Israel has lost over 900 dead in traffic accidents. It must also be remembered that during this same period, Israel has absorbed over 90,000 new immigrants. Losing 328 Israelis, with all the pain involved to the individual families and even to the nation as a whole, is not an existential question. Finally, it must be remembered that over 200,000 Palestinians have emigrated during the last 18 months. Arafat has decided on war, not on peace. He has decided on guns and not bread and butter for his people. If Arafat does not allow the Palestinians to live in peace with Israel, they will choose to live in peace elsewhere. This is the third and final consideration of Israeli Prime Minister Ariel Sharon. The only question remaining is this: For how long will this situation continue?

Chapter VII
APRIL 2002 NEWSLETTER

Victor Mordecai's Monthly Message

The Emperor's New Clothes

In March-April, 2002, as Israeli tanks, troops and helicopters do the job of neutralizing terrorists and suicide bombers, Jerusalem is perceived by the world as a burdensome stone. The world press lauds the daily demonstrations by Arabs-Moslems throughout the world. Anti-Semitic acts such as the arson of synagogues and Jewish property in France and Belgium have become rife. This vandalism against Jews is reminiscent of events preceding the Holocaust. It is precisely a new holocaust by Muslims against Jews that I have been predicting and warning about since my first newsletter of October 2001. The Moslem plan is to kill Jews everywhere very soon.

Few in the world condemned the suicide bombings which took over 100 Israeli lives in the month of March alone, yet when Israel took the only action it could to defend its civilians, the whole world, including the US, our supposed ally, pounced on Israel demanding that it desist from doing precisely what must be done to stop the terrorism. Soon the Jews will start dying in the US and other countries of the Diaspora, and no one will condemn it. On the contrary, Israel and the Jews will be blamed for all the tribulations the world is going through.

Not only is Israel being pressured not to complete the job it set out to do to eradicate terrorist infrastructure, now talk has resumed of an imposed settlement forcing the Israelis to return to the abortive borders of June 5th, 1967. This appears under the guise of the supposed "peace plan" of Saudi Prince Abdullah, much praised by US President George W. Bush and his top advisors, all big players in the oil business.

UN Resolutions 242 and 338, bandied about all the time by the media, that Israel should hand over land for peace, never ever called on Israel to go back to the borders of 1967. On the contrary, they called for new borders, which are described in the resolutions as "secure, recognized and defensible," not the '67 borders, which then Secretary of State Henry Kissinger and then Israeli Foreign Minister Abba Eban described as "Auschwitz Extermination Camp borders."

How strange it is then, that so many respected world leaders such as US President George W. Bush and British Prime Minister Tony Blair and others swallow hook, line and sinker the Saudi proposal which would lead to the undoing or suicide of the State of Israel? And when Israel disagrees about committing suicide it is condemned.

Is this something new? Are these the new clothes of the Emperor?

In my books *Is Fanatic Islam a Global Threat?* and *Christian Revival for Israel's Survival,* I relate an experience that changed my life forever. In April 1991, I spoke before the Dallas Council on World Affairs, the Dallas branch of the Council on Foreign Relations. I presented a lecture on the realities of Israel's security needs and explained that Israel had fulfilled 93% of UN Resolutions 242 and 338.

Israel in June of 1974 gave up half of the Golan to Syria as part of the Disengagement Talks led by Henry Kissinger. And then in 1981, Israel handed back Sinai a 3rd time to Egypt for a peace agreement. Half the Golan represented 2% of the total of lands Israel was forced to take in wars of self-defense and Sinai 91%, hence 93%.

I explained that for Israel to survive, it must keep its troops on the Jordan River, the other half of the Golan Heights and Gaza. Any retreat from those borders would be tantamount to the "Dutch boy pulling his finger out of the dike." We could give land up to the Palestinians for their autonomy, but withdrawal from the above three borders was like committing suicide militarily. It could not and would never happen.

I also told the honorable well-heeled Dallas people that if the Arabs wanted peace, they needed to compromise. We compromised 93%. The Arabs should compromise 7%. (By the way, in 1994, we made peace with Jordan, giving it lands in the Arava valley — another 2% — and we gave Arafat 2% of land for his autonomy areas. So Israel has already given up 97%. Now the Arabs have to compromise only 3%!) [By the way, in June 2000, then Israeli Prime Minister Ehud Barak offered the Arabs 98.5% and Arafat's response was to walk away only to return later with his guns firing as part of this new intifada al-Quds in September 2000.]

Their answer to me was: "We don't care about 91% or 93%. Israel must return to the borders of 1967. We don't even care about UN Resolutions 242 and 338. Israel stands alone and the only thing that made America great was oil, the steady price of oil and the steady supply of oil. And we're not going to let the Jews get in the way."

My Christian friends there that night answered before I could: My patron Eric Gustavson from Cleburne, Texas, said: "You call yourselves Christians? What made America great is not the barrel of oil. What made America great was Jesus Christ!" His daughter Carol Burton said: "Besides, it says in the Bible: Those who bless Israel are blessed, and those who curse Israel are cursed."

That night changed my life forever. Until that night I hated the cross. I really wasn't sure either whether or not I really liked the Christians. Then it dawned on me that the Christians were not our best friends. They were our only friends.

I answered the Dallas Council people by saying that 6 million Jews died in the Holocaust because of the cynical manipulations of anti-Semitic Americans such as Under Secretary of State Breckenridge Long, who made sure to it that Jews in Nazi-occupied Europe would never get visas to the US to escape Hitler. He even blocked the German refugee ship St. Louis from disembarking in Havana, Cuba, with over 800 Jewish German refugees with valid visas to Cuba in May 1939. This was because of loyalty to the Arabs, their petroleum and petrodollars. Hitler was not alone. He had the Moslems, the British Colonial Office with their "White Papers" blocking Jewish immigration to Palestine and the US State Department under Roosevelt as his accomplices in the killing of 6 million Jews for a barrel of oil during and before WWII.

In 1998, I received a testimony from a pastor who was a sailor in his first lifetime career about 20 years ago. This testimony is in my second book, *Christian Revival for Israel's Survival*. The US Navy was considering him for promotion. During the interview to test his loyalty to the US, he was asked what he would do if he were captain of his ship and ordered to launch a nuclear strike at Tel Aviv. He laughed and answered: "I'm a Christian. God is not a liar. He would never allow Israel to be nuked. Secondly, I wouldn't want to be on that ship, because God would take out the nuclear weapon, and the ship, and everyone aboard." Very soon, he found himself out of the Navy and became a pastor. I am not talking about a Soviet, or Arab or Moslem ship. I am talking about the US Navy nuking Israel.

During my cross-country travels to over 400 churches in the US, this testimony has repeated itself many times from many pastors who were in the Navy in their first lifetime careers and were asked this same question of loyalty. The US has interests: money, oil and global. Israel and the Jews have always been really rather marginal. US Administration praise of Israel is merely lip service.

I will never forget September 11th, 2001, a day that will live in infamy — even worse than the Japanese attack on Pearl Harbor. All of a sudden, we were all in the same boat, or so it seemed. The alarm went off, but somebody in Washington pushed the "snooze" button.

But I will also never forget that two weeks before September 11th, George W. Bush signed a secret agreement with Saudi Arabia that Israel would be delivered an ultimatum by which it would be forced to return to the borders of 1967, the Auschwitz Extermination Camp borders. Then two weeks later, God judged America. (By the way, I take this opportunity to suggest to my readers to get the book by John McTernan and Bill Koenig: *Israel: The Blessings and the Curses*. The book basically researches newspaper articles reporting terrible disasters — floods, tornados, earthquakes, and terrorism — that happen every time to America when it goes against God, the Bible, and Israel.)

Very simply, those who attacked the US on September 11th were the radicals, the revolutionary Moslems. But Bush and those like him do their multi-trillion dollar business not with the revolutionaries, but rather with the "evolutionaries," those kind Saudi businessmen who instruct American schools on how to ramrod Islam down the throats of American schoolchildren when the Bible and the God of Abraham, Isaac and Jacob are forbidden in US schools. He consorts with those who have controlling stock interests in banks, corporations, the media and Wall Street. He succumbs to the State Department with the blood of six million Jews on its hands, as well as millions of black Christians in the Sudan and countless other Christians slaughtered, enslaved and persecuted by the Moslems throughout the world, never mentioned by the US media and State Department.

So why would Israel be an exception to the rule today? Just as Serbia was sacrificed to the Moslems on a gold platter, so will Israel be. Just as Pristina, Kosovo, the Jerusalem of the Serbian Orthodox Church, was surrendered to Islam, so would Jewish Jerusalem be. Just as Slobodan Milosevic is described by CNN as one of the worst war criminals since WWII and is now on trial in The Hague, Netherlands, so too, will Ariel Sharon be described, even though we did not harm civilians, but only armed terrorists shooting at us and blowing themselves up in restaurants, hotels, and synagogues. It doesn't matter. The game is sold out to the petrodollar and oil supplies. Israel is the sacrifice on the altar of Saudi oil.

Saudi Arabia is in control. Its so-called peace plan rejects UN Resolutions 242 & 338 and calls for a full and total withdrawal to the impossible suicide borders of 1967.

Yasser Arafat, to whom Israel and the world were so generous, rejects UN Resolutions 242 & 338. It was all a lie on his part. He succeeded and is still succeeding in pulling the wool over everyone's eyes except ours. The US, like Arafat, it seems, rejects UN Resolutions 242 & 338 when it accepts the Saudi plan. Everyone, it seems, wants Israel to commit suicide.

Such delusional, inept, and self-serving thinking by the leadership of the West brings us back to the Neville Chamberlain approach of sacrificing the Sudetenland to the Nazis, which inevitably led to the destruction of Czechoslovakia. Not only is Israel not Czechoslovakia, but such delusional thinking by President Bush will lead to a nuclear cataclysmic war. This is because the Arabs/ Moslems feel, and with good reason, that Bush is with them and against Israel. Bush himself through such behavior will bring about an Armageddon war making the losses of WWII pale in comparison. At the same time, the Moslems will not spare America. Remember September 11th, 2001, anyone? America is still the ultimate and primary target of globalist, imperialist, expansionist Islam.

So when US President George W. Bush said just a few days ago that the US was Israel's best friend, and that Britain's Tony Blair was a friend of Israel, I took it with a few grains of salt. The Saudi plan is that Israel will be sacrificed for a barrel of oil. Britain and the US are again accomplices to the planned Islamic genocide of the Jews. But rest assured. It will never happen. God in Heaven will never let it happen. The time has come to say clearly: The emperor has no clothes on. Not in Ramallah, Riyadh, Washington or London.

MILITARY INTELLIGENCE

El-Solayil Missile Base — Saudi Desert

Article by Ronen Bergman in
Israeli Hebrew daily *Yediot Ahronot* of
March 27th, 2002

The El-Solayil desert oasis has been turned into a military base. Over the last few years, launch pads have been added. Access roads, command centers, a huge residential neighborhood. In addition a total territory of 1,400 square kilometers has been added, including unlimited bunkers for the storage of long-range missiles. The most recent peace initiative bestowed upon Saudi Arabia the image of moderation, but is only one side of a duplicitous game it is playing. Intelligence sources are disturbed, but official Israel, under heavy US pressure, is keeping silent.

The computer at the command center of the CIA at Langley, Virginia, USA, chooses random code-names for subjects and operations it is following. "Deep Blue" is the code-name for a cluster of worrisome pieces of information that have been received at the Agency since the beginning of 1988. The source of most of this information — eavesdropping conducted by the National Security Agency (NSA) for monitoring signals of the administration and the military of China. According to these signals, Saudi Arabia has been conducting advanced negotiations with China for the purpose of purchasing dozens of ground-to-ground missiles capable of carrying nuclear payloads.

The intelligence communities of the US and Israel were thunderstruck primarily because until that stage, they knew nothing about this. At the CIA and at the technical level of the Israeli Military Intelligence research division, compasses were taken out and radii drawn. The missiles that the Saudis intended to purchase, CSS-2 as they are called in the professional language, Dong-Feng 3, have a range of 2,500 - 3,500 km. The whole Middle East, parts of the former USSR and, of course, all of Israel are under the range of this missile.

The US and Israel did not understand why Saudi Arabia, professing a moderate political stance, needed this missile, that at that time represented China's vanguard atomic offensive weapon. The concern increased when these reports were reconfirmed by the generous financial support the Saudis were providing for the development of "the first Islamic bomb," as Pakistan's atomic program was described.

Israeli and US intelligence undertook broad, all-encompassing operations with a double objective: collecting details regarding the purchase and an attempt to learn what the Saudis really intended to do with the missiles. The operation was partially successful. It turns out that the Saudis purchased 120 missiles, and with them 12 launchers. A special surprise was in store for the US, when it became clear that the Saudi negotiator was none other than US State Department favorite Prince Bandar bin-Sultan, the charming ambassador in Washington.

The Saudis paid a fortune for the missiles. The Chinese received from their Saudi interlocutors the feeling that money would not be an obstacle and that Prince Bandar would pay any amount that would gain entry for his country into the prestigious [atomic-ballistic — VM] club.

The Blooming of the Desert with Missiles

The first CSS-2 missiles arrived in June 1990 and were deployed in two places south of Riyadh: most at the giant complex built north of the El Solayil desert oasis, about 500 km from the capital, and a smaller quantity at Al-Jofar, 100 km from the city. The remainder of the missiles arrived later.

About two weeks ago, the "Ikonos," the best civilian

photography satellite in the world, took a series of photographs at the behest of *Yediot Ahronot* over Al-Solayil. The pictures sent down from the heavens, and shown in this article for the first time, proved that over the last few years the Saudis have invested tremendous amounts in developing the "King Khaled" secret military city.

Compared to previously available pictures of the region, taken by the French satellite "Spot" in 1995, the intensive construction in the region stretching over an area of hundreds of square kilometers in the desert is clearly visible. The Saudis added missile launchers, approach roads, command centers, a huge residential area, a mosque for engineers and members of the staff, as well as a new and tremendous area, full of incalculable bunkers with conventional and non-conventional weapons, with a storage capacity of over 60,000 cubic meters. East of Al-Sulayil, out of the range of the cameras, is a Saudi Air Force base with two squadrons of Tornado jet fighters.

The enormous missile base has a support area and two launching areas 6 km apart from each other which are positioned in narrow and hidden ravines.

There are 33 buildings in the support area. Eight of them are buildings large enough to store the CSS-2 missiles that are each 24 meters in length. The launch area includes scattered buildings and a concrete launch pad.

In each of the two launch areas, a 50-meter-long unidentified building covered over with earth was located. So were two underground missile storage warehouses, as well as garages and two large support buildings.

In comparison to the photographs taken in 1995, a large expansion is noticeable in the administration and residential areas. It is possible to clearly see command installations, residential areas, a large mosque, soccer field, a spacious park, car parking lots and more. The airstrip of the local airport has been lengthened to over 3km [2 miles].

The weapons storage compound, spread out on over 1,400 square kilometers, is much too large to be merely a CSS-2 missile base, and it evidently serves other secret purposes. It is possible to identify clearly more than 60 fortified buildings for weapons storage.

For a long time, it was not clear to American intelligence where the Saudis were hiding their missiles. At first it was thought they were at the Al-Harj Air Force Base complex, about 50 km south of Riyadh. Only ground level intelligence and pinpoint satellite surveillance led the CIA to the secret military city of Al-Solayil. The "Ikonos" pictures were received according to the coordinates that were obtained beforehand by American intelligence.

The updated information, already in the hands for some time of the Israeli and US intelligence services, was the cause for not inconsiderable headaches. This was reinforced after September 11th, when it became clear to everyone, really to everyone, that it could happen, and there are those who are sorry today about the obedient line Israel adopted regarding Saudi Arabia because of US pressure.

All Enemies and Opponents Are Bought Out

The purchase of the missiles was part of a general Saudi trend to achieve military power, which turned it at the beginning of the 90's into the biggest purchaser of weapon-ries in the Third World after Iraq.

The US Administration felt betrayed. For only a few years after the great efforts by President Reagan, to ratify the sale of AWACS early warning aircraft to the Saudis, all of a sudden this deal pops up, contrary to the declared policy of Riyadh, and on the surface with no practical purpose.

The furious Americans asked for clarifications. The Saudis explained that they needed the missiles in order to defend themselves from Iran (then thought of as the most serious regional threat), and that it was decided to purchase them from China, after the US refused to sell them F15 fighters in 1985. In the end, it is true that 24 planes were sold to them but the missile project, said the Saudis, was already under way.

King Fahd promised that Saudi Arabia would not place chemical or nuclear warheads on these missiles, nor would they use them in a first strike. In order to lessen concerns even more, Saudi Arabia signed the nuclear non-proliferation treaty (NPT). The king promised not to take part in the development of atomic bombs, and also promised that after the missiles were in place, military activities at the Al-Solayil area would cease.

Fahd, how should we say, did not exactly keep his word. The Saudis promised they would allow US inspectors at the Al-Solayil site, if Washington would promise that Israel would not attack them, but in the end, they refused to allow inspections at the site.

After the Gulf War, the Saudis became the "underdogs" and succeeded in diverting the anger elsewhere, especially at Iran and Iraq. Neither did Israel in discussions with other countries raise the Saudi issue.

In 1990, when the missiles began arriving at Al-Solayil, Israel wanted to stir up a storm but the US was satisfied with assurances by King Fahd, and instructed Israel to maintain a low profile. Israel sufficed with a protest, but this was just a drop in the ocean compared to the campaigns it was waging against countries such as Syria and Iraq.

In the case of Saudi Arabia, details about its involvement in the Pakistani atomic project became known, and that Saudi Arabia was bankrolling terrorist organizations. It was also clear that the House of Saud was beyond any doubt corrupt to the foundations and lusted for unrestrained power, buying out any and all enemies and opponents. The US kept silent and forced Israel to do the same.

For the Saudis, September 11th reshuffled the deck. Many in the US in and out of the Administration felt free to get off their chests something that had been accumulating for a long time. Four months ago, it was Pentagon strategist Richard Perle who said: "In my opinion, the Saudis are not part of the solution. They are part of the problem.... We had all reasons to assume that they were grateful for our saving them during Desert Storm — and we were wrong."

The Pentagon did not limit itself to declarations. Updated photos arriving from "Ikonos" point to massive building of American bases in the Gulf. For example, the giant airbase at Qatar was intended to replace at least partially the bases in Saudi Arabia.

Putting the Eggs in All the Baskets

Publicity about what is happening in Saudi Arabia, together with the enormous anger following September 11th, caused a deterioration of the prestige of the Saudi regime, which was supposedly Western and enlightened. Leading analysts in the US press published highly critical columns about the royal house.

But the Saudis were quick to recover. Dr. Uzi Arad, formerly head of the research branch of the Mossad, and political adviser to Prime Minister Netanyahu, knows the subject from up close: "The Saudis operate a well-oiled lobbying and propaganda machine in Washington. They correctly identified the shortfall as a result of the terrorist attacks and were quick to counterattack.

"The publication by Thomas Friedman about Prince Abdallah's initiative must not be seen as merely incidental, but as part of a much wider sophisticated process which was intended to restore the status quo ante showing Saudi Arabia again to be a moderate and pragmatic country, and to turn it into a primary axis between the US and the Arab countries."

The new political initiative, with its virtual Middle Eastern innovation, does not, from the Saudi perspective, conflict with its continued support for terrorism, well-oiled kowtowing to regional powers, as extreme and crazy as they might be.

This is basically a duplicitous game, the only purpose of which is the continued hegemony of the Saud family in the Arabian peninsula, by means of putting the eggs, and there are many of them, in all the possible baskets.

Professor Yossi Kostiner, Head of the School of History at Tel-Aviv University, has been dealing for years with the Saudi regime: "What we are dealing with here is very tough tribal/male-oriented politics. The Saudis are placing the emphasis on defending the regime, by means of diplomacy, shrewd politics and caution, and not necessarily by means of force."

In his words, "US forces in the Gulf as well as the emergency facilities, intended for receiving additional forces, are intended for protecting the kingdom from a military challenge, primarily from Iran or Iraq. Iraq attacked Saudi Arabia with missiles, and Iran took over control in 1992 of the Island of Abu Musa, at the entrance to the Persian Gulf, and it is administered since then by both countries."

In spite of the confidence in the strength of the US, and that it will not allow Saudi Arabia to be conquered, there is an attempt by the Saudis to flatter the Iranians, in order to keep the latter as a regional counterweight to the Iraqis.

Beyond the danger of a frontal military confrontation, the Saudis identify other threats to the security of the Saud dynasty: a revolution from within, or terrorism supported by groups like Al-Qaeda or from states like Iraq.

"The Saudi desire to ensure quiet with the help of flattery or much money is directly opposed to US policy in the region. In spite of this, the Americans acquiesced to the relations with Iran, and also later swallowed the Saudi support for terrorism."

The duplicity of the Saud family expresses itself in nearly all fields. For external purposes, the Saudi administration puts on a display of enlightenment, Western behavior, and its representatives are most active in European diplomatic communities and in the US. The Saudi oil barons often give orders in London and New York. But, on the darker side, there is another reality, and the relationship with Iran and Iraq is an excellent example of this.

At first, Saudi Arabia explained its purchase of Chinese missiles as a reaction to Iranian aggression towards Saudi Arabia. When asked whether he would give orders to use the missiles, King Fahd responded: "If we are forced to, we will. Our patient opposition should not cause the Iranians to think that we are weak. We are hoping they won't make problems for us, because we don't want to test the will of our people to defend themselves."

On the other hand, Saudi Arabia has over the years adopted a position of compromise toward Teheran — and this position became stronger with the election of Khatami as president. The Saudis today support Iran financially, issue fraternal declarations with the Khomeinistic Islamic regime, and oppose any US initiative to attack it.

The same applies to Iraq. In spite of the hatred felt by the leadership in Riyadh toward Saddam Hussein, whom they see as a megalomaniac who broke the basic rules of the tribe, and in spite of Saddam's attack on Saudi Arabia with missiles and threatening to invade their territory, like he did in Kuwait, the Saudis today are doing everything they can to torpedo the expected American attack on Iraq.

Massive Support for Terrorism

For years, Saudi Arabia was not in the center of Israel's concerns. The US, on the other hand, knew well what was going on there, and according to assessments by Israeli sources well acquainted with CIA, it was clear that there was a system of commissions between the princes and themselves, as well as toward outside elements. The Americans saw clearly just how corrupt things were, and the ease with which it was possible for officials in the Riyadh regime to earmark giant budgets from this clause to another clause in order to cover themselves.

An investigation published about three months ago in the *New Yorker* revealed US National Security Agency eavesdropping tapes during the 90's. The broadcasts paint a picture of a regime that is growing increasingly corrupt, distancing itself from the people, from the religious. A weak and frightened regime, it is ensuring its future by paying off hundreds of millions of dollars in protection to extremist organizations seeking its overthrow.

In 1996, Saudi funds supported Usama bin Laden's Al-Qaeda, as well as extremist organizations in Afghanistan, Lebanon, Yemen, central Asia and throughout the Persian Gulf.

According to the *New Yorker*, in 1994, Mohammed Al-Hilawi, first secretary of the Saudi delegation to the UN, defected and sought asylum in the US. According to his lawyer, Michael Wilds, he brought with him 14,000 internal government documents, showing royal family corruption and human rights violations and support for terrorism. He claimed that he was in possession of proof that the Saudis had provided technical and financial assistance to the Hamas, and a meeting was held in the office of his lawyer with two FBI agents and an assistant District Attorney. "They were given samples of the documents, and we put them on the table," Wilds said. "But the agents refused to receive them." The lawyer and his client did not hear from the federal agencies ever again. Al-Hilawi, who won asylum, now lives in hiding.

From a series of secret internal memorandums of the FBI, made available to *Yediot Ahronot*, it turns out that in 1992 it was already then clear to American intelligence that Saudi Arabia was a supporter of Hamas. Thus, for example, in a memorandum written by FBI special agent Robert White, of the Anti-Terrorism Task Force of the FBI in Chicago, that in 1993, Mohammed Saleh, one of the heads of the Hamas in the US, received $110,000 from a mysterious Saudi association by the name of Faisal Financial, registered in Geneva, Switzerland, to his account number 8060700 at the "National Bank of Chicago." Behind the association, according to the FBI, is a group of Saudi banks, with the full knowledge of the regime in Riyadh.

In another case mentioned in the memorandum the Hamas asked to circumvent strict US laws against organized crime and money laundering. For that purpose, the members of the associations entered into complex and Gordian business deals in real estate, the only purpose of which being the transfer of funds into the US, without this being registered as such in the bank computers, and being exposed to the scrutiny of the FBI.

"The Koran Institute," identified by the FBI as a front organization of the Hamas, undertook a series of money transfers under the direction of a Saudi businessman, Yassin Kadi, the president and owner of "Kadi International," which serves actually as a front for the Saudi government. With the completion of the deal, $820,000 was transferred from Mr. Kadi, who created a labyrinth of front companies, to the "Koran Institute," and from there to the Hamas.

Professor Kostiner: "There is no doubt that the Saudi administration knows exactly what the Hamas is. They pay ransom to many organizations, and according to the information in my possession, they actually had a working arrangement with Al-Qaeda. True, Bin Laden was expelled from Saudi Arabia, and his citizenship was revoked in 1994, but his family, which continued to maintain close relations with him, allowed him to continue to work, and in exchange, Al Qaeda did not act against Saudi Arabia.

[Victor Mordecai: According to the book *Usama bin Laden: The Man Who Declared War on the US* by Yosef Bodansky, US President Bill Clinton cut the same deal with Usama bin Laden by which the US in the mid-1990's paid off Bin Laden with megabuck taxpayer dollars for Al Qaeda to take its terrorism elsewhere. This also helps to explain the cover-up regarding the Islamic connection to the Oklahoma City bombing in April 1995 and the shooting down of TWA800 in the summer of 1996. Clinton wanted the US economy to prosper, and so he paid "protection" to Usama bin Laden to ensure "industrial quiet." The Saudis did it. The Europeans did it. Clinton did it. The only problem is that the chickens came home to roost with the attacks on September 11th.]

"The Saudis have been doing this for a long time — all the way back to the 60's, in other words, since the money, the big money, began to accumulate in their coffers. They buy out their enemies, they bribe and reconcile, and alongside this, they support Islamic causes. In the 1970's they succeeded in this way to avert PLO attacks against Saudi Arabia.

"To a certain extent, the Saudis got themselves into a trap. The moment they paid ransom once, they could not refuse the next time, and they created a list of individuals and organizations now on the payroll for industrial quiet."

And when Saudi involvement was required for the investigation of attacks, this help was not given happily. Examples are not lacking.

On April 7th, 1995, the Americans were sure that Imad Mughnieh, operations officer for the Hizbullah and No. 2 most wanted in the world, was that close to being apprehended, tried and perhaps given the electric chair. That same day, he was flying with MEA (Middle East Airlines) from Khartoum, Sudan, to Beirut, Lebanon, with a scheduled stop in Riyadh. Sources in the FBI told us that the Saudis foiled the plan and prevented the plane from landing in the kingdom, claiming that there was a malfunction in the airport's technical computer.

An extreme lack of cooperation was also noted during the investigation of the attacks against the US Army base at

Dhahran in 1996, where 19 American soldiers were killed, as well as a year before at the Khobar Towers, where 7 people died. FBI and CIA teams arriving to investigate the incidents reported a cold Saudi attitude, hiding evidence, and a feeling that from Riyadh's perspective, it was preferable to bury the whole affair quietly. The Americans solved the riddle of the attacks, carried out by the "Saudi Hizbullah." The royal family really did have that to hide.

The attack on the USS *Cole* in 2000 was perpetrated by Saudi citizens of Yemenite origin. Here, too, the Saudi security services did not assist in solving this case.

But the peak was after September 11th when the Saudis refused to assist in checking the backgrounds of 19 men, half of whom were Saudi nationals, who took part in the attacks on the World Trade Center and the Pentagon. This group is just a tiny part of the thousands of Saudis who have joined the extremist organizations throughout the world.

Bribery Opens Up All the Pants

Beyond America's need for Arab support, there is another matter causing it to be hesitant in any matter involving Saudi Arabia: big Saudi money that has been "invested" in Washington, DC, over the last 30 years. Fahd's regime was a big financial contributor to the aggressive campaign waged by the Reagan administration, headed by the CIA head, William Casey, against what appeared to be a Russian presence in South America, and then in the war of the US against the Soviets in Afghanistan.

Even when the oil revenues decreased considerably, the Saudis had enough money to be able to approach the right elements in the American capital. A senior American official said this week: "A Saudi diplomat once smilingly quoted to me an Arab saying: 'Bribery opens up all the pants.' It would be interesting to conduct a survey about the number of senior people in the administration during recent decades who have not slipped into their pockets, or into organizations for whom they were seeking favors, Saudi money.

"This is not clear or blatant bribery. The Saudis can finance for this or that secretary a festive lecture at Harvard University, and pay him $50,000. If he is not able to receive these monies during his term of office, he is assured of a career as a lecturer when he retires." (Look at former president Bill Clinton today.)

The Saudis and their friends in the oil industry play an extraordinary role in the Texan administrations of the Bushes. For example, the Texas company Haliburton has a number of subsidiaries active in Saudi Arabia. This company was run for many years by Vice President Dick Cheney.

During the Clinton Administration, the situation was similar. The Saudi government donated $24 million to Arkansas University, which was close to the President's heart. The Saudis also acquired Boeing aircraft in the billions of dollars, and assisted his administration in a number of initiatives of his in the Middle East.

According to Bob Barr, formerly a senior operations person in the CIA, the CIA was asked during that time not to conduct any dangerous intelligence gathering operations in Saudi Arabia, and in effect became almost completely blind to what was taking place among the royal family.

Barr was appointed in 1993 to CIA station director in Dushanbe, Tajikistan, on the border with Afghanistan. He relates that they watched hopelessly the Islamic fundamentalists who preceded the Taliban, who were supported by the Saudis, as they were building the training camps, mobilizing supporters and were conducting campaigns in countries bordering the former USSR. His reports and warnings were received with apathy.

The Saudis never scrimped anywhere in the world, and they displayed a special involvement in parts of Yugoslavia.

They were the first to respond positively to requests by the leader of the Moslem majority in Bosnia, Alija Izetbegov-itch, for financial aid, and they assisted in undermining the embargo that prevented Bosnia from arming itself legally. The result: Today there are more religious Moslems in Bosnia than there were in 1992, and what used to be historic mosques became again active worship mosques, and not only museums for tourists. New, shining mosques are being built, usually in the kitsch style of the Persian Gulf. Thus, for example, the new Saudi mosque in Sarajevo, which looks like a space station, is so different from the local tradition. Also, Islamic educational centers have popped up one after another, in Sarajevo and other cities.

The number one organization for financing terrorist activities in Bosnia is the "Supreme Saudi Committee for Welfare." On October 18th, 2001, hundreds of peace force soldiers surrounded the Committee for Welfare offices in Sarajevo, shot the locked doors open, and broke in. Large trucks brought to the site were loaded up with the contents of the offices — computers, documents, lists, pictures, videotapes. Everything, including $200,000 in cash that was hidden away in a safe, was confiscated.

From a meticulous search of the documents, it was revealed that Saudi private and governmental sources had sent, through the Committee for Welfare, more than $800 million since the end of the civil war in Bosnia. There were clear lists as to what to do with $600 million, and "according to the material that was confiscated, we fear very much that the rest of the money was used for terrorist purposes," said senior sources in the Bosnian government.

Stocks in the "Islamic Bomb"

As for the Pakistani atomic project, more is hidden than visible. The excellent relations between Pakistan and Saudi Arabia stretch out to many additional aspects of intimate military cooperation, including Pakistani military visits to Saudi Arabia, unilateral declarations of the regime in Riyadh in favor of Islamabad.

American and Israeli intelligence investigations regarding this affair began in the middle of the 80's, when it became clear where Pakistan, a poor country, was obtaining the enormous amount of funds needed for the project. From the Saudi perspective, this was a continuation of the traditional policy of supporting religious objectives ("The Islamic Bomb"), involvement in important projects in the area and flattering an influential power that would soon become a nuclear club member.

On November 22nd, 1990, President George Bush, Sr., received a highly classified document which dealt with the possibility of arming Chinese missiles with Pakistani nuclear warheads on Saudi soil. The Saudis, according to the information, feared Saddam Hussein so much that they demanded from the Pakistanis that they deliver the Saudi share or "stock" in the atomic project.

To this day, it is not clear if this information was accurate or false. Everyone agrees that the scenario is not impossible. According to the information that has accumulated in the US, the Saudis not only paid between half a billion to one billion dollars to the Pakistani atomic project, but they also made sure to "grease" the hands of one private person, the chief scientist, Ahmed K. Khan, who is also connected with the Iranians.

A Non-Conventional Warhead Aimed at Population Centers

The CSS-2 missile (Dong-Feng 3) is the main weapon of the Chinese non-conventional arsenal. It is based primarily on the Russian missile R-12/SS-4. (In spite of the fact that the Russians refused to sell the missile to China, the latter attained the technical details necessary, evidently through espionage, to produce the missile.) The missile was test-fired for the first time by the Chinese at the Shuang shi tso site in 1967.

The missile is propelled by liquid fuel, which is relatively easy to store, in four engines with a propulsion force of 64 tons. The missile may be launched directly from within the storage facility (such as Al Solayil) or from a mobile launch pad.

The missile was designed to carry a nuclear, chemical or biological warhead as well as conventional warhead, and was intended to provide an answer to a possible threat from the USSR. It is not an accurate missile, and has a range of error of 2.5 km. In light of this, the missile is not intended for pinpoint targets but rather large targets such as highly populated areas.

This missile is also used by the Chinese for launching satellites into space, and there are at least two versions of this missile. The first has a range of 2,650 km and flies at an altitude of somewhere between 100 to 550 km and carries a single nuclear warhead weighing 2,150 kg.

In 1983, the Chinese initiated a program to lengthen the range of the CSS-2 to 3,500 km. The payload, according to some reports, can include 3 nuclear warheads.

The last experimental launch took place on August 21st, 2001, when China conducted the largest-scale war games in the last decade. The Dong Feng 3 was fired from the test grounds in northern China, and US military satellites followed it until it landed near the Mongolian border.

When the sale of the missiles to the Saudis was leaked, the then Deputy Foreign Minister, Wu Shuwa Qien, adamantly defended the sale: "The Saudi government has promised us they will not transfer the missiles, will not use them in a first strike, and will only use them in self-defense. We believe Saudi Arabia will keep its word."

"The sale of the missiles," added the minister, "would contribute to stability in Saudi Arabia in particular, and the Middle East in general."

About a thousand Chinese engineers participated in building the site, and today as well, there are at the site on a permanent basis, Chinese engineers responsible for the ongoing maintenance of the missiles. A thirty-year contract between the two nations was signed.

The Best Satellite in the World

The Ikonos satellite, which provided *Yediot Ahronot* with the pictures for this report, is the best commercial photography satellite in the world. This is the first commercial satellite that collects photographs with a resolution of one meter (yard). In other words, one can identify objects on the ground the size of which is one meter, on condition that they are distant from other objects, and have special visual characteristics. Individual human beings cannot be seen.

The "Ikonos" was built by Lockheed Martin and is operated by the "Space Imaging" company.

The pictures were analyzed by John Pike, CEO and owner of "Global Security," and Tim Brown, senior researcher of the company.

Saudi-Funded Terrorist Net in Florida

March 20, 2002 from John Loftus

For twenty years I have served without compensation as a lawyer for federal whistleblowers within the US intelligence community. In the last year, I have received highly classified information from several of my confidential clients concerning a Saudi covert operation. The Saudi relationship is so sensitive that, for more than a decade, federal prosecutors and counter-terrorist agents have been ordered to shut down their investigations for reasons of foreign policy.

I am filing a lawsuit in Hillsborough County Court to expose the manner in which Florida charities were used as a money laundry for tax-deductible terrorism. The complaint cites specific testimony including highly classified information that has never been released before. Simply put, the Saudi Government was laundering money through Florida charities run by USF Professor Sami Al Arian for the support of terrorist groups in the Middle East. Through the Al Arian network and others, the Saudi Government secretly funded Al Qaida, Hamas and Islamic Jihad.

The Saudi purpose was twofold: the destruction of the State of Israel and the prevention of the formation of an independent Palestinian State. Two particular terrorist groups, Hamas and the Palestinian Islamic Jihad, were specifically chosen and funded by the Saudis for their willingness to undermine Arafat's Palestinian Authority. The secret Saudi goal was to create such animosity between Israel and the Palestinian Authority that it would wreck any chance for the creation of an independent Palestinian State. Their tactics specifically called for the intimidation or murder of those Palestinians who were willing to work with Israel for peace. To put it bluntly, the covert Saudi network in Florida funded the murders of fellow Muslims for the crime of wanting to create the first democratic Arab state.

Whatever harm the Israelis may have done, they did build an excellent public education system, including several universities, for the benefit of their Palestinian neighbors. That was the problem. While literacy in the Arab world is below 50%, in Israel it is 97%. Israel is the only place in the Middle East where an Arab woman can vote. After 50 years, Israel has created the first Arab class exposed to democracy, literacy and Western values. To the Saudis, a democratic Palestinian nation would be a cancer in the Arab world, a destabilizing example of freedom that would threaten Arab dictators everywhere. As King Fahd said, "Next to the Jews, we hate the Palestinians the most." The harder the Israelis and Palestinians worked for peace, the more money King Fahd poured into his murder for hire program.

The Saudi Government has already begun its spin operations, claiming that this terror network was a rogue operation financed by a radical Saudi businessman without the support or knowledge of the Saudi Government.

The truth is that many of the Saudi princes, notably Prince Bandahar and Prince Alwaheed, are good and loyal friends of America who want to lead Saudi Arabia into the modern world. Unfortunately, they are now in the minority in their own country. King Fahd is on his death-bed, and his nephew and heir apparent, Crown Prince Abdullah, depends on the most radical southern and eastern clans for his political base. The southern faction is the center of popular support for Al Qaida and the Taliban because it is the home of the most extreme Muslim sect, the Wahabbis. Ninety-nine percent of the Muslim world rejects the Wahabbi religious tenets as utterly repugnant to the teachings and examples of the Prophet as written down in the Hadith.

Since most Wahabbis are functionally illiterate, they cannot read about this conflict on their own. Typically, they memorize a few passages of the Koran taken out of context, and never read the accompanying Hadith for explanation. For example, the Wahabbis are taught by rote that Jews are sub-humans who should be killed as a religious duty. In contrast, the Hadith explains that the prophet Mohammed honored Jews, married a Jewish wife, forbade forced conversions of Jews, always bowed in respect when a Jewish funeral passed, and promised that good and faithful Jews would go to Paradise just as good Muslims and Christians would, and that the Jews would have their Holy Place in the west (meaning Jerusalem) while Muslims would have their Holy Place in the east (meaning Mecca). Illiteracy is a weapon of oppression.

[Victor Mordecai disagrees regarding the Hadith. One Hadith teaching is that on the day of judgement, all Jews will be killed by the Moslems. They will hide behind rocks and trees, and on that day, Allah will give mouths to the rocks and trees, and they will call out: "Oh, Muslim pursuers, there is a Jew hiding behind me. Come and kill him!"

Secondly, according to the Hadith, Jesus Christ comes back a second time as a Moslem. After killing the anti-Christ, who is a Jew according to the Islamic teaching, Jesus the Moslem goes up to the Temple Mount in Jerusalem and prays as a Moslem with 400,000 other Moslems. He then comes down with 400,000 Moslems, breaks all the crosses, destroys all the churches of the Christians and the synagogues of the Jews, and on that day of judgement, all the Jews and Christians who have not embraced Allah as the greatest of gods, Mohammed as the greatest of prophets, and the Koran as the greatest of all the books will be put to the sword by Jesus the Moslem.]

The Saudis, and their Wahabbi proteges, the Taliban, have decreed that women cannot work or even sit in the front seat of a car. In contrast, the Hadith records that the Prophet worked for his wife, and that she drove her own caravans in international commerce. The Prophet forbade racism; the Wahabbis practice it, especially against their non-Arab Shiite minority. The Wahabbis (both in Saudi Arabia and the Taliban) discriminate viciously against women. The Prophet, who lovingly raised three daughters, insisted that women should have substantially equal rights in contract, ownership, and divorce. The Muslim faith envisioned by the Prophet in the Koran and recorded by his contemporaries in the Hadith is a religion that practices tolerance towards all races and religions [Victor Mordecai disagrees], stresses the extreme importance of literacy and education, and elevates the status of women to unprecedented levels in many societies. This is the gentle, peaceful Muslim faith practiced everywhere in the world, except in Saudi Arabia and the Taliban provinces of Afghanistan and Pakistan.

Muslim scholars speak derisively about the primitive Wahabbi apostasy, but rarely in public. The reason for this deafening silence is simple — most mosques in the world are impoverished and depend upon Saudi subsidies for their operation. In return, however, the Saudis have gained a foothold for proselytizing and radicalizing the Muslim youth through religious education in the form of militant Wahabbism. Children learn to hate because they are being taught that way.

The Saudi charitable network in America that began with religious education evolved into other areas over the decades. The Saudis dabbled with funding anti-Semitic hate groups as a means of breaking down American support for Israel. After the fall of communism, the Saudis took over funding the most militant terror organizations for direct attacks against Jewish and Palestinian supporters of the peace process. Year after year, members of the intelligence community warned that a rising wave of terror was coming. Oliver North wrote in his autobiography that every time he tried to do something about terrorism, he was told to stop because it would embarrass the Saudi Government. John O'Neill quit his job as head of FBI counter-terrorism for the same reason. Jonathan Pollard went to jail. [Victor Mordecai: Jonathan Pollard is still in jail since 1986. His crime, revealing the Iraqi plans to attack Israel with biological weapons, something his superiors decided to hide from Israel. Free Jonathan Pollard now!]

Federal agents in Tampa, who had known about the Saudi-Sami Al Arian connection since 1990, were ordered to drop the investigation in 1995. The Saudi influence-buying machine had effectively shut down any threat of criminal prosecution. Those Americans, including a former President, who lobbied for the Saudis have a lot to answer for. So do the Saudis. With the explosive growth of Al Qaida and their Taliban allies, the Saudis finally recognized that they had gone too far. As Usama Bin Laden laughingly related on videotape, he was approached prior to the attack on the twin Trade Towers by his relatives, who offered him $300,000,000 to cancel the operation. Apparently, the Bin Laden family really had not broken off all ties and knew exactly what was coming. So, my clients say, did the Saudis.

Six months later, a much chagrined Prince Abdullah belatedly announced that the Saudis would release the names of the terrorists which their charities had "unwittingly" funded, but only in Somalia and Asia. The main Saudi charities in Herndon, Virginia, and the Al Arian network in Florida are still untouched. My clients are betting that the American influence peddlers hired by the Saudis will succeed once again in derailing a federal investigation. They came to me for help in exposing the cover-up. That is why I am filing this lawsuit.

In the months to come, the American public may finally begin to learn why the Saudi-Sami Al Arian terror networks went untouched for so long. It wasn't an intelligence failure. It was a foreign policy failure. The orders were not to embarrass the Saudi Government. Year after year, the cover-up orders came from the State Department and the White House. The CIA, the FBI, and the Justice Department just did what they were told. No one intended the harsh consequences of letting the Saudis get away with it again and again. Only after September 11, when the Treasury Department found the financial transactions linking the Saudi charities directly to Usama bin Laden, did American officials realize the extent of their betrayal. We are not alone in our grief and anger. Saudi money sabotaged every Israeli initiative to make peace. The bewildered Palestinians may finally realize that they have been stabbed in the back by an Arab brother. The rules have changed after September 11, but the bottom line remains the same: If we want to stop terrorism, we have to tell the Saudis to stop funding it.

(John Loftus is the president of the Florida Holocaust Museum, a former federal prosecutor and author of several books, including *The Secret War Against the Jews*. He is an Irish-Catholic.)

Saudis Pledge Up to $20 Million for Clinton Library

Saturday March 30, 2002; 11:31 a.m. EST

Disgraced ex-President Bill Clinton, whose disdain for national security over the last eight years is widely believed to have rendered the U.S. vulnerable to last fall's terrorist attacks, is set to collect millions of dollars from Saudi Arabia, home to fifteen of the nineteen 9/11 hijackers.

Estimates of Clinton's expected Saudi jackpot range from "less than $1 million to $20 million," according to columnist Robert Novak, who cites high-ranking members of the Saudi royal family as the source for the information.

In addition to the hijackers, al Qaeda terrorist mastermind Usama bin Laden is a Saudi national, and most of his family now live in the country.

Ostensibly U.S. allies, Saudi leaders have refused to allow American pilots to use U.S.-built airbases in the country to fight the war on terrorism, and have been described as uncooperative in 9/11 related investigations.

On Thursday Saudi Crown Prince Abdullah planted a kiss on the cheek of a top Iraqi official during a Mid-East Arab summit, in a move widely seen as a slap against the Bush administration, which has identified Iraq as a member of the "Axis of Evil."

Clinton's Saudi windfall comes in the form of a pledge to his presidential library foundation in Little Rock, Ark. A library spokesman would neither confirm nor deny the donation.

Former senior Clinton advisor Dick Morris has described the library donor account as a "slush fund" which the former first family will divert to their own personal use.

The ex-President was also paid a $750,000 speaking fee when he traveled to Saudi Arabia three months ago, Novak said.

The Saudi pledge follows what Novak describes as "a similar gift to the elder George Bush's presidential library." The Bush library lists the Saudi contribution among "gifts of $1 million and above." The donor is identified as the family of the Saudi ambassador to the U.S., Prince Bandar bin Sultan.

Novak did not say whether the Bush donation was accepted before or after Sept. 11.

[Victor Mordecai: President George W. Bush grew up in a modest home in Midland, Texas. Today Bush Sr. is valued at $16 billion. I wonder where that money came from, certainly not from his salary as President. The bottom line is that senior US leadership in Washington has been bought out by the Islamic petrodollar with the Saudis in the lead. This augurs evil for Israel, the US and the world. That was the purpose of this April 2002 newsletter.]

Chapter VIII
MAY 2002 NEWSLETTER

Victor Mordecai's Monthly Message

In last month's newsletter (April 2002) I emphasized the duplicitous at best and totally hostile intentions towards the West at worst of the Saudi regime. In this newsletter I feel led by God to emphasize the fruits of Saudi Arabia's duplicity: international terrorism.

In my very first newsletter of October 2001, I related my experiences in Edmonton, Canada, regarding fanatic Islam's plans to murder Jews and certain Christians anywhere there are Islamic population concentrations capable of carrying out these satanic orders, even as far away as Edmonton, Canada, halfway to Alaska.

During the week of April 11th - 18th, 2002, we witnessed declarations by Islamic leaders in Norway and Denmark to kill Jews anywhere and everywhere they can be found. Leaflets to this effect were printed and distributed in these two countries and aroused a furor among the respective populations of those countries.

Also during this week, Islamic Al Qaeda terrorists detonated a natural gas truck bomb outside of a Tunisian synagogue in Djerba killing 17 people, 10 of whom were German tourists. The Tunisian government at first described the explosion as a "tragic accident," but within a very short time, the German federal government exposed taped conversations between the suicide truck bomb driver (of French citizenship) and his operator, a German convert to Islam in Germany. So the cat is out of the bag. The German government has declared this an Al-Qaeda attack. (The German government also arrested four Al-Qaeda members in Germany connected with this attack. It seems they were under surveillance for some time and were also connected to the 9/11 attacks in the US. It also has to be remembered that the 19 suicide bombers were trained in Germany prior to the attacks. The French government now has also asked to send investigators to find out about the French connection to this attack.) The only question now asked is: Was this an attack against a Jewish synagogue (which is nothing new) or was this an attack against German tourists visiting an Islamic country (also nothing new) or was it both? My guess is both.

Meanwhile, the anti-Semitic attacks in Europe in the last month are up into the hundreds. The governments of Europe until now have been unwilling or unable to do anything about them, fearing the stirring up of an Islamic hornets' nest in Europe with incalculable damage that could cause.

One of the reasons for Jean Marie Le Pen's success in the first run-off ballot for president of France, coming second after Jacques Chirac on April 21st, 2002, was the inability or unwillingness of the Chirac-Jospin coalition to deal with the threat of radical Islamic demographic growth in France. This, more than anything else, points to the backlash by the French voter against Jospin and the indifference toward Chirac. As Islam continues to grow from eight million in France, so, too, will the rightwing backlash. The same applies to Georg Haydar in Austria and other rightwing candidates throughout Europe.

Finally, on April 18th, a small private plane piloted by a 70-year-old Swiss man that took off from Locarno, Switzerland, flew to Milan, Italy, reported trouble with the landing gear, and was told by the control tower to fly west and to circle around toward the airport again after the landing gear problem was straightened out. But instead, the old pilot flew directly north toward the downtown of Milan and crashed his plane directly into the center of the 27th floor of the Pirelli building in Milan, the biggest building in Italy. Sound familiar? Of course, the Italian government called this a "tragic accident," but I don't buy into this. Some questions arise:

Didn't the pilot know the difference between west and north? If the tower told him to go west, why did he go north straight toward the downtown of Milan and straight at the tallest building in Milan? Didn't he see that he was headed straight toward the building? Did he want to die? Are we sure he was alone? Could it be that someone in Locarno, Switzerland, forced his way onto the plane and forced the 70-year-old pilot to fly to Italy against his will? If the suicide commandeer wanted to target the Pirelli building, isn't it natural that he would come up with some excuse to cover up his real intentions — such as landing gear problems? Could the suicide terrorist who commandeered the plane have gone straight toward the Pirelli building without some ruse to buy time, or could Italian Air Force have been scrambled to shoot down the plane?

At first, there were reports of 3 bodies: the pilot, a cleaning woman in the building and a woman on the ground who was hit by debris. Then there were reports of 3 bodies: the pilot, and two women on the 27th floor. There were also reports of the aviation fuel explosion causing much damage and a terrible fire on the 27th floor. Maybe there were more bodies involved that might have been burned to ash? How do we know the pilot was alone? And if, as final reports put it, the old man was in debt and wanted to commit suicide, why did he go to all the effort of flying 100 km away and crashing his plane into a building in Italy? Is there a cover-up here in order to bury the whole affair?

In my newsletter of December 2001, I relate a testimony I collected as part of my travels around the US. A man dressed in a black "ninja" type outfit tried to commandeer an ambulance plane at Deming Airport in New Mexico. Due to some quirk, the hijacking failed and the hijacker escaped into the New Mexico desert. He kept saying "Salama." (Ma'as Salama in Arabic means "good- bye.") This leads me to think that perhaps this is a new strategy of Islamic terrorists to commandeer planes flown by innocent pilots and then to crash them into whatever target deemed appropriate.

The final question is: Why Italy?

For that, I refer my readers to my very first newsletter of October 2001. In it, I quoted the Friday, September 28 issue of the *Jerusalem Post* quoting Italian Prime Minister Silvio Berlusconi, who contends that Western Civilization is superior to Islamic culture. Speaking at a news conference after talks in Berlin with German Chancellor Gerhard Schroeder and Russian President Vladimir Putin, Berlusconi said:

"We must be aware of the superiority of our civilization, a system that has guaranteed well-being, respect for human rights and, in contrast with Islamic countries, respect for religious and political rights." Berlusconi added he hoped the West would continue to conquer peoples, like it conquered Communism.

According to Amr. Moussa, secretary general of the 22-nation Arab League, Berlusconi's remarks in Berlin crossed the limits of reason. "We do not believe there is a superior civilization, and if he said so, he is utterly mistaken." The conservative Italian premier's comments were quickly condemned by other Italian politicians as the US is trying to build a coalition with Islamic countries to stamp out terrorism in the wake of the September 11th suicide jet strikes on America. Was this tit for tat? Was this Italy's version of the WTC because of Berlusconi's remarks? My guess is yes.

CURRENT EVENTS AND ANALYSIS

The following is the translation of an article by Isaac Ben Horin in the Friday weekend magazine of the Israeli Hebrew daily *Ma'ariv* of March 29th, 2002.

America Continues to Close Its Eyes

Washington — Ziyad Halil is living proof of the connection between the Hamas and Al-Qaeda. This is one of the proofs shown below in order to present the organizational, financial and operational cooperation between the Al-Qaeda, the Palestinian terrorist organizations and the Hizbollah. This is stark evidence showing the continuing helplessness of the US and the shallowness in Israel's information campaign.

Whoever wants to explain to the American public about the direct links between the Al-Qaeda, the Palestinian terrorist organizations, and the Hizbollah doesn't have to go too far. Proof of this can be found in the non-classified documents of Israeli military courts as well as in the federal court in NY, where the trial is taking place of the blind Sheikh Abdul Rahman and Ahmed Yousef, who were among those behind the first bombing attack on the World Trade Center in 1993. Six people were killed and 1,000 were injured in that first attack. Later, another trial was held against Usama bin Laden, who was indicted for the attacks on the US embassies in Kenya and Tanzania in 1998, which claimed 200 lives and injured 4,000.

Halil, a Palestinian-Jordanian with US citizenship, was arrested in Jordan on December 29th, 1999, after state security services uncovered a plot to carry out attacks during the millennium celebrations in the US and Jordan.

He is a member of Hamas, and until his arrest, he was the creator and website master of the official Hamas Internet website: www.palestine-info.net based in Orlando, Florida, where he lives. He also operates the site of the "Palestine Times," the Hamas Internet monthly, as well as the "Muslim World Library," a group based in London zealously defending the Hamas. Halil lectured in American universities on behalf of the "Islamic Association for Palestine" of the Hamas.

But Ziyad Halil is also an agent of Usama bin Laden. He is the man who purchased computers and satellite communication cell-phones, as well as electronic surveillance equipment for the Al-Qaeda leadership. He is the one who personally traveled to Afghanistan to deliver to bin Laden his famous satellite communications cell-phone, with which he ruled the world and gave instructions to blow up the US embassies in East Africa.

After his arrest in Jordan, Ziyad Halil was released and returned to the US. Today, he moves about freely and operates the Hamas Internet site without hindrance. By the way, he is not the only one linked to bin Laden and to the Palestinian terrorist organizations, and he continues to move about freely in the US.

A Letter From a TV Network

There is another terrorist connected to a Palestinian terrorist organization and bin Laden who lives in North Carolina, near the capital, Washington, D.C., and the Pentagon that was attacked on September 11th, 2001. His name is Tarik Hamdi. He also is moving about freely and is a living example of the plan to obfuscate the distinctions between the Palestinian terrorist organizations and Al-Qaeda.

Hamdi is an Iraqi immigrant who studied at Tampa University in Florida toward the end of the 1980's and the early 1990's. In an interview with the *St. Petersburg Times* in Tampa during the Gulf War, he admitted he had a deep commitment to "Arab and Palestinian issues."

From the beginning of the 1990's, he was connected to a group in Tampa which created the headquarters of the Palestinian Islamic Jihad in the US. There were figures there such as Sami Al-Arian, and Ramadan Shallah. When the leader of the movement, Fathi Shkaki, was assassinated in Malta, on October 26th, 1995, it was Shallah who flew to Damascus to take over.

For years, the FBI has been investigating the activities of the Islamic Jihad in Tampa and the collection of funds at mosques, as it were, for charitable purposes. Partners to these activities were Hamdi, his wife, and Wafa Huzain. When the FBI investigation "began to warm up," the couple moved to North Virginia in 1994 and continued their activities for the Hamas, but at the same time, Hamdi became active on behalf of Usama bin Laden.

His involvement was revealed in a classified document that was just recently declassified during the trial of bin Laden in NY regarding his role in the blowing up of the US embassies in East Africa. On March 20, 2001, the prosecutor called to the stand witnesses such as Marilyn Morelli, a salesperson who testified about the sale of a satellite phone to Ziyad Halil, for use by bin Laden. The purchase took place on May 11th, 1998, a few months before the attacks in East Africa. True, Ziyad purchased the equipment, but he mailed the equipment to the address of Tarik Hamdi in the town of Herndon, Virginia, and it was the latter that made sure to it that the cellular apparatus made it to bin Laden.

In this trial, Hamdi's name is mentioned also regarding a letter from the ABC television network on May 13th, 1998. The letter, asking to interview bin Laden, was sent through Hamdi to Muhammad Atef, bin Laden's senior military assistant, also related by marriage through his daughter to the arch-terrorist's son. Atef was the most high ranking Al-Qaeda member to be killed in the American bombings in Afghanistan after the attacks of 9/11.

The connection of ABC with Atef was revealed by the letter to have been "through Tarik Hamdi in Washington." The interview finally did take place in May 1998. And who was it that flew with John Miller and the TV crew to Afghanistan to interview bin Laden? You've got it, Tarik Hamdi, who took advantage of the opportunity to bring a spare cellular battery with him for bin Laden.

Target Surveillance in Kenya

From Hamdi the Iraqi, we go on now to Ali Muhammad the Egyptian, the man who helped bin Laden to get his people established in Nairobi, in preparation for carrying out the attacks on the US embassies. Ali Muhammad was a former Egyptian military officer that immigrated to the US and lived in Santa Clara, California. Because of his past the US military mobilized him to teach special operations forces courses on Islamic culture. But throughout those years, his loyalty was to bin Laden, and he passed on to bin Laden information regarding US Special Forces.

The name Ali Muhammad first surfaced during the investigation into the first bombing at the World Trade Center in 1993. It soon became apparent that he trained everyone, including Al-Said Nosair, who murdered Rabbi Meir Kahane at the entrance to a hotel in NY, as well as Ahmed Yousef and the other involved in the WTC bombing.

Investigative reporter Steven Emerson wrote about him and the US Army ceased to employ him, though there was on the surface no incriminating evidence against him. Five years went by before the FBI was onto his trail, following the explosions at the embassies in East Africa and a list of phone calls by Ali Muhammad and he was arrested. He confessed and cooperated with investigators.

In his confession in court, he told about his role in taking bin Laden from Afghanistan to the Sudan and then taking him back to Afghanistan. He was also the man who arranged for the first meeting between bin Laden and Imad Mughnieh, head of Hizbollah's overseas attack apparatus.

From his testimony arises the direct connection between Al Qaeda and Hizbollah, and joint training exercises in camps in Lebanon, Afghanistan and South America. Members of Hizbollah trained those of Al-Qaeda on how to carry out massive bombing attacks. In practice, it was the Hizbollah who blew up the Khobar Towers in Saudi Arabia in 1996, an attack killing dozens of US soldiers.

The following are quotes from Ali Muhammad's testimony in NY Federal Court on Oct. 20, 2000:

"In 1992 I taught basic military training and the use of explosives to members of the Al-Qaeda in Afghanistan. I also taught them about military intelligence and about how to form operational cells. I helped the Al-Qaeda to establish a presence in Nairobi, Kenya, and I worked with some others on the project.

"Abu Obeida was responsible for the Al-Qaeda in Nairobi. We established a car business in order to create a basis for income. Wadiya Al-Hajj set up a charitable organization. We had code names: My name was Jeff. Al-Hajj's name was Norman.

"Towards the end of 1993, bin Laden asked me to begin to conduct surveillance of American, British, French and Israeli targets in Nairobi. These targets were chosen in revenge for US involvement in Somalia. I took photographs, made drawings and wrote a report.

"I returned to Khartoum and presented bin-Laden with my photographs. Bin Laden took the photograph of the US embassy in Nairobi and pointed to a probable place where a truck bomb could penetrate the embassy.

"In 1994, after an attempt to murder bin Laden, I went to Sudan to train his bodyguards. I trained the Al-Qaeda in surveillance and in evading surveillance. At the beginning of the 1990's, bin Laden's deputy, Ayman Zawaheri, visited the US twice to fundraise for the Islamic Jihad. I helped him to do this.

"I was aware of the links between Al-Qaeda and the Islamic Jihad on the one hand, and with the Hizbollah on the other. I was responsible for the security during a meeting held in the Sudan between bin Laden and Mughnieh of the Hizbollah. The Hizbollah provided Al Qaeda and Islamic Jihad with explosives training. Iran provided the weapons for the Egyptian Islamic Jihad. Iran also used the Hizbollah to provide explosives designed to look like rocks.

"At the end of 1994, I was in Nairobi. Abu Hafez met me and instructed me to conduct surveillance of possible US,

British, French and Israeli targets in Senegal. At the same time, I received a phone call from the FBI asking me to talk to them about Abdul Rahman's trial. I returned to the US, spoke to an FBI agent but I didn't tell him everything I knew. I reported on this meeting to Abu-Hafez, and I was told not to return to Nairobi.

"After the explosions in 1998, I planned to go to Egypt and from there to Afghanistan to meet bin Laden. Before leaving the US, I was invited to appear before a jury in New York to give testimony. There I was arrested."

Terrorist Roof Organization

Last October, US President George W. Bush presented a second list of organizations and people whose property had been frozen and were prohibited from maintaining economic activities. Included in this list was a Saudi businessman by the name of Yassin Al-Kadi because of monies he transferred to bin Laden and to Al Qaeda. But Kadi also transferred monies to the Hamas, not only to bin Laden.

After Israeli Prime Minister Itzchak Rabin banished the Hamas leadership to Lebanon, Kadi headed efforts to financially rehabilitate the terrorist organization. In a complicated financial undertaking, including land purchase deals in Illinois, the Saudi businessman released $820,000 to the bank account of the "Institute for the Study of the Koran" headed by Muhammad Saleh for the translation of the Koran.

Saleh, who acted on behalf of Musa Marzouk, head of the Hamas, was sent to Israel with money to be handed over to activists in Gaza and the West Bank. In January 1993, Saleh was arrested and the affair was uncovered.

A source in Washington, well acquainted with this affair, said, "This isn't surprising. Monies collected by the charities are given out to everyone, to bin Laden, to the Hamas, to the Islamic Jihad and to the Hizbollah. The Administration included in the list of economic sanctions two Saudi charitable organizations, 'B.I.F.' and 'Global Relief,' because of monies they transferred to bin Laden. But these organizations have branches in the Palestinian territories as well. Or, for example, the 'Qatari Charity Fund,' which turned out during the trial of the embassy bombings in Africa to be a bin Laden organization with a branch in Gaza. These groups will finance terrorism and it doesn't matter where. They are in Israel, and they will finance the Palestinians. If it's somewhere else, they will finance whoever they want to carry out terrorism," this source said.

At the trial of Jamal Al-Fadal (for the first bombing of the WTC) in 1997 in New York, background information provided by the prosecution showed that Al Qaeda was an umbrella organization including the Palestinian Islamic Jihad and some other Jihad groups from other countries.

The father of this idea of a roof organization was Abdullah Azzam, a Palestinian who had been expelled from Jordan to Pakistan because of his extremist ideas. Bin Laden listened to a speech of his during the course of the war in Afghanistan, was turned on, and together they established what was to become the Al-Qaeda.

The vision of Azzam was "Now we liberate Afghanistan and afterward, Palestine." Bin Laden had other ideas. At the beginning of the first intifada tapes of Azzam's speech were heard. In 1987 and 1988, he traveled to the US to fundraise "in order to buy missiles and weapons of war."

But he was murdered in December 1989 when a car in which he was traveling in Afghanistan blew up. There were those who blamed Israel for his death. To this day, his pictures are displayed together with those of Ahmed Yassin in demonstrations of the Hamas, and he is mentioned at the Internet site of the organization.

Israeli Arabs Are Being Mobilized

Azzam died but his vision of Palestinian youths arriving to train in training camps in Afghanistan would be realized in a decade.

From Israeli military court files in Hebron, it is possible to learn about Saad Hindawi, a 27-year-old from Halhoul, who was arrested in February 2000, and about Basel Dakah, a 26-year-old from Tulkarem, who was arrested in March 2000, after they returned from training camps in Afghanistan. More telling about the links between Hamas and Al Qaeda, however, is the story of Nabil Ukal, a 27-year-old from the Jebaliya refugee camp.

In October 1997, Ukal went to Pakistan and for months went through arms training, karate and military fitness at a camp in the mountains of Kashmir. From there, he was transferred to Afghanistan and was trained in explosives and missile launching in the city of Jalalabad. In July 1998, Ukal returned to the Gaza Strip via Jordan, met with Hamas leader Sheikh Ahmed Yassin and suggested creating a terrorist infrastructure. Yassin gave his blessings to his independent activities with a direct link to him and funding circumventing the military wing of the Hamas.

Ahmed Yassin made it clear to him that the link would be through a man by the name of Id Al-Bik and a bank account was opened to pay for his military activities. The messages would be given to him every Monday after the afternoon prayers. At the end of 1998, Yassin deposited $5,000 in this bank account.

Ukal approached Muhammad Abu Labda, a Hamas activist, and told him about the training he had undergone and suggested that he undergo such training. They made contact through the Internet with the Al-Ansar organization, where Ukal was trained in Pakistan, and through the Internet they received instructional material about making bombs.

The two planned to carry out a number of attacks in marketplaces and military installations by means of cellular remote controlled bombs. They also planned to kidnap soldiers and to keep them hostage for a long time as bargaining chips

Ukal also decided to mobilize an Arab-Israeli squad and to send them for training in Afghanistan. Abu Labda said he knew two residents of Umm el-Fahm, members of the Islamic movement, who came to his house for visits and that he could mobilize them. About a week later at Abu Labda's house, one of the Israeli Arabs expressed his willingness to join the Hamas and mentioned the names of another five Israeli Arabs who would be ready to carry out any mission of the Hamas.

Ukal decided that he and Abu Labda needed to go for further training in Afghanistan and to be trained in remote controlled explosives. In April 2000, Ukal again met with Sheikh Ahmed Yassin and notified him about his intentions to go to get instructional materials for bomb-makings. As an alibi, the two went to a hospital in Gaza and received recommendations to receive further treatment in Jordan. On June 1st, 2000, the two traveled together with a Hamas activist ID Abu Siha, to the airport of Gaza, and there, Ukal was arrested.

One Ukal was arrested, but there are many more that have succeeded in evading arrest, something which allows us to understand the overall picture of an international terrorist connection, and the dimensions of the terrorism with which Israel must deal at this time.

PRIVATE INVESTIGATION

Sharon Is More Merciful Than Saddam Hussein

Article by Fuad el-Hashem in April 8th, 2002, edition of the Kuwait daily *el Watan el Kuwaiti.*

It is nothing new for me as a Kuwaiti citizen that I should hear all kinds of headlines that reporters provide for us over the TV screens such as Ramallah being a "ghost city," that Bethlehem is a "ghost city," and one sees only military vehicles. Because I saw with my own eyes and experienced all that happened when the Iraqi army entered Kuwait in August 1990, and turned the capital into a real ghost city. One did not see anything other than military vehicles, and I think that only God knows that the Palestinian people should prostrate themselves with thanks to God, morning, night, and all the time that their enemy is the Israeli army. Because the situation of the Palestinians is much better than that we experienced with the Iraqi army, a savage army multiplied many times more savage than the Israeli, so much so that all the Israeli army does to the Palestinians compared to what the Iraqis did to Kuwait is child's play.

The Palestinians feel the pain and suffering in their war with the Israelis, but they have a consolation and this ameliorates their situation in that they are facing a foreign army, speaking a foreign language, and their faces are not Middle Eastern. But our suffering (the Kuwaitis) was double. We were between a rock and a hard place. The Iraqi army Republican Guard was the rock and the hard place was the Arabic language, the Islamic religion, the same history, and geography with us.

I understand the feeling of the Palestinians when an Israeli soldier puts the end of the barrel of his gun in their faces but: what would your feeling have been, Arab Palestinians, if the soldier putting the end of the barrel of a gun in your face spoke Arabic, and was of the Arab nation, of the same Islamic religion, and had the same history and geography and destiny? And above and beyond this, the Iraqi soldier tells you his lies about the Ba'ath Party, one Arab nation, and the same eternal message.

I tell you, Palestinians, that you need to get down on your knees and to pray to God, morning, night and all day because Israel has biological, chemical and nuclear weapons, but doesn't use them. Israel didn't even threaten to use these weapons against the Palestinians. And had it been Hassan el-Majid, commander of the Iraqi army, who surrounded the Jenin refugee camp and not Israeli Army Chief-of-Staff Mofaz, it wouldn't have taken more than five or six days, but rather the mustard gas would have been used by order of Meguid on the first day, to kill, not only the people, and the plantlife, but even the cats running between the houses and garbage bins and the rats in their holes.

The cries of the Kuwaiti people rose to the heavens in August 1990 for the Arab nation to save us from the total destruction of the criminal brother Saddam Hussein. And the Palestinians came out in Amman, Jordan, with demonstrations of happiness calling on Saddam as follows:

Bil Kimawi ya saddam, min el-Kuwait ledamam.

"With chemical weapons, Oh Saddam! From Kuwait with their blood!"

Here are some other things the Palestinians said:

Just yesterday, Hajj Ahmed ul-Kutan praised the Palestinian victory, but in history, eleven years ago, Sheikh Bayud al Tamimi yelled from the minaret of the Mosque, and said:

"Allahuma ehraq arduhum, wa lah tut fi nar abarihim.

Allahum shattit shamluhum wansur Saddam Hussein alla el qaum azalimin.

"Allah will burn their land (Kuwait), and the fires will never be extinguished."

"Allah will scatter them, and give Saddam Hussein victory over this bastard nation" (Kuwaitis).

From the 18 months of intifada, there were 1,700 Palestinian shahids (martyrs), compared to six hours of Iraqi invasion from that morning of 2nd Av (August 1990) and the criminal Saddam Hussein army killing 1,000 Kuwaiti martyrs. Ariel Sharon is more merciful than Saddam Hussein. Shaul Mofaz is more merciful than Hassan Majid and Izzet e-Douhuri and Taha Yassin and all the other gangs of the Baghdad rulers.

MILITARY INTELLIGENCE

Islamic Infiltration From Mexico Into the U.S.

From worldnetdaily.com

The numbers of unauthorized immigrants smuggled across this porous border dumbfound the imagination. To date, the U.S. Border Patrol has apprehended 158,782 illegals in 2001. By the Border Patrol's own admission, it catches one alien in five, and admits that around 800,000 have slipped across the U.S. line this year. The local ranchers, who have been watching the border for several generations, strongly disagree. They contend the agency only nets one in 10, and estimate that in 2001 over 1.5 million unlawful immigrants have crossed into America in what the Border Patrol calls the Tucson Sector.

Another agent, of supervisory rank, stated, "The smuggling traffic of Mexicans has really slowed. We are experiencing a tremendous increase in OTMs," border lingo for "other than Mexicans." When queried about the ethnic make-up of the OTMs, he answered, "Central and South Americans, Orientals and Middle-Easterners." Middle-Easterners? "Yeah, it varies, but about one in every 10 that we catch is from a country like Yemen or Egypt." Border

Patrol spokesperson Rene Noriega stated that the number of other-than-Mexican detentions has grown by 42 percent. Most of the non-Mexican migrants are from El Salvador and other parts of Central America, she said, but added that agents have picked up people from all over the world, including the former Soviet Union, Asia and the Middle East.

According to Border Patrol spokesperson Rob Daniels, "Ten Egyptians were arrested recently near Douglas, Arizona. Each had paid $7,000 to be brought from Guatemala into Mexico and then across the border." According to the San Diego *Union-Tribune,* hours after the 9-11 attacks on the World Trade Center and the Pentagon, an anonymous caller led Mexican immigration agents to 41 undocumented Iraqis waiting to cross into the United States.

The Associated Press reported that Mexican immigration police detained 13 citizens of Yemen on Sept. 24, 2001, reportedly waiting to cross the border into Arizona. The Yemenis were arrested Sunday in Agua Prieta, across the border from Douglas. Luis Teran Balaguer, assistant head of immigration in the northern state of Sonora, said, "The evidence indicates that they have nothing to do with terrorist activities."

The Agua Prieta, Mexico, newspaper *El Clarin* clearly did not agree with Balaguer's assessment. The editor, Jose Noriega Durazo, claimed in a front-page *El Clarin* headline, "ESTUVIERON AQUI TERRORISTAS ARABES!" (The Arab terrorists were here!)

El Clarin quoted Agua Prieta police officials as identifying the 13 Yemenis as terrorists. Reportedly, the Mexican immigration police returned the Yemenis to a federal detention center near Mexico City, but new information would indicate that they were "released" and returned to Agua Prieta.

Carlos X. Carrillo, assistant chief U.S. Border Patrol, Tucson Sector, told WorldNetDaily in a telephone interview Monday that nine Yemenis were reportedly holed up in a hotel in the border town of Agua Prieta, Sonora, Mexico, across the border from Douglas, Ariz. "We have passed this tip to the FBI," said Carrillo.

When pressed for more information, he said he could not confirm the number of OTMs or Middle-Easterners apprehended while crossing the American/Mexican border.

"We are under OP/SEC and cannot divulge this," the chief said. (OP/SEC is a counter-intelligence acronym for operations security.)

Terrorists are well aware that the 4,000-mile border between the U.S. and Mexico is easy to cross, with its vast unmonitored stretches. Their crossing directly into Arizona is of special concern.

Arizona appears to have been the home of a "sleeper cell" of Usama bin Laden's worldwide terrorist organization, with a select group of operatives living quietly in bland apartment complexes and obtaining flight training, in preparation for the Sept. 11 attack. The organization's known history in the state goes back nine years. Terror experts say the activities of at least three part-time Arizona residents fit the pattern of the al-Qaida terrorist network.

A Border Patrol field patrol agent, who spoke anonymously, confirmed the presence of the nine Yemenis. The agent said, "They can't get a coyote to transport them and they are offering $30,000 per person with no takers."

Rural citizens here have met with savage recriminations for exerting their legal rights. Immigration advocacy groups howl in protest, as does the Mexican government. Their lawyers have demanded that the ranchers be prosecuted for false arrest, kidnapping, intimidation, criminal assault and violation of civil rights, anything lawyers can come up with to advance their clients' interests. Illegal immigrants have now sued some Cochise County citizens in American courts.

Ben Anderson, a retired U.S. Army colonel who lives in Sierra Vista, Ariz., has made a detailed study of the border danger since the flood of illegals began through Cochise

County in 1997. "There is only one way to handle this," the colonel says firmly. "In a world now filled with biowarfare agents, backpack nuclear devices and chemical weapons like Sarin gas, we must militarize the border. There is no other way to stop the flow."

Chapter IX
JUNE 2002 NEWSLETTER

Victor Mordecai's Monthly Message

It is with great pleasure and apologies that I present my readers with my much belated June 2002 newsletter. It is never my intention to appear with a late newsletter, but obviously, if I must drive all alone throughout the US and Canada for 9 weeks, returning only on June 26th, it is a given that the newsletter will come out in July. I hope to compensate my readers with interesting if not critical information.

I have now been at home in Jerusalem for three weeks and have sifted through two months of Israeli newspapers, English as well as Hebrew. Sometimes I feel that the preparation of this newsletter is like working in a gold mine. In order to get to the gold you must dispose of much worthless earth. Then when you find the gold, you must refine it and purge the dross attached to the gold.

I am fortunate to receive emails from dozens of caring people throughout the world, Christians, Hindus, Jews and Moslems. Many of the emails include articles not readily available to anyone else. Together with the newspapers, emails, as well as scoops I receive from wife, Rachel, who monitors the Arabic language media here in Jerusalem, I am fortunate to come across some remarkable information. I praise God for enabling me to carry the burden of my travels abroad eight months of the year and then to return home to Israel to "re-sharpen" myself, recharge my batteries with the new information constantly streaming in.

I also praise God for being with me on my travels, protecting me and opening new doors in the Christian, Hindu and Jewish communities, all threatened by Islam and wanting to hear the message.

One small sign of God's presence was in Barstow, California. After five difficult days of driving from New York to California with radio and TV shows en route, I was crossing the Mojave Desert in southern California with the sun setting. I was six hours behind schedule in reaching Oakland, where a Judeo-Christian Zionist conference was to be held. The Sabbath was rapidly approaching, the sun was setting and I realized there was no way I could complete the drive to the San Francisco Bay area.

So I called the Chabad rabbi in Berkeley, who was also one of the speakers at this conference and who had been kind enough to extend to me an invitation for Sabbath hospitality with him and his family. I told him I would have to stop in Barstow because the sun was setting. I asked him if he could advise me regarding synagogues in Barstow. He checked his computer and said that there was a conservative synagogue in Barstow.

I arrived at the conservative synagogue just as the sun was setting and just in time for Kabbalat Shabbat (receiving the Sabbath). As soon as we finished praying, I checked into the Ramada Inn just across the street.

Entering the Ramada Inn, I was greeted by a stunningly beautiful, elegantly dressed black woman, who said to me: "Welcome to Barstow. How are you today?"

I took it for granted that this lady was part of the hotel reception staff. In a very tired and gruff spirit I responded: "I have just driven from New York to California in 5 days. After a shower and after I'm in bed, I'll feel a lot better."

When I approached the reception desk, the receptionist asked both of us: "What can I do for you two?"

Kind of taken aback, I answered: "Ladies first!"

The black lady requested a bottle of drinking water for her pastor.

The receptionist referred her to a second floor dispensing machine. I immediately detained her, asked her about her pastor and to which church she belonged.

She said, "It doesn't matter, just a non-denominational charismatic church."

I retorted: "Well, I'm a Jew from Israel. I speak in Christian churches about the threat of Islam. Non-denominational charismatic churches are my favorites!"

Her eyes opened wide. She said to me: "I know you. I know that voice. I just received yesterday a cassette you made called the 'Legacy of Hate.' I listened to it three times already. You drive from coast to coast speaking in churches. Your wife's name is Rachel. She is from Egypt, and she taught you everything you know about Islam. Your name, your name is.... Avi Missler!"

I almost fell over. It was like being struck with lightning. You tell me: What is the likelihood of driving across the entire US, stopping at an unscheduled stop in the middle of the Mojave Desert and meeting a beautiful woman who had just heard my tape three times the day before and knew exactly who I was.

For me, it was a sign from God that God was with me anywhere I went, even in the desert.

I told this wonderful Christian woman that I made this tape with Chuck Missler at Koinonia House in Postfalls, Idaho, on July 11th, 2001, two months before the infamous attacks on 9/11. The tape predicted the attacks, but it was only ten months later that she received the tape, and just the day before I arrived in Barstow, California. Was it some coincidence or a divine appointment?

Sunday morning I continued the drive north to Oakland to participate in Rosemary Schindler's Judeo-Christian Zionist conference, then flew with a bunch of the leaders to New York for a parallel conference organized by Ina Perfido, then flew back to San Francisco, continued driving north along route I-5, spoke for two weeks in Oregon, one week in the Spokane-Coeur d'Alene area, and then after a short visit to Port Orchard and Bellingham, I crossed the border into Vancouver, British Columbia, Canada.

During the ten days in Canada, I was blessed to meet with new groups as well as second time visits in Victoria, Surrey, Maple Ridge and Edmonton. It was also my first time on Canadian Christian TV with the Miracle Network in Lethbridge, Alberta (just across the border from Great Falls, Montana, USA). I then drove back west into the Canadian Rockies in order to speak a second time in one month at Chuck Missler's Koinonia House in Coeur d'Alene, Idaho, then across to Great Falls, then on to Denver, Colorado; Kansas City; Springfield, Missouri; Philadelphia, Mississippi; and finally back to New York and home to Israel.

If your head is not spinning, mine certainly is, and this is the way my travels have been for over eight months of each year for the last eight years.

All this work has been to alert the world, but especially the US and Canada, of the threat of Islam.

In 1995, I came out with the first edition of my first book *Is Fanatic Islam a Global Threat?* I self-printed only 1,000 copies and it was really just a pamphlet of 63 pages. When they were sold out, and time came for a reprinting, I decided to add another 30 pages of information I had gathered. The second edition of 93 pages was expanded and revised. These 1,000 copies also sold out in six months.

By 1996, I had begun working closely with Dr. David Allen Lewis in Springfield, Missouri, and his son-in-law Neil Howell. When the time came to reprint the 3rd edition, revised and expanded, it was now really a book of 170 pages with much new information. These 1,000 copies sold out in a month.

The fourth revised edition, printed in 10,000 copies in May 1996, was up to 200 pages, and the 5th and final edition was expanded to 286 pages instead of 332 pages because we shrunk down the letters to save on the paper. Of this fifth and final edition, we have so far printed 30,000 copies in English.

I sealed this book, deciding not to expand, revise, or change it again in any way. But by the spring of 1999, it became clear that I needed to write a new book because of the barbarous attack of

Bill Clinton and the globalist allies of Islam on Yugoslavia. My first book dealt more with the Islamic threat while my second book, *Christian Revival for Israel's Survival,* dealt with the binary threat of Islam and the globalist harlot riding the dragon (Revelation 17). In total, I self-printed 20,000 of this second book.

A total of 43,000 of the first and 20,000 of the second book were self-printed. I would dare say therefore that the sum total of my work for the last 12 years has been to reach about 50,000 people, which is really rather paltry for so much effort.

But this trip was different than all the previous trips because one day, my booking agent, Bette (1 800 728 1779), called me to advise me that Pastor Chuck Smith of Calvary Chapel Costa Mesa had called her asking me to speak in his church. God willing, I will be in his church on August 7th.

Though I had previously spoken in over a dozen Calvary Chapels in the US and Canada, this was the first time I was to be honored by speaking in the main church of Pastor Smith. This group of churches (I hate to use the word denomination) loves Israel, the Jews, and is a vanguard church in the US and Canada. There are about 1,000 churches with about a million Christian believers.

For years, now, I was frustrated at merely preaching to the choir, going to pretty much the same 50,000 people all these years. Now, God has given me, hopefully, another confirmation to Barstow.

Now over a million believers will hopefully be exposed to a message so critical to the defense of Israel, America and the world. This is a big breakthrough, God willing. I hope that Israel and I will be blessed by this connection to the Calvary Chapels and that "those who bless Israel will be blessed" as well.

My dream is that after the Calvarys, one by one, all Christian denominations in the US and Canada will become adherents to Christian Zionism and supporters of the Jewish State of Israel. Then America and Canada will continue to protect and maintain the blessings that God has bestowed upon them and which made America and Canada the greatest countries on earth. This is called Christian Revival for Israel's Survival (as well as the survival of America, Canada and the rest of the world).

CURRENT EVENTS AND ANALYSIS

2000 Cyberattacks Against GPO in Last Week

(Dan Diker on page 4 of *Jerusalem Post*,
May 29th, 2002)

The Government Press Office Internet site was attacked 2,000 times in the last week, GPO director Danny
Seaman told Jerusalem Post Radio yesterday.

"The recent cyberattacks could have destroyed the
government's official photo archives containing the entire
pictorial history of Israel," he said, adding that the archives
are fortunately backed up off-line.

Seaman said GPO officials don't know the source of
the attacks but believe that they were premeditated.

He noted that additional funds are sorely needed to
create much better on-line security. "We are not protected
against worms and viruses as we should be," he said. "It's
all a question of government priorities."

[Victor Mordecai comments: The GPO, where I
worked in 1989-90, is part of the prime minister's office. The
only conclusion about the "premeditated" attacks is that only
the Islamists could have a possible motive for these attacks.
The lesson of Islamic cyberattacks is mentioned in both my
books: *Is Fanatic Islam a Global Threat?* and *Christian
Revival for Israel's Survival.*]

ADL: Saudi PR Sullied by Continued Incitement

(Article on page 2 of *Jerusalem Post* of
May 8th, 2002)

Washington — The government-sponsored Saudi
press continues to spread anti-Semitism and anti-American
hatred, according to the Anti-Defamation League, which

today pointed to numerous examples of incitement in the Saudi media appearing as recently as May 1st.

"While the Saudis are spending millions on their public image campaign in the Western world, they are still spreading crude, ugly, classical anti-Semitism and anti-American hatred among their own people," said ADL national director Abraham Foxman.

"Despite the Saudi government's efforts to portray themselves as a moderate regime and a facilitator of peace in the Middle East, the message conveyed by the state-controlled newspapers of Saudi Arabia is just the opposite. There is no message of moderation or support for America in the war against terrorism. Articles, editorials, cartoons, and op-eds are often deeply critical and mocking of the US and its leadership and hateful toward Jews and Israel," Foxman said.

At the ADL's annual National Leadership Meeting, held in Washington, DC, League leaders cited ongoing incitement and hatred in the Saudi press as "a major issue of concern, and an impediment to peace in the Middle East."

"It is anathema to peace to have this kind of crude, hateful incitement continuing in the Arab world," Foxman said. "Saudi leaders must speak out and denounce the hate, and must stop providing an environment where incitement against Jews, Americans, and Israel can flourish." The ADL, which monitors news reports from the Arab world, has compiled numerous examples from between late March and May 1st, 2002, where the Saudi press expressed strong anti-Semitic or anti-American sentiments.

The following excerpts appeared in the Saudi government controlled press during that time frame:

"Mr. Bush, if you truly believe that Sharon, the indiscriminate murderer and oppressor of Palestinian youths, children and elderly men, is a man of peace then it is the end to peace... I also warn you that Muslims and Arabs look forward to the hour when Allah removes from their rulers' hearts their fears of you. Then they will open the road to Palestine for a jihad which will ultimately lead them to the Paradise they yearn for, even as you fear death" (Editorial, English-language *Arab News*, April 20, 2002).

"I need to tell the President of the United States, 'Mr. President, for God's sake don't talk like an evil man who cannot escape from an evil choice. It is better to be dumb than to speak like an evil accomplice who financed Zionist warlords and launched an evil crusade against Muslims everywhere....'" "The bitter truth, of course, is that the Bush White House is not interested in understanding the realities of history. White House involvement is driven simply by the domestic political need to keep Zionist opinion sweet back home, in the face of this year's mid-term elections. Therefore, any American voting the Republican ticket is effectively marking his voting with Palestinian blood" (editorial, *Arab News*, April 18, 2002).

"The Americans, who also have the power to rein in Sharon, are willing dupes for his terrorist rhetoric, and anyway have a political system shot through with Zionist sympathizers. Even if Bush actually understood what was going on, his political masters would never dare enrage the US Zionists and thus jeopardize a second term for their man in the White House" (editorial, *Arab News*, April 7, 2002).

"The Israelis know that they are in no shape to take on the whole Muslim world. For this reason they are depending on their Zionist assets in the US to thoroughly demonize Islam and the Muslims, and in the process reinvigorate a 'Crusader' mentality throughout the West" (News article, *Arab News*, May 1, 2002).

"Why are they (the Jews) hated by all the people which hosted them, such as Iraq and Egypt thousands of years ago, and Germany, Spain, France, and the UK, up to the days they gained power over the capital and the press, in order to rewrite history?" (article, *Ar-Riyadh*, April 15th, 2002).

"Life stopped in 'Israel' yesterday for two minutes

[Holocaust Memorial Day siren] while the warning siren whistled all over the occupied territories of Palestine, in memory of the 6 million Jews, about whom 'Israel' lies, saying that they were killed in the Nazi crematoriums during WWII" (Article *Ar-Riyadh*, April 10, 2002).

"Far from shying away from behavior that has made the world draw analogies between them and the Nazis who persecuted their Jewish brethren during WWII, the Israeli Army yesterday launched a campaign of mass executions against the Palestinians.... Once again, Israel's economic, political, and military backer, the US, remained silent in the face of such an outrage" (news article, *Arab News*, April 1, 2002).

Saudi Arabia's American Captives

(Article by William McGurn in *Wall Street Journal,*
reprinted in *Jerusalem Post* of June 12, 2002)

When Pat Roush wants to show off her daughters, she reaches for an old Christmas photo. It's the classic family snapshot: two happy little girls in front of the tree, holding matching Pound Puppies — gifts from Santa — over their heads.

Exactly one month later, Miss Roush would lay out their black Mary Janes and party dresses for a birthday bash the girls had been looking forward to. It was a party they would never make. Kidnapped by their estranged father, seven-year-old Alia and her three-year-old sister, Aisha, were already on their way to Saudi Arabia.

That was 1986, and the sisters, now young women, remain there still. They have not seen their mother since, except for one heart-wrenching two-hour meeting in 1995 where Alia, clad in the black abaya, begged her mother, "Please, Mama, don't leave us here!" In the meantime, Alia has been married off; each has been converted to Islam; and both remain under an effective life sentence in a land whose law forbids them to leave without the written permission of a father or husband.

Wahhabi Yoke

"I'm proud America has liberated Afghan women from the Wahhabi yoke," says Miss Roush, referring to the brand of Islam Usama bin Laden and the Saudis pushed among the Taliban. "But what about America's own daughters? When does liberation come for my girls?"

Good question. Until very recently hers was only another hard-luck tale. But 9/11 has dramatically changed the backdrop. For 16 years, the Saudi desk at the State Department has told her, "Let's look at this from a Saudi's point of view." But tomorrow the House Government Reform Committee will hold hearings that will finally look at her case from an explicitly American point of view.

Plainly the testimony will not be kind to Saudi Arabia, now in the midst of a PR campaign designed to persuade Americans that 15 of 19 hijackers carrying Saudi passports should be nothing between friends. But the grilling may be more embarrassing to State, especially when Congress hears how Americans in distress were treated when they cried out — often literally — for help. A taunt from a representative of the governor of Riyadh to Miss Roush sums up the signal received by the Saudis: "Your State Department won't help you, and your government doesn't want you."

Alia and Aisha's tragedy began on a snowy Super Bowl Sunday in 1986 just outside Chicago. By that time Pat Roush had split with her Saudi husband, Khalid al-Gheshayan, whom she had met as a student in California; Gheshayan's record during his years in America shows several arrests and a hospital diagnosis of alcoholism and paranoid schizophrenia.

Though Pat had secured a divorce and custody of the children, she did let her husband see his daughters when he returned to America. On the day in question, she was readying herself for the birthday party in the girls' bedroom. She glanced at Alia's Brownie handbook on a nightstand, and suddenly felt a hollow pain in her stomach. When she called Gheshayan and he didn't answer, she raced over to the building where he'd taken up residence.

In the grocery store below, a young child told her, "He took them away in a taxi and they didn't want to go." Days later, her husband would call to tell her their daughters were in Saudi Arabia. A few months later, the office of a Saudi governor would make a tape — in the presence of the US consul general — in which a glazed-looking Alia said, "I hate the United States" and "My mother hates me and my sister."

Since then Miss Roush, a nurse, has spent almost every waking moment badgering diplomats, pushing for legislation, putting holds on ambassadors, picketing the Saudi Embassy, even hiring mercenaries. With a few brave exceptions, however, American officialdom has seen her as a nuisance. How much easier their jobs would be if this woman would simply write her daughters off.

Still, twice she has come close to getting them out. The first time was in 1986, when pressure from Illinois Sen. Alan Dixon resulted in a deal that would have reunited the two tiny Americans with their mom. But the deal broke down after the higher-ups in Foggy Bottom cabled the ambassador that he was not to be present at the deal, on the grounds that the US must "maintain impartiality."

The second time came under the girls' other champion, Ambassador Ray Mabus. Appointed by Bill Clinton, the former Mississippi governor made no bones that he wanted the girls back in America, referring to Gheyashan as a criminal, cutting off all US visas for his family and pushing hard for a resolution. He too worked one out, but left for America before it was seen through, never dreaming that it would all come crashing down in his absence.

"This was never about Saudi law and customs," says Mr. Mabus. "It was about American law. This is a man

[Gheshayan] who voluntarily put himself under American law, got married under American law, was divorced under American law and then broke that law."

The governor adds that his push for the rights of these American citizens never hurt the bilateral relationship. To the contrary, he believes that "one of the main jobs of embassies is to protect American citizens and uphold American law."

And lest people think that Miss Roush exaggerates, the House will hear supporting testimony from other women caught in the Saudi vise. Exhibit A is Dria Davis. When Dria was just 11 years old, she too was held in Saudi Arabia by a father who wouldn't let her return to America. When she begged the US Embassy for help, they told her there was nothing they could do. "I was confused," she says. "I just kept asking, 'Why?'"

Tomorrow, Congress will play tapes Dria's mother secretly made of emotional phone conversations during her daughter's captivity, with Dria tearfully relating how her father shrieked at her, calling her a "bitch," and screaming for her mother to "get me out of here, they are going to kill me." Abused by her father, abandoned by her country, this intrepid teenager ultimately pulled off her own escape, via Baharain, when she was just 13.

When set against the larger war on terrorism, the plight of a handful of American women may appear small potatoes. And there is undoubtedly any number of people who regard Miss Roush's campaign for her daughters a distraction from larger issues. But after 16 years, the answer to that should be obvious: If not now, when?

The State Department understandably bristles at the accusation that it is indifferent to the plight of fellow Americans such as Alia and Aisha. But the problem is not that the State hasn't done anything. The problem is that everything the State Department has done has been done within the parameters set by Saudi law. Thus do we signal that our "special relationship" is more important than two American daughters — and then we are surprised that the Saudis are so uncooperative in, say, the Khobar Towers investigation.

At the official level, the American response is always that this is a complicated matter. But privately the whispers are that all it would really take is for President Bush to let Crown Prince Abdullah know he wants his two citizens to come to America, where they can then decide for themselves where they want to live without fear of reprisal. As one State representative conceded to a congressional staffer, in terms of US representation, Alia and Aisha would be better off if they were convicted criminals.

The bitter irony is not lost on Miss Roush. "In Peru, President Bush raised the case of Lori Berenson," she sighs. "If an American woman convicted of aiding guerrillas is worthy of the President's concern, shouldn't he be able to say something about two American women serving a life sentence even though they've never done anything wrong?"

Saudis Boycotting US Goods on Perceived Pro-Israel Bias

(Article from Reuters news service in
Jerusalem Post of Friday, June 21st, 2002)

A boycott of United States goods by Saudis angered by Washington's Middle East policies has led to a sharp fall in US exports to Saudi Arabia, diplomats and economists said yesterday.

Official US figures show exports plunged 33 percent to $2.8 billion between September, the month that suicide-bombers, most of them Saudis, attacked the US, and March. In the first quarter of 2002, exports fell 43% to $986 million from $1.74 billion a year earlier.

Many Saudi consumers have shifted to European and Japanese products, encouraged by campaigners wearing Palestinian checkered head scarves who have distributed leaflets at mosques, schools, and shopping malls, a resident said. They urge Saudis to boycott US household items, vehicles, food and beverages, fast-food restaurants, and tobacco in protest at Washington's perceived pro-Israel bias and anti-Saudi campaigns by some US senators and media following the September 11 attacks.

"The reason [for the drop in exports] is definitely political. The boycott of made in USA products is a major contributor to this sharp drop," said Bisher Bakheet, managing director of Bakheet Financial Advisors.

Oil *Power* Saudi Arabia is the biggest energy supplier to the US, with two-way trade estimated at $20b. Saudi exports to the US also fell 36% to $2.44b during the first quarter year-on-year from $3.83b., but economists attributed the drop to lower oil prices and output curbs in line with OPEC efforts to defend revenues. According to diplomatic sources, although US exports accounted for only a fraction of its global trade, the steep decline appeared to show the depth of anti-US sentiment in the conservative Muslim kingdom, which is a staunch supporter of the Palestinians.

The US Embassy in Riyadh said Saudis shunning American products was worrying. But it cited other factors, including the appreciation of the dollar and shrinking defense contracts from US firms, the kingdom's biggest arms suppliers.

"The fact is that the impact of the boycott is very significant.... Yes, we are concerned. But exactly how big this impact is, is very hard to determine without a detailed study," said Charley Kestenbaum, the US Embassy's commercial officer.

[Victor Mordecai comments: The rise in value of the Euro over the dollar and the steep slide on Wall Street over the last few months shows, I believe, a shift from Saudi investments in the US to the European Union. This is a tactical and strategic threat to the US posed by the Saudis. The Saudis, in effect, are now waging economic war on the US.]

Saudi Arabia Considers Free-Trade Accord with Iraq

(Bloomberg news service article in *Jerusalem Post*
on p.11 — June 27, 2002)

Saudi Arabia is considering signing a free-trade agreement with Iraq to promote inter-Arab trade, the *Arab News* daily reported, without citing a source. Saudi Arabia would become the 11th Arab country to reach such an accord with Iraq, joining states like Egypt, the United Arab Emirates, Qatar, and Oman, the paper said. Iraq attacked Saudi Arabia during its 1990 invasion of Kuwait. Saudi businesses have sold more than $1b of goods such as foods, chemicals and medicines to Iraq since 1996, through a United Nations-supervised program using the proceeds from Iraqi oil sales. The UN imposed economic sanctions after Iraq's 1990 invasion of Kuwait.

Any normalization of relations between Iraq and the rest of the Arab world, particularly the oil-rich Persian Gulf monarchies, will make it more difficult for the US to secure support for its campaign to remove Iraqi President Saddam Hussein.

[Victor Mordecai comments: Saudi Arabia is an ally of fellow Moslem and Arab Iraq. Even Iran, an erstwhile enemy of Iraq is now an ally. The enemy of the Arab world now is Christian America.]

PRIVATE INVESTIGATION

In my October 2001 newsletter, the first of its kind, I revealed a typical example of the kind of private investigation I carry out during my travels around the US, Canada and other countries.

It was during a visit to Edmonton, Canada, in the summer of 1999 that it was revealed to me in a synagogue that the Moslems of

Edmonton would be required to kill the Jews and certain Christians in Edmonton upon the receipt of orders from the Middle East.

It has been barely a month since I was a second time in Edmonton, June to be precise, and it was revealed to me that the synagogue had been fire-bombed by a young Moslem militant from the local community. The Moslem was given only one year in jail and everyone tried to paper over the problem.

When I left Israel in late April to undertake this very trip, it was at the same time as a number of anti-Semitic attacks throughout Europe as well as scary newspaper articles from different countries pointing to the plans of international Islam to murder Jews not only in Edmonton, Canada, but anywhere and everywhere.

I carried with me an article from the March 1st, 2002, *Jerusalem Post* which appeared on page A13 entitled:

UK Moslem Cleric Appears in Court

London (AP) — A Muslim cleric accused of urging his followers to murder Hindus, Jews, and other nonbelievers appeared briefly in court yesterday, and was ordered held pending a further hearing in May. Abdullah el-Faisal, 38, of east London, is charged with inciting others to commit murder under the rarely used Offenses Against the Persons Act 1861.

The defendant's lawyers say el-Faisal, who denies the charge but has not yet entered a formal plea, is a respected religious leader whose comments have been taken out of context. El-Faisal circulated cassettes of sermons in which he called on Muslims to kill non-believers, prosecution lawyer Sally Walsh said at a hearing on February 21st.

Prosecutors said copies of the tapes were found in el-Faisal's east London home, along with notes for sermons and duplicating equipment. The cassettes — one titled "No Peace With the Jews" - were also for sale in Muslim bookshops.

Further to the above article, it was indeed during this same period that the police in Berlin, Germany, asked Jews not to wear the kipa, or Yarmulke (skullcap head-covering) or the Star of David type jewelry or any form of identification designating people as Jews, because the German police would then be incapable of protecting the Jews who, according to the police, were being targeted for destruction in the streets of Germany by the Moslems who were "out gunning for them." This report was on Israel Radio.

Another report on Israel Radio was that the Islamic leaderships in Denmark and Norway had called upon Moslem believers in those countries to kill the Jews wherever and whenever they could find them.

Of course, the Moslems in France were behind the vast majority of attacks on the Jews, their synagogues and property. There were hundreds of incidents just in the year 2002.

The murders of two Jews at LAX airport in June were perpetrated by an Egyptian Moslem with no police record.

The Moslems outnumber the Jews in the US and Canada by over 3 to 1. They are not afraid to die as they kill Jews, and for them going to jail in America is a picnic, at least definitely better than the lives they have outside of jail. That's the nature of Islam.

A second interesting aspect of this recent trip to Canada was that I appeared in a church in Edmonton in which the pastor introduced me by saying that until the night before my appearance, he had had second thoughts about me speaking because of the "radical" nature of my message. But it just so happened that the night before I spoke, CBC TV in Canada showed a movie called *The Recruiter,* a movie about Islamic terrorism in Canada. The pastor had no second thoughts about me speaking in his church after he saw this CBC documentary.

The third and final interesting tidbit of private investigation happened as I was crossing the border back into the US. First, there was no traffic at the border crossing while in the past, it was a busy border crossing. People are just not traveling so much any more. The US border inspector asked me what my nationality was. Since I expected that question, I already had my US passport ready and flashed it in front of his eyes.

He said to me: "I want to hear you say it." So I said it. He then checked every box and suitcase in my van. When he saw my books on fanatic Islam, we started to talk and we talked for 20 minutes. Again, there was no traffic at the border.

He finally explained to me that the reason he asked me orally to tell him what my citizenship was, was that the Moslems are using white people (like Johnny Walker Lindh, the Taliban of Marin County, California) including Europeans who have converted to Islam to infiltrate the US as terrorists. This was racial profiling in reverse!

MILITARY INTELLIGENCE INFORMATION

Iran Confirms: "We've Successfully Launched 'The Shihab3'"

Translation of article by Itamar Eichner and staffers of Israeli Hebrew daily *Yediot Ahronot* of Monday, May 27th, 2002.

Concern in Israel Regarding the Missile, Capable of Hitting Any Spot in Israel; Peres: Iran Is "The Mother of Terrorism"; The US Warns Russia and China: Stop Military Cooperation With the Iranians.

There is great concern in Israel regarding the successful launch of the Iranian "Shihab III" missile, a missile with a range of 1,300 km. The ramifications: It can reach any spot in Israel.

Israeli Foreign Minister Shimon Peres warned yesterday that Iran is intending on developing missiles with even a longer range — of up to 10,000km (6,000 miles). He described Iran as a "dangerous state, the mother of terrorism, who finances and trains the Islamic Jihad to attack Israeli civilians." The foreign minister also expressed his concern about the weakening of the moderates in Iran. Peres said this after a meeting in Jerusalem with the Czech Foreign Minister Jan Kavan.

Iran yesterday confirmed reports of the successful launch of the "Shihab 3." Radio Teheran quoted Iranian Defense Minister Admiral Ali Shamkhani, who said, "The purpose of this test was to improve the accuracy and the payload carrying capability of the missile."

Army Intelligence Expert Warns of Nuclear Equipped Iran

(Article by Greer Fay Cashman on page 4 of the *Jerusalem Post* of Thursday, June 20th, 2002)

If September 11th was a watershed, a nuclear-equipped Iran will be much worse, Col. Miri Eisen, head of doctrine in the IDF's Combat Intelligence Corps, warned yesterday.

Eisen, speaking in Jerusalem to a World Keren Hayesod solidarity mission, noted that by the end of the decade Iran will be nuclear.

The Russians, North Koreans, and Chinese are all making it easier for Iran to reach nuclear capabilities, she said, adding that Iran presently has missiles that can reach Israel and India. By the end of the decade, Iran's missiles will be able to reach the rest of the world, she cautioned.

Eisen is part of Israel's new preemptive offensive. Instead of responding to Palestinian allegations against Israel, she brings up Israel's issues, stating what terrorism is, citing corroborative facts.

"The impact of what we managed to do in North America has been huge," said Eisen. "Within a four-week period, all polls showing that people who believed Arafat to be a terrorist and unreliable went way up." [Victor Mordecai comments: This includes Victor Mordecai!]

One of her own strengths, said Eisen, is that she has spent the whole of her military career in intelligence, and has the background to counter any charges brought against Israel.

Following her American success, she will now direct her attention to Europe. "We certainly have to focus there — in each country in a separate way."

The biggest myth about terrorism, said Eisen, is that some person wakes up in the morning, feels overwhelmed by occupation, and miraculously finds a bomb. Terrorism is not spontaneous, Eisen concluded. "It is not a reaction; it is organized."

Eisen listed ideology, people, weapons and money as the four separate components of terrorism. "Terrorism costs — and it costs a lot of money," she said. "Money makes terrorism go around."

The money given by the Saudi Arabians to Hamas has gone mainly for explosives, she said.

As for training in terrorism, one of the key centers is Syria in which 13 terrorist organizations are headquartered. Most terrorists are trained in Syria, she said.

While the army can do something about weapons, explosives, and terrorists, ideology is where it hits a brick wall. "The ideology is the one thing the military can do nothing about."

Over the past three-and-a-half months, she said, the IDF has uncovered 82 explosive labs in six cities and has arrested 27 suicide bombers who did not explode. Of 44,000 light weapons given to the Palestinians as part of the Oslo agreement, the IDF has recovered 5,000.

"If ideology and education don't change, the present reality won't change," said Eisen, who is convinced that things can change if the ideology does.

Easier said than done? Maybe not. Eisen quoted a would-be suicide bomber who was interviewed on television. When asked why she wanted to be a suicide bomber, her reply was: "Because President Arafat asked us."

"And if President Arafat tells you not to?" queried the interviewer.

"Then I won't."

Study: Syrian Textbboks Drenched With Anti-Semitism

(Article by Melissa Radler on page 3 of the *Jerusalem Post* of June 27th, 2002)

New York — Virulent anti-Semitism, calls for Jihad, and support for the elimination of Israel are entrenched in every level of Syria's school system, according to a study of 68 Syrian school textbooks spanning grades 1-12 released by B'nai B'rith International on Tuesday.

Conducted by the New York-based Center for Monitoring the Impact of Peace, the 30-page study entitled "Jihad, Jews, and Anti-Semitism in Syrian School Texts" found that Syrian children are taught to hate Jews and Israel with such ferocity that genuine reconciliation between the two peoples appears unlikely anytime soon.

The study also highlights Syria's contradictory roles in the international arena. Listed as one of seven sponsors of international terrorism by the US State Department, Syria holds the rotating presidency of the United Nations Security Council, and it co-chairs its Human Rights Commission, based in Geneva.

Among the many examples of anti-Semitism and anti-Israel sentiment cited in the study, which examined government-funded texts only, is an excerpt from a 10th grade social studies text that describes Zionism as "a racist-imperialist-colonialist-aggressive-expansionist political movement." In an 11th grade reader, Zionism is called the "new Nazism" and a "model of racist evil." Eighth-graders are taught that "It is known that the Jews of today do not have any connection to Palestine," and sixth-graders learn that "The Prophet (Muhammad) knew about the treacherous intention harbored in the Jews' souls."

By age 15, Syrian children read in their Islamic studies textbooks that Jews deserve to be liquidated: "Co-existence with them or having them as neighbors is an enormous danger that threatens Islamic and Arab existence with destruction and extinction.... Their criminal intention should be turned against them by way of their elimination." Calls for "martyrdom" and terrorism are also tracked in the study. An Islamic studies text for grade-5 students describes praising Palestinian youth for "rushing towards death, trying to reach it ahead of one another," and 6th graders learn: "There is neither excuse nor forgiveness for the one who refrains from jihad for the cause of God, for the purification of Palestine of the Jews."

US Congressman Rep. Eliot Engel (D-NY), who cosponsored the Syria Accountability Act along with House Majority Leader Dick Armey (R-Texas), joined B'nai B'rith leaders at the study's release in Washington on Tuesday. "How can we have hope for peace in the future if Syrian children of today are growing up to passionately hate Jews and Israel? This report highlights the dangers the world will continue to face unless Syria makes some drastic changes now," he said.

B'nai B'rith executive vice president Dan Mariaschin said the study highlights the dim prospects for peace between Israel and Syria.

Report: Syria Preparing to Build Extended-Range Scud

(Article by Arieh O'Sullivan in *Jerusalem Post* of
Friday June 21st, 2002)

Syrian defense industries have completed the development of a longer-range Scud-C ballistic missile and are preparing to start serial production, the London-based *Jane's Defense News* reported yesterday.

According to the report, the assembly line could produce as many as 30 missiles a year, doubling the current Scud-C production. The extended-range Scud-C variant has a range of 700 km and uses an engine similar to that of the standard Scud-C, but has an increased-diameter fuselage, allowing it to carry more fuel and achieve a greater range, the *Jane's* report said. It added that it was capable of carrying a 700 kg payload designed to contain biological and chemical weapons.

Senior IDF officials said that the Syrians have been steadily investing in their surface-to-surface missile arsenal. Their main efforts now are to extend the missiles' range and protect them from air strikes in elaborate mountain tunnels. These missile sites are spread out across Syria and are designed to allow arming the missile underground, reducing the time they are exposed to attack on their launchers.

The liquid fuel powered Scud-C rockets are based on a North Korean missile; *Jane's* reported, that Iran provided the liquid fuel technology and material.

Israeli security experts note that a longer range Scud-C missile would allow the Syrians to deploy them further away from the battlefield. It would also make them faster, which could hamper attempts by the Israeli-made Arrow anti-ballistic missile interceptor to hit them.

Geostrategy-Direct Intelligence Brief

UK Lists Saudis as Missile Threat Arsenal of Chinese Weapons Seen as Emerging Danger To London

Posted: May 16, 2002
5:00 p.m. Eastern

Editor's note: WorldNetDaily brings readers exclusive, up-to-the-minute global intelligence news and analysis from Geostrategy-Direct, a new online newsletter edited by veteran journalist Robert Morton and featuring the "Backgrounder" column compiled by Bill Gertz. Geostrategy-Direct is a subscription based service produced by the publishers of WorldTribune.com, a free news service frequently linked by the editors of WorldNetDaily. © 2002 WorldNetDaily.com

Britain fears that Saudi Arabia's arsenal of Chinese missiles could pose a threat to London by the middle of the decade, according to a report by the British Ministry of Defense.

It was the first time in years that a Western government report listed Saudi Arabia as a missile threat and acknowledged its arsenal of CSS-2 missiles.

The Saudi missile arsenal was cited in a 1997 CIA report, but not as a threat. Since then the U.S. intelligence agency has not listed Riyadh as a missile state.

Britain has listed several Middle East countries as emerging missile threats and has termed Saudi Arabia as possessing intermediate-range missile capability.

The report, issued jointly with the Foreign Office, said Iran, Iraq, Libya and Syria are developing ballistic missiles that threaten London. North Korea was also on the list.

"A particular cause for concern is the fact that North Korea appears to be willing to sell its missiles to any country prepared to pay for them," the report said. "Were a country in the Middle East or North Africa to acquire a complete long-range ballistic missile system, a capability to target the U.K. accurately could emerge within the next few years."

The report, submitted to Parliament's Defense Select Committee, listed 28 countries as possessing ballistic missile capabilities. They included such Middle East states as Egypt, Israel, Saudi Arabia, the United Arab Emirates and Yemen.

"We recognize that threat depends on both capability and intention," the report said. "We currently have no evidence that any state with ballistic missiles has the intention specifically to target the UK. But intentions can change rapidly, and the fact is that the proliferation continues of weapons of mass destruction and their means of delivery. We believe that all responsible nations need to remain alert and take action to deal with the potential threat."

The CSS-2, known as the DF-3 by the Chinese military, has been described as a single-stage, mobile, liquid-fueled, intermediate-range ballistic missile capable of delivering a single nuclear warhead. It has a range of about 1,500 miles. In the late 1980s, China upgraded the CSS-2 but is not believed to have provided Saudi Arabia with the more advanced model.

The British report said the government of Prime Minister Tony Blair has not decided on whether to obtain a missile defense system. It said the government will soon release an unclassified report of British readiness against the missile threat.

"It is still premature to decide on acquiring an active ballistic missile defense capability for either deployed forces, for whom we already have considerable capabilities for passive force protection against weapons of mass destruction, or for defense of the UK," the report said.

"But we have for some years been monitoring developments both in the potential ballistic missile threat and in the missile defense technology available to counter it, which is evolving rapidly."

Victor Mordecai comments: In my April 2002 newsletter, I decided to translate an article by Ronen Bergman in the Israeli Hebrew daily *Yediot Ahronot* of March 27th, 2002. The article describes in depth the Chinese built and maintained missile base in the heart of the Saudi Arabian desert at the "El Solayil" Oasis.

The thrust of the article is that the Saudis now possess up to 120 CSS-2 Chinese missiles with a range of up to 2,000 miles and with possibly/probably nuclear tipped warheads provided by the Pakistanis.

In the April newsletter, there is also a map of the Middle East showing the range of these missiles. India, Israel, Turkey, Kuwait and Qatar are all within range of these missiles.

Stage II, it seems, is for the Saudis to extend the range of these missiles to cover all of Europe including London. And this is the reason for the British concern. Saudi Arabia, not Iraq, not Iran, has now become a strategic, tactical threat to the world.

The June and July newsletters are intended to help expose the threat of Saudi Arabia to the civilized world today and to give food for thought to the wise as to how to deal with the Saudi threat.

Chapter X
JULY 2002 NEWSLETTER

Victor Mordecai's Monthly Message

One of the frustrations of being only one person and not a dozen human beings is that I cannot both research and produce a monthly newsletter, which requires a sedentary life, and travel eight months of the year all over the world to preach the same message. I don't even have time to answer letters mailed to me by "snail mail" and give the individual attention needed to friends and potential supporters.

The information provided in these newsletters since October 2001 includes newspaper articles appearing in the Hebrew and English language Israeli press, as well as Arabic and foreign media. Newspapers accumulate in my home and during my short R & R visits to the homeland, that's when I do my reading and preparation of newsletters.

In fact, the July 2002 newsletter, which is now being written in February 2003, is based on articles collated and read in September. The birth of my second grandchild, the visit of my father, who is eighty-eight, one month of High Holidays, as well as one full week's participation in the Christian Embassy's "Feast of Tabernacles" and the extended sickness of my mother-in-law, and her death in January 2003 were tremendous obstacles to producing the newsletters over the last six months.

In spite of the tardiness of this July newsletter, to be followed, God willing, by the August and September newsletters for
2002, I have chosen "evergreen" articles which have stood the test
of time and are relevant, perhaps even more so today in February
2003 than they were six months ago. Though I don't like to write
newsletters in retrospect or hindsight, because that is cheating, my
purpose is not so much to be original, but to provide my readers
with truthful information that is relevant to the survival of Western
Civilization.

My monthly message for July 2002 will be based on my
first visit ever to Norway and Finland during that month of July.
For twelve years, I have been preaching my message in certain
countries such as the US, Canada, Mexico, Israel, Switzerland,
Russia and Greece. But by far, my emphasis has always been the
United States of America.

The reason for this was that I always believed that Washington, DC, was the key to war and peace in the Middle East. I still
believe that. I felt that any effort invested outside of the US was
wasted time, because after all, it was only Washington, DC, which
counted. I should not fritter away my time outside of the US.

However, thanks to Mr. Malcolm Hedding, Director of the
International Christian Embassy of Jerusalem (ICEJ), and Leif
Wellerop, the leader of the Norwegian branch of the ICEJ, as well
as Ulla Jarvilehto, leader of ICEJ Finland, I decided to accept their
invitation to visit Scandinavia in July 2002.

I was in for a big surprise. In my meetings in Norway and
Finland, I was told in no uncertain terms that Israel was neglect-
ing its friends in Europe and there was much work to be done to
improve Israel's image in Europe in general and in Scandinavia
in particular.

Before my visit to Scandinavia, I had felt that Europe was
a lost cause. It seemed from the Israeli media that the European
Parliament was an anti-Israel, anti-Semitic monolith. The "Europeans" were against us. All the more reason not to waste time with
the Europeans and to focus on what really counted: the US.

But what I discovered was that in a recent anti-Israel decision, the European Parliament voted by 263 against Israel and 213 in favor of Israel. The margin was 50 votes or about 10%.

My "discovery of America" was that of the 263 votes against Israel, the majority of these were based not on anti-Semitism, but on ignorance as to the realities of the Middle East. My Norwegian and Finnish interlocutors said that provided with the truth, the EU parliamentarians could and would change their votes in favor of Israel, but only if more of an effort was made to reach them. To continue to ignore these parliamentarians would mean continuing negative fallout for Israel.

My friends said to me, "If only there were a few dozen more people like yourself and your wife, we could within months turn the European Parliament around and in favor of Israel." I am not trying to flatter myself here, but to say that there are hundreds and probably thousands of Israelis who could travel to Europe to do the job. With a little imagination, effort, and ideological grounding, Israeli spokespeople could meet with these European parliamentarians one on one and offer them the truth as to what's really happening with the Islamic nations bent on destroying Israel.

I think that the biological and chemical weapons of the Moslem terrorists being found every day in countries like the UK, France, Italy and Spain will eventually also show the European Union that it is not only Israel's existence which is being threatened by Islam, but theirs as well.

It is not enough to let the Moslems do all the work to show how menacing they are. And if we want to put a stop to US President George W. Bush's "Road Map" to a Palestinian state, which would lead to the annihilation of Israel, then maybe we do need the European Union Parliament vote to be in favor of Israel.

President George W. Bush has decided to deliver Israel an ultimatum forcing it back to the indefensible borders of June 5th, 1967. He is basing his strategy on four pillars: 1. US. 2. European Union. 3. Russia. 4. UN.

Knock out one pillar (the European Union). Bush is left with Russia and the UN.

Since Russia also has its own never-ending wars with Islam (Russia has been fighting Islam for over a thousand years), Russia is not necessarily an enemy of Israel, but probably an ally.

Knock out that pillar (Russia) from Bush's Road Map strategy, then he is left only with the US and UN.

Since the UN is comprised of 1/6 Moslem peoples and 5/6 "everybody else," I don't even "write off" the UN. The people of India represent 1/6, the Buddhist nations are 2/6 and the Judeo-Christian world is 2/6 of the earth's population.

This leaves only Washington, DC, of George W. Bush as the last of four pillars to threaten Israel. Knock out the other three pillars of the "Road Map to Palestine Plan" and spark a Christian Revival in the US, thus sending the right message to President George W. Bush: Christian Revival for Israel's Survival. Whoever touches Israel touches the apple of God's eye. Whoever blesses Israel is blessed. Whoever curses Israel is cursed. Pray for America. Seek the peace of Jerusalem by preventing the creation of a Palestinian state whose only objective is the annihilation of the Jews.

CURRENT EVENTS AND ANALYSIS

I. Egyptian Suppression of Democracy

Egyptian Rights Activist Again Gets Seven-Year Jail Term

Article by Nadia Abou El Magd on page 5
of *The Jerusalem Post* of July 30th, 2002

CAIRO (AP) — Egyptian-American academic and human rights activist Saad Eddin Ibrahim was sentenced to seven years in prison yesterday for embezzlement of foreign funds, receiving foreign funds without authorization, and tarnishing Egypt's image — a case international human rights organizations have condemned as politically motivated.

The State Security Court's verdict and sentencing

yesterday came at the end of a retrial an appeals court had ordered on procedural grounds. The 63-year-old Ibrahim, a sociology professor at the American University in Cairo and an outspoken human rights and democracy advocate, was sentenced last year to seven years on the same charges he faced in the retrial.

The US Embassy in Cairo and Amnesty International were among those expressing disappointment and shock at the verdict. The US has occasionally chided Egypt for its poor human rights record.

Chief Egyptian government spokesman Nabil Osman refused to comment on the case.

Ibrahim was composed as he listened to the verdict. Moments later, he told the Associated Press he believed the verdict was "politically motivated" and said he would appeal again.

His wife, Barbara, said, "The rule of law died today in Egypt." Their daughter, Randa Ibrahim, a lawyer, said she had not expected a verdict so quickly because the judge had given the impression he was going to take time to study defense arguments. Instead, the verdict came right after defense attorneys finished their arguments yesterday.

The verdict was "quite a shock. From the beginning of the case we were saying the charges were politically motivated," Sara Hamood, a London-based Amnesty International official, said in a telephone interview.

Negad Borai, a leading Egyptian lawyer and political reform advocate, said the verdict revealed "that Egyptian laws are autocratic by nature."

The US charge d'affaires in Cairo, Gordon Gray, issued a statement expressing "disappointment" at the verdict and reiterating US concerns about the "fairness of the process."

Twenty-seven co-defendants, most staff members of a think tank Ibrahim founded and ran since 1988, were convicted of bribery and fraud charges and received sentences ranging from one-year suspended sentences to three years yesterday.

Most of the 24 given one-year suspended sentences had received similar sentences in the last trial and had not been attending the retrial hearings.

Ibrahim and the three co-defendants who did not receive suspended sentences were transferred from the courthouse to a Cairo prison yesterday.

In his closing arguments last week, prosecutor Sameh Seif said Ibrahim used funds raised through his Ibn Khaldun Center for Development Studies for personal gain and lured his staff into an embezzlement scheme.

At the heart of the case were about 252,000 euros in European Union democracy-building grants. The European Union had said in an affidavit it did not believe its grants were misused. One of the main defendants said he was forced during his pretrial imprisonment to falsely accuse Ibrahim of embezzlement.

Among the democracy projects the Ibn Khaldun Center created was a documentary meant to encourage voting. The script argued election fraud, which observers say has marred Egyptian voting, is less likely when citizens participate. Prosecutors claimed the documentary tarnished Egypt's image with its references to fraud.

A report Ibrahim did on the status of Copts (Christians) in Egypt also was cited by prosecutors. Egypt's government is sensitive to criticism about the treatment of Coptic Christians in the country.

II. Imprisonment of Syrian Democracy Proponents Upheld

Article on page 5 of *The Jerusalem Post*
of July 2nd, 2002

Damascus (AP) — A Syrian appeals court has upheld the conviction of two pro-democracy legislators sentenced to five years' imprisonment, their defense counsel said yesterday.

The dismissal of the appeal "consecrates the Syrian authorities' decision to suppress and silence any opposition voice or any voice that calls for ending widespread corruption and to save the country from economic, political, social and moral backwardness," attorney Anwar al-Buni said in a statement to reporters.

Lawmakers Mamoun al-Homsi and Riyadh Seif had appealed against their conviction in separate trials in March of inciting rebellion, disseminating lies, and trying to change the constitution by force.

Buni said the appeals court issued its ruling early yesterday. The court did not immediately make the ruling public.

"The criminal court verdict was correct and legal," Buni quoted the ruling as saying.

He added that the decision had killed Syrians' hopes for "honest, independent and evenhanded justice in Syria."

Seif and Homsi were among a group of pro-democracy activists detained in August and September 2001 for taking part in political discussion groups in private homes.

Their activities were part of a quiet push for reform in Syria, which has long been a virtual one-party state with little tolerance of dissent.

III. Egyptian Conspiracy Theories and the Jews

Article by Arieh O'Sullivan on page 2 of
The Jerusalem Post of July 16th, 2002

Alexandra — Just a 45-minute flight from Ben-Gurion Airport, Alexandria is Egypt's second-largest city.

It's a cleanly swept Mediterranean pearl of a place with broad avenues and a marvelous boulevard on the sea front. Its mix of colonial-era buildings and simple cement apartments make it look like a once beautiful lady who had matured...awkwardly. Still, at 2,334 years old, she looks good for her age.

On her northern shore is the Ras e-Tin Palace. Faced in a white marble with six large solid granite columns at its entrance, it was from here that King Farouk was sent into exile nearly 50 years ago.

The only remnant of his rule is the letter "F," painted and carved throughout the palace's gaudy, gilded halls and mirrored ballrooms.

Today, President Hosni Mubarak uses it to greet foreign dignitaries and it is decked out in its full splendor with plenty of colorful flags snapping in the wind.

A strange thing happens when you get too many journalists inside a flashy palace on a hot summer day in Egypt. Conspiracy theories start to fly.

The Israelis wanted to know why there is not even one blue and white Israeli flag anywhere on what is supposed to be an official visit by Minister of Defense Binyamin Ben-Eliezer. Were they all stolen? Is it because they had all been burned in a street protest, as one Egyptian reporter quipped? In fact, "Israel" and "Israelis" don't even exist there. Except for a polite few, the Egyptian security and journalists all referred to us as "the Jews." Judging from the security checks we had to go through, they trusted us about as much as our own Shin Bet. You have to be careful with the Jews, you know. They run the world.

And if there was any lingering doubt about their fertile minds it was soon put to rest when the press conference with Ben-Eliezer began.

An Egyptian television reporter who gave her name as Annette Simeri took the microphone and with a straight face asked: "Is it true that the Israeli government reached an agreement with the American administration based on freezing the situation on the ground until the American elections take place in November, in return for Republican

Congressmen getting all of the Jewish support?" The Israeli journalists laughed. The members of the Israeli delegation chuckled and Ben-Eliezer himself cracked a broad smile. But the Egyptian reporters saw nothing funny about what they considered a very, very serious allegation.

"This is just an illusion. This is the first time that I heard such crazy things," Ben-Eliezer said, shaking his head.

Questioning the TV reporter afterwards on the source of such a fantastic story, she just said: "Oh, I read it someplace. I can't remember — a wire service or something." The fact that an apparently professional journalist can take such folly seriously and even venture to query the visiting Israeli defense minister about it is more than just an amusing peek into their minds. It is scary.

IV. Go Down to Egypt

Editorial on page 8 of *The Jerusalem Post* of
July 16th, 2002

So Transport Minister Ephraim Sneh, Knesset Speaker Avraham Burg, and now Defense Minister Binyamin Ben-Eliezer have gone down to Egypt to confer with Egyptian President Hosni Mubarak, all within the space of a week. For what?

Ostensibly, the topic of conversation is the reform of the Palestinian Authority and a reduction in the level of violence, both of which are areas where Mubarak is thought to have the power to play a constructive role. Indeed, he does have that power. But it is power he has conspicuously failed to exercise for years, choosing instead to cultivate the image of honest broker with the US while playing the part of spoiler against Israel. With their visits to Egypt, the Labor Party's current batch of wise men has merely helped Mubarak further along this path.

This is foolish. It is also dangerous. Our supposed ally in the struggle for Middle East peace demonstrates its hostility to us at nearly every turn. Often, it does so in extraordinarily petty ways. Contrary to ordinary protocol, Israeli flags are not flown when Israeli diplomats confer with their Egyptian opposites as Sharm el Sheikh. The Israeli embassy will not be serviced for its workaday needs by Egyptian plumbers, bricklayers and the like. Israeli doctors must be flown to Cairo to treat embassy personnel, as Egyptian doctors refuse to do so.

Then too, when two Egyptian journalists showed up at our Cairo embassy's Independence Day celebration last year, they quickly found themselves evicted from their professional guild. There is little by way of academic contact because the Egyptian intelligentsia operates under similar threat. The state-run Egyptian media gives its colleagues in Baghdad a run for their money when it comes to rantings against Jews. Meanwhile, Egypt refuses to send an ambassador to Tel Aviv, in contravention to its obligations under the Camp David Accords, or maintain ordinary trade relations with us, except to the extent that they can profit from our reliance on their natural gas.

All this may be dismissed as merely what's to be expected from an Arab autocracy that must keep its radical domestic critics at bay, and a reasonable price for Israel to pay for a secure southern frontier. Yet the southern border is not secure. Palestinian weapons are every day smuggled through tunnels running beneath the Egyptian and Palestinian sides of Rafah, and the Egyptian government does little to help Israel prevent the smuggling.

Egypt's military — the recipient of billions in American largesse — continues to see Israel as its principal strategic adversary, and trains to fight accordingly. The Ariel Center estimates that as much as 30% of Egypt's gross domestic product is steered toward military expenditures, about the same as the Soviet Union during the Brezhnev era. Most worrisome, the Egyptian military is equipped with state-of-the-art American equipment, including Harpoon missiles, F-16's, and M1-A1 tanks, all of which goes far to reduce Israel's qualitative edge.

Reasonable people must ask what Egypt, a country with massive and growing economic problems, intends to do with all this expenditure. To defend itself against Yemen? Or Libya? Yet instead of drawing appropriate conclusions, successive Israeli governments have been silent, presumably in hopes that by not calling attention to a problem they might make it go away.

The same, it must be said, goes for US policy toward what Fouad Ajami has called its "runaway ally." Mubarak has not only snubbed the US when it suited his convenience — most recently, by refusing to meet with Secretary of State Colin Powell during his visit in May — he has also put himself squarely in the way of US efforts to see both Yasser Arafat and Saddam Hussein deposed. Yet for this he has been repaid with indulgence: weekend visits to Camp David, forgiveness of Egyptian debt and, of course, undiminished economic and military assistance.

Of course, if Israel continues to act as if Egypt plays a positive role in the region, the US is likely to follow suit. Yet indulging bad behavior has never yielded good results. At some point, Egypt must be made to pay a price for failing to deliver on its end of the bargain. Just the threat of diminished US military support would go far to achieve this result. Israelis can do their part by refusing to play a part in Mubarak's charade.

V. Saudi Newspaper Editor "Apologizes" for Purim Blood Libel

Article by Dan Izenberg and Gil Hoffman on page 4
of *The Jerusalem Post* of March 20th, 2002

A Saudi Arabian newspaper editor yesterday issued

a backhanded apology for a column published last week which resurrected the medieval blood libel against Jews by claiming they use the blood of Christian or Muslim "mature adolescents" to prepare special Purim pastries.

Al Riyadh editor-in-chief Turki al-Sudairi wrote that the article, written by Umayma Ahmed al-Jalahma of King Faisal University, was "not fit to print." The paper had been sharply criticized by the US government before *Al-Riyadh* published the apology.

On Monday, the Voice of America aired an editorial praising Saudi Arabia for its peace initiative, but criticizing it for not doing more to reduce Israel-Arab tensions.

"In the meantime," said VOA, "there is something that Saudi Arabia and other countries could do right now to ease tensions in the Middle East. They could stop newspapers, radio and television stations, especially those controlled by the state, from inciting hatred and violence against Jews."

Directly referring to the blood libel column, published on March 10th, the VOA editorial added: "No one who is not blinded by hate for Jews could ever believe such nonsense."

Al-Sudairi wrote: "I checked the article and found it not fit for publication, because it was not based on scientific or historical facts, and it even contradicted the rituals of all the known religions in the world.... The information included in the article was no different from the nonsense always coming out in the yellow literature, whose reliability is questionable. The understanding of this serious mistake escaped Ms. Al-Jalahma, as did the understanding that Jews everywhere in the world are one thing, while the Jews belonging to the Zionist movement that wants to annihilate the Palestinians are something else and completely different."

In the article, which was translated into English and disseminated by the Middle East Media Research Institute, al-Jalahma wrote: "During the Purim holiday, the Jew must prepare very special pastries, the filling of which is not only costly and rare — it cannot be found at all on the local and international markets. Unfortunately, this filling cannot be left out, or substituted with any alternative serving the same purpose. For this holiday, the Jewish people must obtain human blood so that their clerics can prepare the holiday pastries. In other words, the practice cannot be carried out as required if human blood is not spilled!"

The Foreign Ministry called the blood libel "a Nazi-like anti-Semitic rumor, whose only purpose is to incite hatred against Jews and the Jewish people." The ministry noted the apology and expressed the hope such an accusation will never be published again in the Saudi press.

"Israel wishes to establish friendly and peaceful relations with its neighboring countries — relations based on friendship and not on racist stereotypes," a ministry spokesman said.

Deputy Foreign Minister Michael Melchior, who founded the International Commission for Combating Anti-Semitism, welcomed the apology, but said it is too bad the paper used it to continue attacking Israel.

"Anti-Semitism is the most stubborn and ancient hatred in the history of humankind, and it has brought about vicious results," Melchior said. "We are shocked that the new anti-Semitism that originates in the Arab world has revived the abominable blood libels of the past. The lies and incitement in the Arab media undermine attempts for normalization and create an anti-Semitic image that will prevent another generation from living in coexistence in the Middle East."

VI. Al-Qaida Spokesman Makes New Threats on American, Jewish Targets

Article by Salah Nasrawi on page 5 of
The Jerusalem Post of July 11th, 2002

Cairo (AP) — A key al-Qaida spokesman has made a new threat to attack American targets and urged Muslims the world over to "kill enemies of God everywhere."

"Al-Qaida will organize more attacks inside American territory and outside, at the moment we choose, at the place we choose, and with the objectives that we want," al-Qaida's chief spokesman, Kuwaiti-born Sulaiman Abu Ghaith, said in an audio recording aired by an Islamic web site believed to be close to the terror network blamed for the September 11th attacks.

"We are coming back, God willing, from where you cannot expect us," said Abu Ghaith in the interview broadcast on www.jehad.net.

The new targets, he said, will be "American and Jewish... our arrogant enemies."

There is no way to verify the authenticity of Abu Ghaith's interview, but US officials said two weeks ago that a recent audio recording by him in which he claimed that al-Qaida leader Usama bin Laden was still alive appeared to be legitimate. Government analysts matched the sound of his voice to previous recordings.

The recording, played on the web site yesterday, appeared to be the same voice.

The Abu Ghaith interview on www.jehad.net is the latest in a series of contacts between al-Qaida and the outside world after weeks of silence. These contacts were made on Islamic-militant oriented web sites whose availability on the Internet has been irregular.

The string of statements coincides with evidence al-Qaida remains capable of planning attacks. Last month, Saudi

Arabia announced it was holding 11 Saudis, an Iraqi and a Sudanese man belonging to a failed plot to shoot down a US military plane taking off from a Saudi air base.

News of the Saudi arrests followed detentions in Morocco of three Saudis who were planning to attack US and British warships in the Straits of Gibraltar.

Referring to the war in Afghanistan that followed the September attacks, Abut Ghaith said in the latest interview that the US-led military campaign has failed to crush the fighters of the Taliban and al-Qaida, claiming that it has instead destroyed Afghan villages and towns.

He said al-Qaida operatives were currently carrying out surveillance operations to pick up new targets.

"Has our battle with America ended? It never ended and will never end because it is not a personal battle but rather a battle between right and wrong... it is a struggle between good and evil," he said.

"America is the head of evil," he added.

Abu Ghaith said bin Laden and most of his top aides were unharmed. "I can assure you that 98 percent of them are well and fine." He also promised, without giving details, that the Saudi-born bin Laden will "soon" appear in a television interview.

"We are living in an age when the enemies of God have successfully killed the spirit of resistance and manhood in Muslims by undermining the Islamic creed," he lamented.

"My message to the Muslim youth is that al-Qaida fighters are not the only ones meant to fight Jews... it is a duty on all Muslims to rise and defend their religion."

Excerpts from the interview were published Tuesday by Algeria's Arabic daily *El Youm*.

In another purported al-Qaida statement on the same web site, another al-Qaida spokesman, identified as Abu Laith al-Libi, warned that al-Qaida was "preparing for a coming period...of guerilla war."

"We have started changing the war to attacks and assassinations and we have succeeded in that with God's help," Libi said without elaborating in the interview, excerpts of which were broadcast by the Middle East Broadcast Center late Tuesday.

VII. Fatah Call for Attacks on US, Zionist Targets

Article by Margot Dudkevitch and Lamia Lahoud on page 1 of *The Jerusalem Post* of July 2nd, 2002

Groups affiliated with Palestinian Authority Chairman Yasser Arafat's Fatah movement yesterday called upon all Palestinian organizations, including the Islamic movements, to attack Zionist and American targets everywhere in response to US efforts "to remove the legitimate leadership of the Palestinian people."

Fatah's military wing, al-Aksa Martyrs Brigades, issued a statement yesterday in which it threatened "to strike at Zionist and American interests and installations" in Israel and throughout the world if the US maintains its opposition to Arafat.

The statement warned US President George W. Bush that it will return to the type of fedayeen operations that prevailed in the 1970's if what they called the conspiracy against Arafat continued.

The statement called for boycotting US Secretary of State Colin Powell and said there is a conspiracy to harm the Palestinian leadership.

VIII. Following Tip of Imminent Attack: Venice Police Step Up Ghetto Security

Article on page 6 of *The Jerusalem Post* of
July 16th, 2002

Venice, Italy (AP) — Police frogmen combed Venetian canals for any bombs, and officers searched handbags and checked identity papers Friday after a reported tip that the lagoon city's ancient Jewish quarter might be the target of terrorists.

An Italian Jewish leader, Amos Luzzatto, a Venetian, said residents of the Ghetto, the neighborhood's centuries-old name, were going about their business as usual despite the concern.

Many Jews live in the neighborhood, which is near the Santa Lucia train station.

Pairs of police stood guard at the six main alleys leading into the neighborhood. At the entrance points, residents and visitors alike were stopped, their handbags or shopping bags searched and their identity papers scrutinized.

Frogmen dived into the waters of the lagoon to search for any explosives, and police boats patrolled the waters. Police officers were posted at many of the bridges which link the city across a myriad of canals.

Italian police have not elaborated on what prompted the measures, but security was stepped up in Venice earlier this year after the tourist destination was named a possible terrorist target.

"The alarm was set off by a tip, I cannot say what kind of tip, whether it was a phone tip or otherwise, that speaks about the Jewish Ghetto districts of Venice and Rome being a target of international terrorism," Luzzatto said.

Venice Mayor Paolo Costa, speaking on Italian state TV, invited all residents to go about their business as usual.

After the September 11th attacks, security was stepped up outside Rome's main synagogue in the Italian capital's Old Ghetto neighborhood, where many Jewish families live. Police with automatic weapons have been posted outside the synagogue for at least two decades following a 1982 terrorist attack on the synagogue that killed a toddler.

The Venice neighborhood, which gave its name to other areas in the world where Jewish communities were segregated, has been inhabited by Jewish residents for nearly 500 years.

In past centuries, Italy's Jews were ordered to live in designated areas. The walls around Rome's Old Ghetto, for example, came down in 1842, after more than 300 years of segregation.

Venice is one of Italy's most popular tourist destinations, and summer finds its narrow streets and many bridges packed with American, Asian and European visitors.

A confidential report by Italy's anti-terrorist police said Islamic militants linked to al-Qaida, Usama bin Laden's terrorist network, made plans for terrorist attacks last year in Italy, according to Italian news reports. Italian officials have indirectly confirmed the existence of the report.

The attack plans were reportedly abruptly frozen two months before the September 11th attacks, and Italian newspapers have quoted Italian investigators as worried that the plans might be reactivated.

The confidential report said one of the terrorist suspects under surveillance visited a Venice church in 2001 and was seen taking photographs.

IX. Chemical, Biological Attack Feared in Turkey

Article on page 5 of *The Jerusalem Post* of
July 11th, 2002

Ankara, Turkey (AP) — Turkish police are on alert over a poisonous chemical or biological substance believed to have been smuggled into the country for an attack that could target the US and Russian embassies, the semi-official Anatolia news agency reported yesterday.

The agency said all provincial police departments were put on alert after the CIA informed Turkish authorities, via the embassy here that the material may be used to target the two embassies and could be used for a mass attack on the Turkish public.

A government official confirmed that the government had been warned about a possible attack involving biological or chemical substances, but downplayed its importance saying police were frequently put on alert against possible attacks, especially since the September 11 attacks. He gave no further information. The US embassy did not immediately comment on the report.

X. Al-Qaida Suspects Die in Shootout

Article by Riaz Khan on page 5 of
The Jerusalem Post of July 4th, 2002

Peshawar, Pakistan (AP) — Four suspected al-Qaida members opened fire after they were stopped at a checkpoint, triggering a gun battle in which seven people were killed, officials said.

The dead included the four al-Qaida suspects — all foreigners — a soldier, a policeman, and a Pakistani intelligence agent, official said. The authorities said explosives were found in the suspects' van, and bomb disposal experts were sent to remove them.

The incident occurred early yesterday at a checkpoint near Kohat, about 70 kilometers southwest of Peshawar. As the checkpoint guards approached the van, the men hurled grenades and opened fire.

Police and troops at the checkpoint killed three of the suspected al-Qaida members in their van, officials said.

The fourth managed to get out and was shot dead as he tried to run away while firing back at the checkpoint guards, officials said.

The officials would not identify the suspects' nationalities. Authorities said the presence of explosives in the van indicated the suspects may have been planning a terrorist attack somewhere in Pakistan.

The al-Qaida suspects were coming from Wana, a remote region near the Afghan border where 10 Pakistani soldiers were killed last month in a gun battle with more than 40 suspected al-Qaida operatives, most of them Chechens.

Since the gun battle, Pakistani troops have arrested 16 suspected al-Qaida fugitives. Earlier police had transferred seven to the prison in Kohat.

Pakistani troops, backed by US intelligence, have been searching the deeply conservative tribal regions along the Afghan border looking for al-Qaida and Taliban fugitives who sought refuge there from US military operations in Afghanistan.

US military officials say they believe most al-Qaida men and senior Taliban officials have fled Afghanistan and are hiding in Pakistan's tribal regions.

The hunt for fugitive al-Qaida and Taliban has generated protests by local tribesmen and Islamic clerics. Fazl-ur Rehman, leader of the rightwing Jamiat-e-Ulema Islam, or Party of Islamic Clerics, warned of riots and civil disobedience if the searches continued.

[Victor Mordecai comments: One of two possibilities exists: Either the al-Qaida, Taliban, and their tribal hosts are completely crushed, or there will be a steady downhill slide for Pakistan from the status of ally of the Western world to enemy.]

XI. Seven Suspected Terrorists Held in Hamburg

Article on page 5 of *The Jerusalem Post* of
July 4, 2002

Berlin (AP) — Seven people, one of whom already was under investigation for links to the cell behind the September 11 attacks, were detained in Hamburg yesterday on suspicion of belonging to a terrorist organization, German federal prosecutors said.

The seven were being questioned after early-morning searches at six apartments and a bookshop in the northern German city. Investigators suspect eight people, along with "further people whose identity is unknown," of forming an Islamic fundamentalist group with the aim of carrying out attacks, the federal prosecutors' office said in a statement.

One person was being questioned in Italy after his home was searched there. Six of the others were picked up in Hamburg in the morning, while a seventh was apprehended in the afternoon, police said.

XII. Report: Atta Met With Other Sept. 11 Pilot in Spain

Article on page 5 of *The Jerusalem Post* of
July 1st, 2002

Madrid (AP) — Spanish police believe suspected September 11th suicide pilot Mohamed Atta met with the other pilot in the Twin Towers attacks and other ringleaders in Spain eight weeks before the attacks to finalize preparations, a newspaper said yesterday.

Atta met in or near the northeastern city of Tarragona on July 10 with Ramzi Bin Shibh, a Yemeni who's now the subject of a worldwide manhunt, and Marwan Shehhi, believed to have flown the second jetliner that crashed into the World Trade Center, *El Pais* said. Atta, an Egyptian, is believed to have piloted the first plane.

The newspaper said it had gained access to a confidential 700-page report in which Spanish police detailed their probe of September 11 preparations in Spain and reconstructed the movements of Atta and other suspects in the terrorist attacks.

XIII. Thailand Suspects Islamic Group in Train Bombing

Article on page 5 of *The Jerusalem Post* of
July 10th, 2002

Bangkok (AP) — An Islamic group is suspected of being involved in the bombing of a train in southern Thailand on Monday in which two security guards were wounded, the national police chief said yesterday — suggesting for the first time a link between Muslims and a rash of violence.

He said the bombing may have been in retaliation for the arrest on Sunday of an Islamic leader, Adoon Hayeed Halor, a former member of the separatist group, the Pattani United Liberation Organization. His followers have banded together as the Islam Pattani Mujahedeen. Authorities said the groups are not linked to the al-Qaida terrorist network.

Muslims are a majority in the south of Thailand, but comprise just 4 percent of the country's 62 million people, who are predominantly Buddhists.

XIV. Dutch Lawmakers Call for Survey of Muslims

Article by *Jerusalem Post* staff on page 5 of
The Jerusalem Post of July 10, 2002

The lower house of the Dutch parliament voted last week to ask their government to commission a study of how mosques in the country are funded, how prayer leaders (imams) are trained, and how many Dutch Muslims are fundamentalists, according to a report in the *Wall Street Journal Europe* which appeared Monday.

The vote came after four Muslim clerks were secretly tape-recorded by a popular Dutch current affairs show, "Nova," praising suicide bombers and calling for the "destruction of the enemies of Islam," according to the report.

An imam in The Hague asked Allah to "take care of" US President George W. Bush and Prime Minister Ariel Sharon, and another in Amsterdam said that "female Palestinian Muslims who offer their lives to Allah should be praised."

The party of slain Pim Fortuyn, who called Islam a "backward religion" which threatens Dutch acceptance of homosexuality and women's rights, received the second most votes in May's election, and is to form part of a new coalition government.

The Dutch internal security agency reported recently that fundamentalists are recruiting young immigrants in Dutch mosques for anti-Western missions in Afghanistan and elsewhere, according to the report in the *Journal*.

The report quoted Miriam Sterk, a legislator from the Christian Democrat Party, as saying, "We need to have freedom of religion, but it is unacceptable that clerics should incite hatred. Imams guilty of encouraging people to commit acts of violence should be expelled from the country."

There are approximately one million Muslims in the Netherlands, out of a total population of 16 million, according to the report.

XV. Moroccans Arrested in Cyanide Plot

Article by Shasta Darlington on page 5 of
The Jerusalem Post of Feb. 21st, 2002

Rome (Reuters) — Italian police said yesterday they had arrested four Moroccans in possession of large quantities of the deadly poison cyanide and maps of Rome highlighting the US Embassy and the city's water supply.

Police said they suspect the men, arrested early Tuesday in an outlying suburb as part of a covert operation, could have been plotting an attack on the embassy or to poison the city's water. They are probing possible links to Usama bin Laden.

Seven Tunisians are on trial in Milan as part of a crackdown on groups suspected of having ties to bin Laden and his al-Qaida network. They are also suspected of plotting an attack on the US Embassy in January 2001.

"The embassy of the United States of America compliments the Italian police and security forces for their excellent work concerning the most recent security threat," said a statement from the embassy.

Deputy Prime Minister Gianfranco Fini hailed the operation: "We should be satisfied because this means that the police force is working hard and controlling our territory." But police chiefs and Italy's leading anti-terrorist prosecutors, who were meeting behind closed doors yesterday, told reporters that leaks regarding the case may have already caused irreparable damage.

Those arrested were found with about 10 pounds of cyanide and a map pinpointing the embassy, charts of Rome's water network, and about 100 counterfeit resident permits, police said. At least two of the men are illegal immigrants.

The Moroccan Embassy said it would comment only after Italy confirmed the identities of the men arrested. "We want to see if they are really Moroccan since in Italy, anyone of color is called a Moroccan," an embassy source said.

The US Embassy, predominantly located on Rome's famed Via Veneto, has been a suspected target for attack on several occasions in recent months.

Even before the September 11th attacks on US cities, the embassy was forced to shut for three days after an intelligence warning of a possible bombing.

Following the attacks on the Pentagon and World Trade Center, the State Department warned again that American symbols in Italy could be targets.

Italy entered the international spotlight in the fight against bin Laden after US investigators said they believed Milan's Islamic cultural center was al-Qaida's main European logistics base. Muslim leaders in Italy have denied the charge.

The four Moroccans, aged 30 to 40, had been followed by police for days and their detention was related to the arrest of three more Moroccans last week, police said.

The Tunisians on trial in Milan have been charged with intent to commit crimes ranging from the trafficking of arms, explosives, and poisonous chemicals to trading in false documents and helping illegal immigrants enter Italy.

Police believe bin Laden sent them to Europe to supervise attacks, including the possible bombing of the US embassy in Rome last January.

Italian justice sources last year released transcripts of telephone conversations in which one of the men on trial in Milan indicated that he was planning chemical attacks in Europe.

In one conversation, the Tunisian told a Libyan associate that there was a plan to "try out" a drum of a "liquid" in France. "This liquid is more efficient because as soon as it opens, people are suffocated," he was quoted as saying.

XVI. Al-Qaida Using Turkey Route to Escape Afghanistan

Article by Selcan Hacaoglu on page 5 of
The Jerusalem Post of Feb. 21st, 2002

Ankara (AP) — The arrest of three suspected al-Qaida members, en route to Israel allegedly for a suicide bombing, has alarmed Turkish authorities who are worried about the infiltration of Islamic militants fleeing Afghanistan.

The suspects — two Palestinians and one Jordanian — were arrested Friday in the eastern city of Van. Police said they planned an attack in a crowded area in Tel Aviv or Ramat Gan, under orders from an Islamic cleric linked to al-Qaida.

It was the first capture of al-Qaida suspects in Turkey.

Authorities increased security along Turkey's mountainous border with Iran and Iraq, an intelligence official said late Tuesday.

A Turkish court formally arraigned the suspects for entering Turkey with fake travel documents late Tuesday, officials said yesterday. Prosecutors are also expected to press terrorism charges.

More checkpoints were erected and paramilitary troops patrolled the area around the clock, said the official. Authorities were also investigating reports that two Tunisian-born Canadians suspected of al-Qaida membership might be in Turkey.

Police in Istanbul were put on alert upon reports that six al-Qaida members were in the city, daily *Hurriyet* said yesterday.

Turkey, a close US ally and NATO's sole Muslim member, has 267 troops serving in the international peace-keeping force in Afghanistan. Turkey also wants to train Afghan military and police officers.

Two US officials were in Van to get first-hand information, the Anatolia news agency said.

All three suspects — identified as Firaz Suleiman, Ahmed Mahmoud, and Mustafa Hassan — fought for the Taliban in Afghanistan, police said. The three underwent military training in a camp run by Usama bin Laden's al-Qaida organization near the western city of Heart, *Hurriyet* said.

The men traveled to Afghanistan to fight among al-Qaida ranks via Turkey, where they obtained fake travel documents.

Mahmoud and Hassan were bearing fake Turkish passports when captured, while Suleiman was in possession of fake Jordanian and Saudi passports, *Hurriyet* said.

Six Turks who allegedly provided the passports to the men were detained in Istanbul.

The Islamic militants were captured after police spotted them in a car at a check point after they crossed the Iranian border. Police fired a warning shot, but the car continued to speed toward Van before smashing into police barricades.

Two other Turks were arrested on charges of human smuggling in Van. Another suspected accomplice, an Iraqi Kurd, is also under interrogation, private NTV television reported.

Police said the suspects planned to travel to Istanbul and then make their way to Israel.

XVII. Suspected 9/11 Mastermind Uncle of Convicted WTC Bomber

Article by Diana Elias on page 5 of
The Jerusalem Post of June 11th, 2002

Kuwait (AP) — Kuwaiti-born Khalid Shaikh Muhammad, 37, suspected of masterminding the 9/11 terror attacks, is the uncle of a man convicted as the chief conspirator in the

1993 World Trade Center bombing, a Kuwaiti government official said yesterday.

The official said Muhammad had an older brother who was a member of Usama bin Laden's al-Qaida network and another brother who died in Pakistan when the bomb he was making exploded prematurely.

US counterterrorism officials believe Muhammad, believed to be in or near Afghanistan, was chief among the bin Laden lieutenants who organized the suicide attacks.

Possible links between the September 11 WTC attacks and the 1993 bombing at the towers that killed six people have intrigued investigators trying to put together a broad picture of al-Qaida's activities.

The Kuwaiti official said Muhammad's sister was the mother of Ramzi Yousef, who was captured in Pakistan in 1995 and sentenced to life in prison in 1998 for masterminding the first WTC attack and for a separate attack on an airliner. US officials have said Muhammad, who is just a few years older than Yousef, worked with Yousef on the 1993 WTC bombing plot and a 1995 plan to bomb or hijack trans-Pacific airliners heading for the US.

Kuwait has said that although Muhammad was born there, he is Pakistani. The Kuwaiti official said Yousef, too, was born in Kuwait. He did not provide further information on Yousef.

US counterterrorism officials believe Muhammad went to Afghanistan to join the anti-Soviet mujahedeen fighters in the late 1980s. Arabs who helped push Soviet occupiers out of Afghanistan have formed the core of Usama bin Laden's terrorist group. Bin Laden himself helped fund and fought with the mujahedeen.

The Kuwaiti official said Muhammad's family traced its roots to Iran and his mother was from the Pakistani province of Baluchistan.

Muhammad left Kuwait to study in North Carolina, "went straight from America to Afghanistan," and never returned to Kuwait, he said.

US officials said last week they believe Muhammad attended Chowan College in North Carolina before transferring to another American university, where he obtained an engineering degree.

Muhammad has been charged for his role in the 1995 airline plot, and remains one of the FBI's most-wanted terrorists. The US government is offering a reward of up to $25 million for information leading to his capture.

Muhammad has not been charged in the September 11th attacks.

[Victor Mordecai comments: In my book *Is Fanatic Islam a Global Threat?* I quote Dr. Laurie Mylroie, an expert investigator who proved beyond any doubt that the conspirators in the 1993 attack on the WTC were financially supported by Saddam Hussein's Iraq. She also proved that Ramzi Yousef was an Iraqi agent. Hence, the connection to the 9/11 attack and Saddam Hussein's support for the Al-Qaida in this attack as well.]

XVIII. Terror Group Says Jihad Is Only Solution to Kashmir

Article by Munir Ahmad on page 5 of
The Jerusalem Post of June 11, 2002

Islamabad (AP) — A terrorist group in Kashmir vowed yesterday to continue armed conflict, saying jihad is the only way to resolve the status of the disputed region.

"There is no chance of a ceasefire since it failed to yield desired results in the past," Salim Hashimi, spokesman for the Hezb-ul Mujahedeen group, told the Associated Press. "Our experience of talks with India is very bitter, and we know that jihad is the only solution to the Kashmir issue."

The announcement came shortly after India said it will resume allowing Pakistani aircraft to over-fly its territory in a move seen as a step toward easing tensions and avoiding war.

New Delhi, which has blamed Pakistani-based militants for terrorist attacks in its territory, said it had monitored "some fall in infiltration" from the Pakistani side of the Line of Control that divides Kashmir.

Hezb-ul Mujahedeen is a major Islamic insurgent group and is part of the United Jihad Council.

President Pervez Musharraf banned five groups in an effort to purge the country of terrorism.

Asked about Musharraf's claim that no cross-border incursions are occurring, Hashimi said: "We don't accept any such Line of Control. We have our own network in Indian-occupied Kashmir, and political decisions taken by the Pakistan government for easing tension with India will not create any problem for us as we know how to survive and face such circumstances. The ongoing armed struggle in Kashmir was launched by Kashmiris, and we will not stop it without getting liberation from the clutches of India."

He said Hezb-ul Mujahedeen's chief, Sayed Sala-huddin, is in touch with all Islamic militant groups to plan strategy in fast-changing circumstances.

PRIVATE INVESTIGATION

Israel Ties El-Arian to Jihad Board

By Michael Fechter in *The Tampa Tribune*
mfechter@tampatrib.com, published June 23, 2002

TEL AVIV — Sami Al-Arian, the professor being investigated by the U.S. Justice Department for alleged ties to Middle East terrorists, helped found the governing council of the Palestinian Islamic Jihad and then served on it, current and former senior Israeli intelligence officials say. The panel is called the Majlis Shura and functions like a Jihad board of directors. It has an unknown number of members and offers advice on such matters as money and organization. It appears to have been formed in the early 1990s, about 10 years after the Jihad's birth.

In addition, the officials say, Al-Arian delivered computer equipment to the Jihad's leader en route to a 1994 meeting of the council in Tehran.

Their revelations for the first time lift the veil on the protracted and secretive investigation into Al-Arian and Tampa's ties to the violence in the Middle East.

Al-Arian denies any involvement with the Jihad, but the officials say they believe his role was in political ideology and fundraising — not in Jihad operations.

Israeli intelligence has provided this and other information tying Al-Arian to the Jihad to federal agents in Tampa, who have been investigating Al-Arian for the past seven years, the officials said. Israeli security agents have briefed U.S. officials on the material in Tampa, and a seven-member delegation of prosecutors and investigators from Tampa traveled to Israel in the fall of 2000 for briefings by the Israelis.

The Israelis say they are frustrated U.S. authorities have not indicted Al-Arian, who is a tenured computer science professor at the University of South Florida but has been suspended from teaching there since Sept. 28.

Al-Arian and his brother-in-law, Mazen Al-Najjar, have long been suspected by U.S. agents of running front organizations for the Jihad — in part through a think tank affiliated with USF that Al-Arian launched in 1991 called the World and Islam Studies Enterprise, or WISE. Federal agents raided WISE's offices and Al-Arian's home in November 1995 after a former WISE director emerged at Jihad headquarters in Damascus, Syria, as the Jihad's commander.

"This is pure nonsense," Al-Arian said of the Israeli allegations in comments made through his attorney, Robert McKee of Tampa.

Al-Arian said he was not in Tehran or Damascus in 1994, nor did he deliver any computer for the Jihad. He said he did travel to Saudi Arabia that year for the Hajj, a pilgrimage Muslims must make to Mecca at least once in their lives if they can afford it.

In February, then-interim U.S. Attorney Mac Cauley issued a statement saying Al-Arian remains the subject of "an active and ongoing investigation." Cauley didn't elaborate, but the Israelis say its focus appears to be whether Al-Arian has violated federal racketeering laws.

The trip by U.S. authorities to Israel in the fall of 2000 included then-U.S. Attorney Donna Bucella. They returned with information about the Jihad's governing board and financial transactions involving the Jihad, the Israelis say.

"If these files were ever opened to the public, if they will do that, there are a lot of Americans who will be very, very disappointed in how the FBI behaved in this case," a senior intelligence official said.

Enough For a Conviction?

U.S. law enforcement officials disagree. The threshold for convicting people in terrorism-related cases is far higher here than in Israel, they say, and — while they understand the Israelis' frustration — this case may dwell in a legal gray area.

Such disagreement is fairly common when investigations in the United States require help from other countries, said Robert Blitzer, the FBI's former chief of domestic terrorism investigations.

"They can do more with less," Blitzer said of the Israelis. "They have a tendency to read an awful lot into a piece of information to the degree that they view it as enough to do something. But we know here it's not enough to get a conviction."

Al-Arian "is a representative of the Islamic Jihad, a known terrorist organization, here in the United States doing his thing in support of that organization, trying to radicalize and bring into the organizational fold more and more Muslims," Blitzer continued.

But that doesn't necessarily mean he's broken U.S. law, Blitzer said.

"They are a part of a support infrastructure for the organization," he said. "That's what this is all about. This is about supporting the political goals of the organization and to collect money and to propagate the organization through proselytizing."

The investigation centers on whether money raised by Al-Arian in the United States was used to finance Jihad terrorism in Israel — in particular an April 1995 bombing attack on a bus that killed eight people in the Gaza Strip, the Israelis say. One of the victims was an American college student, Alisa Flatow, a 20-year-old from West Orange, N.J., who was in Israel studying at a seminary.

Flatow's father, Stephen, said he testified about Alisa's death before a federal grand jury in Tampa in December.

Among other things, racketeering statutes allow prosecutors more flexibility linking criminals acts together even when they're widely separated by time or geography, according to Tampa defense lawyer Todd Foster, who previously served as major crimes chief at the U.S. attorney's office.

Analyzing Foreign Intelligence

Israel also claims Al-Najjar, who has been in federal prison since November pending a final order of deportation, served as a communications conduit between Jihad terrorists in the Israeli Occupied Territories and Jihad headquarters in Damascus.

As recently as 1994, an Israeli intelligence official said, suspects arrested in connection with terrorist attacks in Israel have had slips of paper with Al-Najjar's home telephone number in Tampa written on them.

The suspects said during subsequent interrogations they had been instructed to call the number to report on an attack, the official said. Before Al-Najjar was a contact, the Israelis say, the Jihad used Basheer Nafi, a former WISE director deported by the United States in 1996. Nafi has repeatedly denied any involvement with the Jihad.

It isn't clear whether this allegation is part of a package of secret evidence that was used by immigration officials to jail Al-Najjar as a national security threat in 1997. That evidence alleged an association between Al-Najjar and the Jihad. He spent 3 1/2 years in an immigration detention center in Bradenton.

An immigration judge ordered his release in December 2000 after a U.S. district judge ruled that using secret evidence to keep Al-Najjar behind bars violated his due process rights. His attorneys successfully argued he couldn't defend himself against evidence he couldn't see.

Agents rearrested Al-Najjar in November after the INS issued a final deportation order. His attorneys have sued for his release, arguing immigration law does not allow unlimited detention but gives the government six months to find a country willing to accept the detainee. As a stateless Palestinian, Al-Najjar says he has been unable to find a country willing to accept him.

David Cole, a Georgetown University law professor who represents Al-Najjar, cautioned against accepting foreign intelligence at face value.

"Intelligence agencies try to gather up as much possible information as they can. They will take rumors and innuendos. Part of their job is to determine which are the more credible pieces of information," Cole said.

Undocumented intelligence information isn't good enough for American courts, Cole said.

"What we have been fighting since Day One in this is you have to have a forum where claims can be tested. When we had a forum where these claims could be tested, we convinced a Republican judge there was nothing here. It was a very lengthy rejection of every claim that the government made."

Immigration Judge R. Kevin McHugh ruled that the government failed to present evidence showing Al-Najjar aided terrorists or that WISE, and a related charity called the Islamic Committee for Palestine, were fronts for the Islamic Jihad.

"There is evidence in the record to support the conclusion that WISE was a reputable and scholarly research center and the ICP was highly regarded," McHugh wrote.

Al-Najjar never served in any capacity with the Jihad, Al-Arian said through his attorney. These are old allegations that were refuted by McHugh's ruling, McKee quoted Al-Arian as saying.

"People just don't want to accept that," Al-Arian said.

Turnover, Ignorance Hinder Probe

Israeli officials also said the U.S. investigation has been hampered by interagency squabbling, turnover among case agents and a general ignorance about the Middle East conflict and its players.

One of the Israelis complained about a change in case agents that came shortly after the autumn 2000 trip. The case was progressing well, the official said, but bogged down as new players brought themselves up to speed.

"They knew nothing about the 'Jihad,'" the Israeli said. "I sat with them for about four hours, and I had to review with them all the history that I told to the [previous investigators]. Every time they changed the team, they started from the beginning. They know nothing. They know nothing about the Middle East reality."

At the request of U.S. investigators, the Israelis assembled a package of additional financial records that the

Americans planned to come back for, the Israelis said. But the Americans postponed their return trip due to security concerns — first in December, then in March — and the package still awaits pickup. The Israelis said they wonder why the FBI hasn't sent one of its agents stationed at the U.S. Embassy in Tel Aviv to retrieve the material.

"It could be very useful," one of the Israelis said.

The Israelis have not released any documentation to support their allegations against Al-Arian and Al-Najjar. However, the roles the Israelis ascribe to Al-Arian and Al-Najjar are detailed in a Jihad document agents seized in their 1995 raid on WISE's office. The paper diagrams the structure of the organization, but does not name anyone. The Israelis say this document — which according to an FBI translation was titled "Internal Manifest" — had never before been published and they weren't aware of it until its discovery in Tampa.

Prosecuting and convicting Al-Arian won't stem the violence between Palestinians and Israelis, said Reuven Paz, director of the Project for the Research of Radical Islam in Haifa. Most of the Palestinian Islamic Jihad's money comes from Iran, and its active core is in the occupied territories. Whatever has happened in Tampa was more about ideology and politics than directing operations, Paz said.

"Israel is confronting real terrorism and didn't pay attention to the political activity," Paz said. "If they wanted, the Palestinian Authority could eliminate the whole group in one day. It wouldn't create such noise in the Palestinian population like the closure of even one social structure of Hamas," which runs schools, clinics and mosques in addition to orchestrating terrorist attacks.

Reporter Michael Fechter can be reached at
(813) 259-7621.

[Note: for more information about the Saudi Arabian "state sponsored terrorism" through bogus charities in

Virginia and Florida that were funding Hamas and Islamic Jihad, and for news on the connection of ENRON and the oil companies to the Taliban for a pipeline through the country of Afghanistan, see www.john-loftus.com.]

[Victor Mordecai comments: Professor Sami Al-Arian is mentioned and interviewed in the famous video *Jihad in America* by Steven Emerson, available from the bookstore of this website: www.vicmord.com.]

Louis Farrakhan Launches Anti-Israel Lobby

Article by Michael Freund on page 4 of
The Jerusalem Post of July 9th, 2002

Louis Farrakhan, controversial head of the Nation of Islam, a US-based black Muslim group, plans to establish an anti-Israel lobbying organization to pressure the Bush Administration on Middle East policy, the Libyan News Agency Jana reported over the weekend. According to the report, Farrakhan, who is visiting Beirut, "put forward his plan to confront the Zionist lobby in America.... Farrakhan told officials in Syria and Lebanon that his mission is focusing on establishing a political group of different ethnic groups, to exert pressure on the American administration and its policies, especially in the Middle East. It will also confront the Zionist lobby which infiltrated the American establishment."

[Victor Mordecai comments: In my book *Is Fanatic Islam a Global Threat?* much space is devoted to Louis Farrakhan and his plans to mobilize the blacks, Hispanics, Native Americans and anyone else for that matter who is disgruntled against the US and ready to join forces against the Jews and the Christians in the US. This is being funded by the Libyan dictator Muammar Gaddafi. And of course, Farrakhan totally ignores the genocide of black brothers and sisters in the Sudan by the Moslems.]

Israel Bars Louis Farrakhan

Article by Herb Keinon on page 4 of
The Jerusalem Post of July 1st, 2002

Israel has informed Nation of Islam leader Louis Farrakhan that he will not be allowed to enter the country during his current Middle East tour. Farrakhan, who in the past has praised Hitler and referred to Judaism as a "gutter religion," is in the region "to help solve this [the Middle East] problem."

Before departing for a tour that has taken him so far to Qatar, Yemen, and Jordan, Farrakhan told a press conference, "I believe that we have a spiritual point of view that may be able to connect the three branches of Abraham — Jews, Christians, and Muslims. It is out of this understanding that I truly believe that I am called of God in this serious hour for the sake of peace to do whatever I can to help solve this problem."

One Foreign Ministry official, however, said that considering Farrakhan's previous statements and problematic positions regarding Israel, this is "not the right time" for him to pay a visit.

The official said Jerusalem was worried about a "provocative" visit to the Temple Mount or other mosques that could fan the flames of violence.

Before leaving the US, Farrakhan said he hoped to meet both Prime Minister Ariel Sharon and Palestinian Authority Chairman Yasser Arafat.

Last week, while in Qatar, Farrakhan responded to President George W. Bush's speech by saying the President sought too many Palestinian concessions, which would lead to more frustration and suicide attacks against Israelis.

Israel is not the only country to have banned Farrakhan — Britain did so as well. In April the British courts upheld a government ban on Farrakhan dating from 1986 for making racist and anti-Semitic comments.

Farrakhan Backs Zimbabwe Land Seizures

Article on page 5 of *The Jerusalem Post* of
July 14th, 2002

Harare (Reuters) — US radical black leader Louis Farrakhan, on a three-day visit to Zimbabwe, gave his backing
to President Robert Mugabe's land seizure campaign, state
media reported yesterday.

"Speaking soon after his arrival...Mr. Farrakhan
said he was in full support of President Mugabe's policies,
especially the land issue as it was aimed at correcting a
historical injustice," the state-owned *Bulaway Chronicle*
said in a report.

The Zimbabwean government is pressing on with
its seizures of white-owned farms despite criticism that
the drive is worsening a severe food crisis in the southern
African state.

Nearly 3,000 white farmers have been ordered to
vacate their farms by August 10th to make way for landless
blacks.

[Victor Mordecai comments: On a recent trip to Texas,
I was told by a South African Christian in a Dallas church
that land seized from the white farmers was not being distributed to the landless blacks, but instead was being handed
over to Libyan dictator Muammar Gaddafi. All this while
the famine is getting worse and blacks are starving to death
while Mugabe lines his pockets with Libyan cash.]

MILITARY INTELLIGENCE

Syria Secretly Acquiring Weapons for the Iraqi Army in Eastern Europe

Article by Ze'ev Schiff on page 1 of *Ha'aretz*
Hebrew daily of July 15th, 2002—Translated by
Victor Mordecai

Syria has established a covert apparatus for the acquisition of weaponry and equipment for the Iraqi army. The equipment, mostly purchased from Eastern European countries, arrives at ports in Syria, where it is unloaded and sent in heavy trucks and trains to Iraq. These acquisitions include, inter alia, Russian-made fighter aircraft engines, overhauled tank motors, also Russian made, and anti-aircraft guns.

Reliable sources say that the elaborate business-military relations that have developed between Syria and Iraq since Bashar al-Assad came to power in Damascus may be considered as part of a significant strategic move. This is especially significant from a regional perspective considering the impending US attack on Iraq, because of significant violations of the Iraqi ruler, Saddam Hussein, Security Council resolutions, and the expulsion of UN inspectors. Assessments both in Israel and the US are that if the military relations between Iraq and Syria have already developed as they have, to include covert weapons deals, it is most surely possible that other forms of military cooperation exist between these two countries.

It is known that the Syrian military procurement was conducted, inter alia, among the following countries: Bulgaria and Belarus provided overhauled T-55 tank engines as well as spare parts for T-72 tanks; Russia provided trucks for military use; the Czech Republic sold anti-aircraft guns; the Ukraine and other countries sold 80 engines for Mig 29 aircraft as well as radar systems for these planes. In addition spare parts for Mig 25, Mig 23 and Mig 21 were purchased. Another service provided by Syria to the Iraqis was the transfer of military equipment purchased by Iraq in Hungary and in Serbia via Syrian ports.

As a result of these actions, Syria has unilaterally violated UN Security Council resolutions regarding the embargo on Iraq, especially regarding weapons acquisitions. Syria at this time is rotating president of the UN Security Council. This Syrian move to acquire weapons for Iraq is a flagrant affront to the US and its policy. Washington is now pondering its possible attack on Iraq, including US ground forces in battle. Assessments are that, in light of the impending attack, Saddam Hussein has decided to speed up the purchases for his army, which is suffering from a dearth of spare parts.

Damascus, for its part, is playing a game of duplicity. On the one hand, it poses with its intentions of intelligence cooperation with Washington regarding Al-Qaida, but behind the scenes, it cooperates in weapons acquisitions for Iraq, considered an enemy of the US.

Such a decision authorizing significant military-business purchases of weapons for Iraq must have come from the Syrian president himself. This demonstrates a change by Bashar al Assad from the policy of his father, Hafez al-Assad, regarding his relations with Iraq and Saddam Hussein during the course of many years. And the Iraqis have at least once returned the favor to Israel when the Iraqis agreed for Iranian weapons to transit to Syria over Iraqi soil.

The Iraqis and Syrians established special companies for the purpose of weapons and equipment acquisition. Among those involved in these deals on the Syrian side include Firas Tlas, the son of the Syrian minister of defense, the owner of a big Syrian corporation; Tlas is also involved in the procurement of Iraqi crude oil. The equipment which was purchased by the Syrians in various countries was transferred to the Syrian ports Tartus and Latakia, from whence it was then sent in trucks or trains to Iraq. This was in addition to weapons and parts flown to Iraq in Iraqi military air transport after the Iraqis sent medical supplies to Syria following the collapse of the Zaynoon dam a month ago. Iraqi military air transport conducted 20 flights to Syria with medical equipment and then returned with the military acquisitions.

Chapter XI
AUGUST 2002 NEWSLETTER

Victor Mordecai's Monthly Message

As with the case of my July 2002 newsletter, based on media sources of that month, but written and posted in February 2003, this newsletter also is appearing greatly in arrears and with apologies. Again, it is impossible for one person to do the job of many all at the same time. Better late than never, I suppose.

On June 11th, 2002, I was crossing the border on my way from Edmonton, Canada, to Coeur d'Alene, Idaho, in the USA. As I reached the US border, I noticed that there was absolutely no traffic at that time. This was quite an unusual surprise for someone like me who frequently crosses the US-Canadian border. I drove straight across to the US passport control and a young officer appeared at the window.

"Nationality," he asked me.

Anticipating the question, I had already placed my US passport in my shirt pocket and pulled it out dutifully to show the officer.

"I don't want to see your passport. I want to hear your voice," he nervously said.

Perplexed, I answered him: "American, a New Yawkuh." I emphasized the NY accent.

"Is there a problem?" I asked.

He said, "Terrorists are trying to enter the US. They are blonde, blue-eyed and are the opposite of what one would normally look for in the way of 'profiling'.

He added, "There are Germans who converted to Islam, Chechens and Bosnians, all blonde and blue-eyed, who are not caught by silence, but only when they open their mouths and we can hear that they are not really Americans, but indeed are Moslem terrorists trying to sneak into the US under the guise of being 'Westerners.'"

The emphasis of this month's newsletter will be Islamic terrorism and the Islamic agendas in Germany, Bosnia, Iran, Argentina, the Palestinian Authority, and last but definitely not least, Saudi Arabia, the financier of much of the above terrorisms.

By August 2002, after two years of "Intifada Al Quds,' almost 400,000 Palestinian Arabs had emigrated from Judea, Samaria and Gaza. Facing an economy that self-destructed under Yasser Arafat's malevolent rule, many Palestinians realized they could not continue living in the Palestinian Autonomy areas, could not make a living, and could not protect their children from being "mobilized" as suicide bombers against Israel.

I have written about the plight of the Palestinians under Arafat's Authority in my book *Is Fanatic Islam a Global Threat?* as well as in my previous newsletters, as well as in the *Israel Today* magazine to which I contribute articles.

Leaders in any country can give their people guns and bullets, but they must also provide bread and butter. Not to provide bread and butter means the people starve in the case of North Korea, or flee in the case of the Palestinian Authority.

God has blessed the Middle East region (with the exception of Israel) with great amounts of petroleum. The Saudis, the Iranians and the Iraqis could be living in a Heaven on Earth scenario if they were not Moslems. Their Islamic religion, a war religion, has them frittering away all their blessings from God by spending their vast wealth on weapons of destruction, profligate living, and spreading the word of Islam all over the earth.

Their peoples do not know democracy, because democracy and Islam are irreconcilable. The welfare of the people — education, health, and food — is not high on the order of priorities. Indeed, the Arabs living in Israel have a higher standard of living than Arabs anywhere else in the Middle East. Life expectancy outside of Israel for the Arabs is low. But weapons of mass destruction abound. There is no democracy. There is no freedom. And, of course, refugee problems are not solved but are enhanced for political reasons. But there is plenty of money to build mosques and spread Islam all over the world, a religion which calls for the annihilation of the Jews and Christians.

Our former Prime Minister Golda Meir once said: "There will only be peace in the Middle East when Moslem mothers love their children more than they hate the Jews."

Unfortunately, this August newsletter is going to show how the Palestinians, the Iranians, and the Saudis are too deep in their hatred of Israel and the Jews to do the right things by their own people, but instead squander their oil wealth on all the wrong things, much to the detriment of their own peoples. And I mourn for these Moslems. I don't hate them. I pity them. But change can only come when they love their children more than they hate us. This will not happen as long as Islam remains their religion. There will not be peace on earth until Islam has been defeated, banished and replaced by Judeo-Christian Western Civilization.

CURRENT EVENTS AND ANALYSIS

1. An Indictment of the Arab World

Editorial on page 8 of *The Jerusalem Post* of
July 3rd, 2002

Yesterday might very well come to mark a turning point in modern Arab history. For the first time in recent memory, a group of prominent Arab intellectuals held up a mirror to Arab society, courageously offering a precise description of what they saw, warts and all. Not surprisingly, the picture they painted, particularly with regard to political freedom and social development, was both unflattering and deeply disturbing.

The findings of the intellectuals came in the form of a survey that was commissioned by the UN and was co-sponsored by the Arab Fund for Economic and Social Development, an institution established by members of the Arab League. Those overseeing the study included prominent Arab personalities, such as Thoraya Obaid, a Saudi national who serves as executive director of the United Nations Population Fund, and Mervat Tallawy, an Egyptian diplomat in charge of the Economic and Social Council for West Asia. As Rim Khalaf Hunaidi, a former Jordanian deputy prime minister involved in preparing the report, describes it to *The New York Times,* "It's not outsiders looking at Arab countries. It's Arabs deciding for themselves."

The bottom line, according to the survey, is that the Arab world is "richer than it is developed." Though the standard of living and life expectancy rates have risen throughout much of the Arab world in recent decades, the report concluded, intellectual life and political freedom remain stultified. Arab women are denied opportunities to advance themselves educationally or professionally, with approximately half of them still unable to read or write. Through its repression of women, stated the report, "the Arab world is largely depriving itself of the creativity and productivity of half its citizens."

The survey also examined how the Arab world has closed itself off to positive outside influences, in the process preventing the cross-border exchange of ideas that is so much a part of Western life and development. Use of the Internet in Arab countries remains relatively low, as many governments clamp down on it out of fear that it will undermine their monopoly on information. Other creative areas, such as filmmaking and writing, are both in decline in the Arab world, the report stated, and little effort is being made to translate foreign books into Arabic. "The whole Arab world translates about 330 books annually, one-fifth the number that Greece translates," the report noted. Even more astonishing, the survey found that the Arab world has translated as many books into Arabic during the past 1,000 years as Spain translated in just one year.

Coming as it does just a week after US President George W. Bush's speech on the Middle East the report could not have been more fortuitous. For, by decrying the utter lack of democracy in the Palestinian Authority-controlled areas, and underlining the urgent need for civil and institutional reform, Bush has done what no other American President before him dared to do: He focused international attention on the lack of democracy in the Arab world. It was a theme he touched upon, albeit more broadly, in a June 1 speech at West Point, where he told graduating cadets that "when it comes to the common rights and needs of men and women, there is no clash of civilizations. The peoples of the Islamic nations want and deserve the same freedoms and opportunities as people in every nation. And their governments should listen to their hopes." The report by the Arab intellectuals complements Bush's message, providing trenchant and detailed confirmation of the President's concerns.

To be fair, it should be noted that there have been a few lone voices over the year who have bravely waged their own battles to pry open the Arab world and inject it with greater freedom and liberty, such as Prof. Fouad Ajami of Johns Hopkins University, or Iranian author Amir Taheri, who shortly after September 11th wrote in *The Wall Street Journal* that "the Muslim world today is full of bigotry, fanaticism, hypocrisy, and plain ignorance — all of which serve as breeding grounds for criminals like [Usama] bin Laden." Others, such as Saad Eddin Ibrahim, one of Egypt's leading pro-democracy activists [see last month's newsletter] have been willing to risk life and limb for the sake of principles that many in the West take for granted. Indeed, Ibrahim has been on trial since last year for producing a film about voter fraud in Egypt's 1995 parliamentary elections.

The importance, then, of the Arab intellectuals' report is that it provides a credible opening that will enable others to step forward and speak out for greater democracy in the Arab world, which remains the last bastion of despotism and dictatorship on the globe. For too long, the international community has been willing to look the other way as basic freedoms and human rights were trampled upon throughout North Africa and the Middle East. The men and women who toiled over the report have provided a damning indictment of Arab society, its ills and tribulations. One can only hope that their plea will not go unheard.

2. UN: Arab Nations Squandered Oil Wealth

Article on page 5 of *The Jerusalem Post* of
July 3rd, 2002

London (Reuters) — The United Nations accused a host of Arab nations yesterday of squandering wealth generated by oil and of depriving their people of basic political freedoms.

The hard-hitting comments were published in the UN Development Program's Arab Development Report 2002.

The report, compiled by Arab experts over the past 18 months, said growth in per capita income in the Arab region in the past 20 years — at an average of just 0.5 percent — was the lowest in the world except for sub-Saharan Africa.

Labor productivity had declined at an annual average of 0.2 percent, it said.

Added together, the gross domestic product of the 22 Arab nations combined is less than a medium-sized European country such as Spain.

"A very large investment in fixed capital formation of over [3 trillion] over the past 20 years has had poor returns in per capita income," the report said.

"Oil revenues are not always reinvested productively in the country, let alone the region. And when such revenues are used in physical capital formation, they contribute little to growth," it added.

The report praised the Arab nations for raising the life expectancy of their peoples, cutting infant mortality, and reducing extreme poverty, but it was critical of the lack of freedoms and opportunity.

"The three main deficits are freedom, gender, and knowledge," said Rima Khalaf Hunaidi, head of the UN's Arab section and leader of the team which wrote the report — the first UN survey of Arabs by Arabs.

The report accused many of the nations from the Maghreb to the Gulf of allowing scant political freedom, keeping women subjugated, and letting education standards drop sharply.

While more people have entered the educational system, the quality of that education has been crumbling, leading to what the report described as deficits in opportunity and capability.

"Given the political commitment, Arab countries have the resources to eradicate absolute poverty in less than a generation," the report said. "Commitment, not resources, is the binding constraint." Some 65 million adults, mostly women, remain illiterate, 10 million children are not enrolled in schools, and unemployment of an average 15% across the region is three times the world average.

"The report aims to start a dialogue in the region — it won't make many friends here. That wasn't the intention," Hunaidi said.

The way forward involved "promoting systems of good governance, those that promote, support, and sustain human well-being, based on expanding human capabilities, choices, opportunities, and freedoms."

3. A Ticking Time-Bomb in Saudi Arabia

Article by Semadar Peri on page 2 of *24 hours*
weekend supplement in Hebrew Israeli daily
Yediot Ahronot of July 31st, 2002 —
Translated by Victor Mordecai

Hard times have hit the Saudis: Many are forced to trade in villas and luxury cars for public housing and more modest vehicles. Tens of thousands of students join the ranks of the unemployed every year. Annual income has dropped from US $20,000 to $8,000. Bin Laden's organization is pictured in the eyes of many as the solution. The rulers in Riyadh fear the rage of the masses will be turned against them.

Saudi Arabia today is a kingdom of sharp contradictions: Islamic fanatics enforcing an absolute law of separation of the sexes from childhood, a new generation of shrewd businesswomen frustrated by the personal discrimination, princes guarding the crème de la crème and diamonds as opposed to unemployed on the verge of desperation. Admirers of Usama bin Laden as opposed to thousands of Americans holed up in military camps far from the big cities.

More than two-thirds (70%) of the more than 19 million residents of Saudi Arabia are youths under the age of 19. About 100,000 male and female students are turned out by the educational system and join the ranks of the unemployed as in recent years. Only a few of them will find a permanent source of income.

Over the last few years, Saudis have been forced to forego luxury homes and American cars for public housing and Japanese cars, which are considered less ostentatious. The level of income per annum has dropped from US $20,000 to $8,000 for those fortunate enough to find steady employment.

And the rest? They already are not traveling the world

far and wide in search of luck. US immigration authorities are placing increasingly more difficult obstacles in the path of those seeking entry visas from the Arab world, especially to people from Saudi Arabia, from whence 15 out of the 19 perpetrators of the 9/11/2002 attacks came.

Those who have remained and no longer enjoy free salaries, according to the recent UN report on the "state of the Arab nation, are ready to commit themselves to dangerously adventurous acts in the Saudi kingdom, in order to close the gap in the face of the wealthy palaces of the princes."

As part of this situation, it is no wonder that the sudden deaths within one week of two princes in line of succession to the throne immediately arouse questions. Prince Ahmed, the son of the governor of Riyadh, died of a heart attack at age 45. Two days later, on his way to the funeral, his cousin Prince Sultan ben-Turki died at the age of 41.

The official announcement spoke of death caused by a traffic accident. But the news agencies wrote about a strange case of "death by dehydration in the heat of the desert," and the prince was described as a lot younger than in the original announcement, being only 25 years old. Gossip had it that he died from an overdose of drugs or alcohol.

The Female Opposition to the Peace Initiative

Margaret S., wife of a British engineer working for the "Shell" Oil Company, who recently returned to the UK after four years of living in Saudi Arabia, told *Yediot Ahronot* about the tension in each of the different spheres of life: "As a result of the encouragement of the authorities, young women have broken into the ranks of the employed and have taken up positions that used to be reserved for university graduates only. Frustrations derived from rights infringements — such as their inability to fly abroad without written consent from their husbands or oldest brother, the forbidding of women to drive, or the forcing of women to eat in a special family section of a restaurant behind a heavy curtain — they take out in their workplace offices."

The women in Saudi Arabia, it turns out, have not only taken the place of men in what was formerly a private preserve for men, now dwindling, but they have even formed an active protest movement against the peace initiative with Israel, presented by Crown Prince Abdullah (the acting king). "At the beginning of the intifada, the Saudis sent planes to bring back wounded Palestinians for hospitalization and medical treatment in Riyadh," tells Margaret S. "Local women came to volunteer in the hospitals. They heard testimonies about the happenings in the territories, viewed the difficult TV screen pictures, and established, much to the chagrin of the royal palace, an outspoken opposition movement to the peace plan.

"If we add to this the stories of hundreds of Saudi students who were 'smuggled' out of the US following the attack on the twin towers of the World Trade Center, we now find in Saudi Arabia a burning hatred for Israel and a despising of the Americans. It was the women in Saudi Arabia who initiated the ban on 'fast-food' establishments and on anything that smacked of 'secular imperialism.'"

The peace initiative of Crown Prince Abdullah suffered two stinging slaps in the face:

Prime Minister Sharon, it is true, requested as did President Katsav, that he be invited to the royal palace "in order to hear from close up just how serious the plan was," but when he was given a totally negative answer, he chose to ignore the plan. Secondly, President George W. Bush, in his recent address, completely ignored the Saudi effort to turn the peace initiative from a newspaper headline to a detailed decision (even if the text was intentionally ambiguous to placate the extremists in the Arab world) — to the flagship plan of the Arab world.

10,000 Were Arrested in the Last Few Weeks

At this very time, the "migration to the north" period is beginning in Saudi Arabia. Anyone who can afford it, and there are still plenty of such people, escapes the burdensome heat of 45-50 degrees Celsius, to go to Europe, Lebanon, Syria or Egypt.

In Spain, France and Britain, shopkeepers are preparing for a band of veiled women who will spread out all over their shops.

In Beirut and Cairo, the Saudis fill up the casinos, stores and comedy shows presented nightly in the theaters which are open. The Saudi intelligence apparatus takes advantage of this emptying out of the kingdom of its citizens to carry out undercover searches: Who is it that insists on staying in the country in spite of the intense desert heat, and why?

The basic work guidelines of the Saudi intelligence apparatus, revealed recently by the commander of the internal security services, reveal a "shadow kingdom" alongside the luxury palaces. The House of Saud fears the realization of a nightmare scenario in which all the sleeper cells and agents of Usama bin Laden spring to life and kick down the regime, burn down the luxury palaces and make sure that the kingdom returns to the bosom of "correct Islam."

According to the assessments of Western intelligence organizations, there are at least 20,000 young Saudis who have already been mobilized into the "bin Laden Brigades" and are waiting for orders. As for the timing, there will be no prior warning. Saudi intelligence thwarted just a few weeks ago the entry of 10,000 "foreigners," as they are described in the official announcement, into the kingdom. Most of them are now under interrogation, with the intention of discovering the addresses from which they were sent and with whom they were to connect up in Saudi Arabia with the purpose of creating underground cells against the regime.

30,000 Princes Are Uneasy

Yesterday morning, the elderly King Fahed left the hospital in Geneva, Switzerland, where he underwent, according to his replacement in Riyadh, Crown Prince Abdullah, a cataract operation in his right eye. Fahed, more than 80 years old, and a living medical miracle, continues to bear the title "Keeper of the Islamic Holy Places," and serves as a buffer in the feuds and power struggles in the kingdom's palaces. As long as Fahed is alive, even if he doesn't do very much, it is possible to buy time in the war over the succession.

On the side of Crown Prince Abdullah, the acting ruler, there is a band of young advisers, which runs the foreign policy and relations with the US. On the side of the third brother, Prince Sultan, minister of defense and of the defense industries, is another band of young advisers, experts and door-openers to the White House, Europe and the Arab world.

The prince who is next in line, Naif, the interior minister, also has his own team of advisers. The same applies to the foreign minister, Prince Saud al-Faisal, who just joined up with the camp of the crown prince. Level B princes came out this week in the dozens in an airlift operation to Geneva, to be close to the bed of King Fahed in the event of his death.

All eyes today in Saudi Arabia are focused on two warning signals to the stability of the regime. What happens the moment the US attacks Iraq? Will the "sleeper cells" spring into action out of their lairs and act as underground cells?

The other question is how to restore Saudi Arabia as leader of the Arab world, a status taken away from it with the death of the Saudi peace plan. A rapidly increasing disruption in the internal calm of the kingdom could provoke the masses to go into the streets. These factors could definitely lead to the fall of the royal regime, and 30,000 princes who live in glaring luxury.

A Sharp Reprimand to a Qatari Minister Who Met With Shimon Peres

It would seem that yesterday's poisonous attack, coming out of Saudi Arabia against Qatar's Foreign Minister Hamed bin Jasem for meeting in Paris with Israeli Foreign Minister Shimon Peres, was unexpected and not flattering to the usual style of the royal palace in Riyadh. The energetic and charismatic minister received compliments such as: "dwarf, cause of damage, and sinking to the lowest levels."

The Saudis reprimanded the Qatari foreign minister, the right hand man and confidante of the Qatari ruler, Emir Hamed bin Alifa a-Tani, because of the "normalization" he demonstrated with "a prominent representative of Sharon." "We feel," emphasized the editorial in the official daily *Al-Watan*, "that this is our duty to address the Qatari minister and to present the facts in their totality. Perhaps the dwarf minister will finally succeed in understanding that to maintain visible relations with Israel means an overdose of dangerous adventurousness. Bin Jasem thinks perhaps that he's smart, but seems to forget that he first and foremost is obligated by resolutions passed in the Arab world."

The Saudi Royal Palace is trying to kill three political birds with one stone. First, they are trying to retaliate against Prime Minister Sharon, whom they accuse of besmirching Saudi Arabia in the eyes of the US after Israel revealed documents which fell into their hands during the "Defensive Wall" operation. The documents reveal correspondences between the ministries of finance in Riyadh and in Ramallah and Arafat's headquarters clearly pointing to generous Saudi funding for families of the shaheeds (martyrs) and for the daily maintenance of terrorists and their handlers.

Another reason for the poisonous criticism of the Qatari foreign minister is the desire of the Saudis to settle bitter scores with the neighboring emirate, which has been playing the game of "yes/no" in all matters concerning the continuation of the activities of the Israeli diplomatic legation in its capital city, Doha.

Also, the popular TV channel Al-Jazeera, which belongs to the Qatari foreign minister and which is managed by his confidantes, is part of the story. Its broadcasts strike at very extremely sensitive nerves in the princes' palaces in Saudi Arabia. It has already been months since the channel's reporters, the most watched TV channel in the Arab world, set foot on Saudi soil.

The reason: a program called "The Opposite Direction." The producers of this program prove every two to three weeks to the crown prince and his advisers that even if they ban Al-Jazeera, the industrious investigators will find experts and analysts from the Arab world that will agree to sit in the luxurious TV studio and to warn about the social gaps, the affliction of unemployment, and the flocking of the masses to the mosques in Saudi Arabia and to report about the ongoing tensions behind the scenes in the royal palaces in Riyadh, Jedda, Mecca, and the resort town of Taif.

The third "bird" the Saudis are trying to kill, at the expense of the meeting between the Qatari foreign minister and Israeli Foreign Minister Shimon Peres, was intended to calm the "man on the street" and, most surprisingly of all, the women in Saudi Arabia. The Saudi authorities are sending a signal that there will be no meetings of any kind with the Israelis until the latter have fulfilled all the conditions set forth by the Saudis. Really, have there been no meetings with Israelis, nor will there be meetings? At least three or four Israelis can now smile amongst themselves.

Victor Mordecai comments: The so-called "Saudi Peace Plan" calls for Israel to return to the borders of 1967 (an impossibility), to uproot all the Jewish settlements in Jerusalem across the Green Line, Judea, Samaria, Gaza and the Golan, in other words, uproot about half a million Israelis from their homes (also an impossibility) and, finally, to take in millions of Palestinian refugees from 1948-49 which would lead to an Arab majority in Israel, meaning the termination of Israel as a Jewish state, also an impossibility. These are the conditions that Saudi Arabia insists Israel must fulfill in order for there to be talks. The Saudis want the destruction of Israel. Now I smile.

One definition of "psychotic" is someone who lives in castles in the air. The above conditions are castles in the air. Therefore the Arabs who agree with these conditions are psychotic in general and the Saudis are psychotic in particular. And anyone who thinks that Israel can or will do business with psychotic people is suffering from delusions, another form of mental illness. The Quartet — US, European Union, Russia and UN — are suffering from delusions because they think that Israel can be forced to fulfill the terms of the Saudi "peace plan." This would mean Israel committing suicide. And if US President George W. Bush leads the pack, he's delusional. In God's terminology, this kind of thinking by the US President, if he's sincere about it, can be very, very dangerous for the people of America and of the world. We must all pray for President George W. Bush not to persist in these delusional plans which so endanger Israel, the apple of God's eye.

4. Boycott of US Goods Hurts Arab Businesses

Article by Bassem Mroue on page 10 in
The Jerusalem Post of July 30th, 2002

Dubai, United Arab Emirates (AP) — Zamzam Cola has new customers in the Gulf and plans to soon expand into more Arab markets. The Iranian company can indirectly thank Israel for its growth.

Zamzam, which previously exported only to Iraq and Afghanistan, is benefiting from a grass-roots campaign by Arabs and Muslims to boycott American goods as a way to punish the United States for its backing of Israel.

Set off by the latest Palestinian uprising, the boycott is especially directed at well-known American products like Coca-Cola and McDonald's. However, economists say the action harms local business, franchises, and employees — but has little impact on mother companies in the US.

"After Arab countries in the region started boycotting some American goods, including Coca-Cola, demand for Zamzam began," said Bahram Kheiri, the Iranian beverage company's director.

He wouldn't give sales figures, but said Zamzam has started exporting to Bahrain and is discussing orders with "about 50 big companies" in the United Arab Emirates, Kuwait, Saudi Arabia, Syria, Lebanon, Jordan, Egypt and Indonesia. Zamzam is sweeter than Coke and has a built-in appeal for Muslims because it takes its name from a holy spring in Saudi Arabia.

The boycott is being urged across the Middle East and North Africa by Muslim preachers, students, intellectuals and — in Saudi Arabia, a main US ally — even some advisers to the Saudi king. The appeal is delivered in mosque sermons, leaflets and Internet sites.

It's difficult to say how hard American companies are being hit by the boycott — and how much of the economic pain is inflicted on Arab businesses selling US products.

Of the six McDonald's franchises in Jordan, two have closed for lack of business — one in the capital, Amman, and one near a Palestinian refugee camp. In Morocco, a government official, who asked not to be identified, estimated sales of Coca-Cola could fall by half in the country's north, a base for Islamic groups. In the United Arab Emirates, sales of the local Star Cola are up by 40 percent in the past three months.

In Dubai, business appears to be down at such American fast food chains as McDonald's, Kentucky Fried Chicken, and Hardee's, and up at local restaurants. In Saudi

Arabia — in a sign of concern at the boycott's effect — prices have been cut up to 50% on some US imports and ads for fast food franchises point out they are Arab owned and managed.

Respected Muslim cleric Sheik Youssef al-Qaradawi issued a religious ruling in the Gulf state of Qatar saying American products should be viewed like Israeli products — which have long been banned in the Arab world. In Riyadh, Saudi Arabia, mosque preacher Sheik Omar bin Saeed al-Badna argued the boycott would be good for the kingdom's economy.

"Boycotting American food and drinks means more business for Saudi, Lebanese, and other restaurants, as well as local producers of soft drinks. This will be good for the majority of Saudis," he said.

The boycott's effect is not that simple, however, according to economists and government officials. They say the action against American products harms local business, franchises, and employees — but has little impact on mother companies in the United States.

"Most of the companies that people consider American are multinational and those who own them are Arabs," said economist Suleiman al-Mazrouei of Emirates International Bank.

Coca-Cola officials said Coke's Middle East operations are run by Arab workers and executives and get materials from local suppliers.

"We, for example, have a bottling partner in the Palestinian Authority area which employs about 320 people. So we are one of the largest employers in the Palestinian Authority area," said Steve LeRoy, Coke's communications director for Central Europe, Eurasia and the Middle East.

LeRoy said Coke was affected by the boycott, but refused to say how much. The international headquarters of McDonald's and Hardee's did not respond to repeated requests for comment.

Samer Tawil, director general of Jordan's Ministry of Trade and Industry, said the effect of the boycott spread beyond boycotted companies to their workers — who could lose jobs — and to their investors, who in Jordan are mostly Jordanians.

In the Emirates, an official at the US Embassy said it was "local agents, sponsors, and distributors, and particularly franchise owners" who were being hurt. The official, who asked not to be identified, said the boycott could discourage foreign investment in the region.

The boycott is not related to the Arab League boycott of companies that do business with Israel, which has largely ended. US laws ban Americans from obeying the Arab League boycott, but no similar measure covers the grass-roots campaign against US products.

The boycott is under way in such strong US allies as Egypt, Jordan, and Saudi Arabia. Earlier this year, Jordan became the first Arab country and fourth overall to sign a free trade agreement with the United States. Under the agreement, tariffs on bilateral trade will be gradually eased, until they are almost completely scrapped in 2010.

In Morocco, US-linked companies were losing business from the boycott even as the country's king, Muhammad VI, was assured during an April meeting in Washington US President George W. Bush would promote a free-trade agreement with Morocco. Critics also say boycott advocates are proposing a simple answer to a complex problem.

Jordanian economist Fahd Fanek said Arabs who find it easy to boycott American soft drinks and fast food joints would likely balk at doing without "American medicines, airplanes, and the Internet," as well as American university education for their children.

5. Follow the Euro Trail

Article by David M. Weinberg on page 9 of
The Jerusalem Post of July 2nd, 2002

Bob Woodward and Carl Bernstein unearthed the nefarious dealings behind Watergate by following the advice of their mysterious source, nicknamed Deep Throat. "Follow the money," counseled Deep Throat. And so they did — all the way up to President Richard Nixon in the White House.

So, too, with the evil Palestinian Authority. The money trail — the path from suicide bomber and terrorist back to his or her paymaster — leads right to PA Chairman Yasser Arafat. More than anything else, Washington sources say, it was the direct funding conduit that runs between Arafat and his Al-Aksa Martyrs Brigade (proud sponsors of many genocide bombings) that convinced President George W. Bush to call for the PA leader's removal.

Which raises the question: Who has been the primary financier of Arafat-the-terrorist since Oslo brought him to our shores eight years ago? Mostly, it hasn't been Israel — although in the days of Yitzhak Rabin and Shimon Peres, we too sinned by propping up the PA with direct payments into a secret Tel Aviv bank account held by Arafat himself.

The Sharon government continues to hold back on some $1.5 billion in various taxes and customs duties collected by the Finance Ministry on behalf of the Palestinian Authority. As suggested in a previous column, Finance Minister Silvan Shalom wisely has begun to use these embargoed funds to cover PA debts owed to Israeli firms and organizations. Last week, he transferred NIS 20 million to Israel Electric.

The PA still owes IE at least NIS 80 million.

Who then has bankrolled Arafat? Washington ceased funding the PA years ago, when its ubiquitous corruption became clear. Arafat's Arab brothers? Naw. They never have substantially put their money where their collective mouth is. Even the biggest talker of all, Saddam Hussein, prefers to transfer his "martyr rewards" directly to the families of suicide bombers, and not through the PA.

The correct answer is the European Union. The EU has been the PA's big-hearted sugar daddy, Yasser's bountiful and boundless papa bear, the deepest honey pot the Palestinians could ever hope for.

As shareholder No. 1 in the PA, the EU has a lot riding on Arafat. So much so that EU leaders are finding it hard to accept that Arafat and Co. have overshot their credit.

In sum, the EU has poured more than $1.4 billion into propping up the PA since Oslo, not including funds contributed separately and directly by EU component countries. This includes everything from food and health services through training and equipping the PA intelligence and police forces.

Since November 2001, the EU has contributed an additional $9 million a month directly to the PA running budget — about 10% of total PA finances.

At the EC Mediterranean Conference in Valencia in April, PA Minister Nabil Shaath demanded another $1.9 billion in "emergency assistance," including $20.6 million for "weapons" and $40.6 million for "support for refugee and martyr families."

In the world of development assistance, these are enormous sums of money — the size of which no other Third World territory or country could ever dream of.

So, where are all the fruits of this lofty largesse? Where are the new neighborhoods for Palestinian refugees? The new infrastructure projects, the successful industrial parks, the small-business incubators and thriving educational institutions — all carefully monitored for quality and efficiency by EU inspectors?

They are buried under the weight of PA waste, corruption, and — worst of all — terrorism and radicalism.

Consider: Brussels has bankrolled and mentored PA television since its inception. It even rebuilt PA-TV antenna towers after Israel toppled them during Operation Defensive Shield. This is the same television that hourly broadcasts messages of jihad against the Jews and praise for the Palestinian genocide bombers.

Consider: The PA school system has enjoyed the investment of more than $300m in EU funds since 1994, including funds for the writing and production of the new, official PA textbooks.

I don't need to tell you that these textbooks deny any ancient Jewish claim to Jerusalem and Israel; that murderer-martyrs are praised; and that Israel is not to be found on any maps in these glorious, EU-financed, educational tomes.

In early May, Jerusalem sent EU headquarters a 100-page file detailing Arafat's funding of terrorist activities against Israel. EU Commissioner for External Affairs Chris Patten's formal response: "We have to date not been shown any hard evidence that the EU funds have been misused to finance terrorism."

Patten's dodge is disingenuous and duplicitous, because money is fungible. Every euro for social welfare contributed to Arafat's budget by the EU frees up other PA funds for terrorism and the purchase of weaponry.

This doesn't seem to bother the EU — when it is dealing with Palestinians.

When dealing with Israel, however, such "fungibility" is unacceptable.

During the first Bush administration, George Sr. coldly told Israel "no" when it requested loan guarantees to absorb Russian immigrants.

Why? Because he didn't like Prime Minister Yitzhak Shamir's spending on settlements. Money is "fungible," the elder Bush intoned, and the EU followed suit.

"We won't be putting money into a society dominated by corrupt leadership that orders and finances terrorism," said President Bush last week.

When will the EU reach the same, inescapable conclusion?

(The writer is director of public affairs at Bar-Ilan University's Begin-Sadat Center for Strategic Studies.)

6. Jobless Palestinians Seek International Help

Article on page 2 of *The Jerusalem Post* of
July 16th, 2002

Reuters — About 500 jobless Palestinians protested outside the United Nations headquarters in Gaza City yesterday to demand international financial assistance.

"We are not beggars. We have the right to live — work and live," they chanted. About 600 unemployed Palestinians also marched outside the Labor Ministry building in Khan Yunis in the south of the Gaza Strip. Unemployed workers have put up tents in cities and refugee camps in the Gaza Strip to press their demands for jobs or for compensation from the Palestinian Authority for being unable to work in Israel. Israeli officials, including Defense Minister Binyamin Ben-Eliezer, have said they intend eventually to raise the number of Palestinians working inside Israel to 30,000 but have linked progress to a halt to violence.

7. Palestinians: $800 Million in Physical Damage

Article on page 2 of *The Jerusalem Post*
of July 16th, 2002

Reuters — The Palestinian Authority estimates that the Palestinian economy has suffered up to $800 million from physical damage caused by 21 months of conflict, Ali Sha'ath, deputy minister of planning and international cooperation, said yesterday. He said estimates of losses suffered because of the violence — including potential losses from planned business projects — range up to $10 billion.

"These estimates reflect what our economy could have gained in two years, but now we have lost these figures forever. We will not be able to compensate [for] them," Sha'ath told a news conference in the Gaza Strip. He did not say how the potential profits had been calculated.

Nigel Roberts, World Bank director for the territories, said the World Bank's estimate of physical damage from September 2000 until the end of December 2001 was $305 million.

"So the figure of $800 million for physical damage [until now] sounds... quite reasonable to me," he said.

8. A Bond of Hypocrisy

Article by Evelyn Gordon on page 8 of
The Jerusalem Post of July 16th, 2002

Last week, the European Union finally convinced me that its bizarre love affair with the Palestinian Authority truly has nothing to do with being anti-Israel.

I always found it hard to otherwise explain why a group of liberal democracies that claims to put human rights above all else should be so enamored of a corrupt, oppressive, terrorist dictatorship.

But it turns out that the EU simply loves all oppressive Middle East dictatorships indiscriminately. Its recent behavior toward Iran leaves no doubt about the matter.

Iran, despite having a typically repressive Middle Eastern regime (albeit theocratic rather than secular), is nevertheless unique — because it also has the only serious pro-democracy movement in the region. Reformists are continually being jailed for criticizing the regime, but after finishing their sentences they go straight back to uttering vocal criticisms.

Student activists who were brutally beaten and jailed during a wave of demonstrations three years ago have regrouped and are now planning university-wide "referenda" on controversial questions such as whether to eliminate the clerics' veto on parliamentary decisions.

And Iran has the freest press in the Middle East — not because the regime permits it, but because stubborn, courageous editors and publishers, despite periodic jail terms, keep opening new papers to replace those that are shut down.

Where else in the Middle East do newspapers receive — and print! — letters to the editor demanding that the government stop funneling money to Hizbullah and start investing in education and job creation instead?

In a country where so much liberal activism is clashing head-on with so much repression, the response of the world's self-proclaimed champion of human rights should be obvious: Fund the reformists and starve the regime.

Yet the EU has been doing precisely the opposite: It has actively encouraged European companies to invest in projects that funnel money to the Iranian government.

In fact, to ensure that European firms were left in no doubt about their governments' desires, the EU even passed legislation making it illegal for European companies to comply with the US boycott on doing business with Iran.

The result is that the EU is now Iran's largest trading partner — and most of these deals put money straight into the regime's pockets.

For instance, three European oil companies — Royal Dutch/Shell, Eni SpA and TotalFinaElf — have invested some $10.5 billion in developing new Iranian oil fields since 1997. These investments cannot be justified as a means of encouraging the Iranian private sector, since they are direct partnerships with the Iranian government. And they have provided Iran's state treasury, which receives 50%-70% of the profits (the rest goes to the foreign investors), with billions of extra dollars in oil revenue to spend on repressing its citizens.

Not content with this, last month the EU's foreign ministers agreed to seek a formal trade and economic cooperation pact with Iran — without imposing any conditions regarding an improvement in Teheran's human rights record.

But the climax came last week, when the Iranian government held its first foreign bond issue since the 1979 Islamic revolution.

Money raised through the sale of government bonds obviously goes directly into the state treasury — meaning it is used to fund the salaries of the police who beat up student demonstrators, and to build the jails into which reform-minded journalists are thrown. (It also pays for the Katyusha rockets and bombs with which Teheran supplies Hizbullah and Palestinian terror organizations, but even the highest stickler would not expect the EU to concern itself with that.)

A bond issue does not even offer the pitiful excuse available to the oil deals: that of creating jobs for ordinary Iranians.

Thus, if ever there was an event in which nations that claim to care about human rights should refuse to participate last week's bond issue was it.

Instead, the 500 million euro ($497.1 million) issue was underwritten by two major European banks, Germany's Commerzbank AG and France's BNP Paribas SA. And 40% of the issue — which was oversubscribed by more than 20% — was snapped up by European (primarily German and British) institutional investors (Middle Eastern buyers took most of the rest).

European hypocrisy has caused great suffering to Israel, as EU money has played a major role in the PA's terrorist war against this country. But Europe's hypocrisy has arguably caused even greater suffering to millions of Iranians, Palestinians, and others — all those whose vicious, repressive governments are propped up with European cash.

Were the EU ever to put its money where its mouth

is — i.e., to make its trade and investment policies at least minimally conformable to its pious platitudes on human rights — it would provide an incalculable boost for democracy and freedom in the region.

(The writer is a veteran journalist and commentator.)

9. Iran Bans Newspaper for Comments on Liberal Cleric

Article on page 5 of *The Jerusalem Post* of
July 14th, 2002

An Iranian court has banned a pro-reform newspaper for publishing comments on the resignation of a liberal cleric, while US President George W. Bush accused "unelected people" of blocking reform in the Islamic Republic.

Ayatollah Jalaleddin Taheri quit as Friday prayer leader in the central city of Isfahan this week, hitting out at alleged abuses of power among the clerical elite. Soon afterwards, the powerful Supreme National Security Council moved to smother the row by banning newspapers from publishing comment on the issue.

The *Aftab-e Yazd* newspaper yesterday quoted publisher Bijan Saf-Sari as saying the press court had banned his Azad daily for violating the order.

Dozens of pro-reform newspapers have been banned in the last three years.

10. Iran Reformists Back Protest Against Dictatorship

Article on page A7 of *The Jerusalem Post* of July
12, 2002

Teheran (AP) — Iran's largest pro-reform party and more than 100 lawmakers have come out in support of a popular cleric who resigned in protest against hard-line authorities, reports said yesterday.

The outpouring of sympathy for Ayatollah Jalaleddin Taheri came despite an order by Iran's Supreme National Security Council banning newspapers from publishing reports about the cleric.

Taheri quit as a prayer leader in the central city of Isfahan on Tuesday, saying that hard-liners in the ruling establishment are "paralyzing" civil and elected institutions in the name of religion, to preserve their power.

The Islamic Iran Participation Front, led by Muhammad Reza Khatami, the younger brother of Iranian President Muhammad Khatami, said Taheri's denunciation of the influence of unelected conservatives reflects the views of millions of Iranians.

No fewer than 125 reformist lawmakers have signed a letter supporting Taheri, newspapers reported yesterday.

Several papers defied the council's ban, devoting pages to comments on Taheri's resignation statement.

The council is Iran's highest decision-making body on security matters. It is headed by President Khatami and its members include the interior and intelligence ministers, top military and police officers, and representatives of supreme leader Ayatollah Ali Khamenei.

11. Iran by the Numbers

Article by Thomas L. Friedman on page 13 of *The Jerusalem Post/New York Times* of June 23rd, 2002

The most striking thing about Iran today is the honesty you can find in the newspapers. Some mornings, they take your breath away. Consider the mainstream paper *Entekhab*, which ran a long piece the other day, headlined "Skyrocketing Figures," that ticked off the following statistics: There are now 84,000 prostitutes operating on the streets of Tehran and 250 brothels, including some linked to high officials. There are 60 new runaway girls hitting Tehran's streets every day — a 12% increase over last year. Forty percent of all drug-addicted women in Iranian prisons have AIDS. Two sisters, ages 16 and 17, recently gave AIDS to 1,100 people in a two-month period. Four million youths under the age of 20 suffer from depression. Unemployment (which is already around 30 percent) is steadily rising.

All of these problems are symptoms of a floundering economy, or, as the newspaper *Iran News* baldly put it two weeks ago: "The nation's entire economic structure is fundamentally bankrupt and in desperate need of urgent and sweeping reforms. Some of the graver and more prominent problems include lack of sufficient foreign investment, mismanagement in all tiers of our economic system, political isolation leading to a deteriorating economic situation, atrocious unemployment and high inflation."

This deterioration is not primarily the result of US sanctions. Iran has plenty of oil wealth and can buy anything from Europe or the black market. It is primarily the result of mismanagement by Iran's theocratic rulers — their corruption, incompetence, arbitrary decisions, religious legal codes and anti-globalization instincts. Which is why the biggest internal drama playing out in Iran today is this: Will the ayatollahs peacefully reform their system, or will it explode beneath their feet from social unrest?

In a poll published by the *Noruz* newspaper last month, 6.2 percent of those surveyed in Tehran said they were satisfied with the current state of affairs, 48.9 percent favored "reform" and 44.9 percent favored "fundamental change."

The problem for Iran's ruling clerics is that they cannot provide enough new jobs without privatizing their state-dominated economy and attracting foreign investment. And they cannot reform the economy and attract foreign investors, who will bring new technology and new markets, without reforming every pillar of their ruling system. This

system includes vast monopolies awarded to their allies —
the bazaar merchants, clerics and children of the clergy — as
well as Islamic charities that serve as front organizations for
huge business conglomerates that pay no taxes and import
everything from cigarettes to cars, duty free. Iran also can't
attract investors, particularly for industry, without some
transparent rule of law, which means curbing the arbitrary
rule of the Guardian Council of clerics and the judges they
appoint, who sit atop the system here, dominating the courts
and parliament.

The Islamic revolution urbanized millions of rural
Iranians and made them real citizens, in a way the shah never
did. "Now they have education, roads, transports and health
facilities," said the manager of an auto-parts company. "Sixty
percent of university students today are girls. But now these
new citizens are looking for a citizens' regime, not a rural
regime. A citizens' regime is a secular government, which
respects the religion of the people but also the rights of the
people."

For the moment, the ruling clerics have enough oil
money — and enough support in the rural areas, in their
seminaries and in the bazaar — to stay on top. But given
Iran's soaring population — there were 30 million Iranians
when the shah left 23 years ago, and there are 66 million
today, with 70 percent under age 30 — something will have
to give if Iran hopes to create enough jobs.

"The establishment has two choices," said the opposition economist Rahim Oskui, "but they have the same result:
Either the establishment will resist international and national
changes — in that case it will crash — or it will become
flexible and adapt. But in that case it cannot remain what it
is now.... [My feeling is] the clergy will reach the conclusion that they will have to secularize the system in order to
survive, but this will take time.... All our modern revolutions
came from inside the country, and given the level of demands
inside the society today, a backward establishment like we

have cannot resist these forces forever — provided there is
no outside interference."

12. The Coming Revolution in Iran

Article by R. James Woolsey on page 15 in
The Jerusalem Post/The Wall Street Journal of
July 30th, 2002

The ruling mullahs in Iran are beginning to look like
the inhabitants of the Kremlin in 1988 or of Versailles in
1788 — the storm that engulfs them may not be here yet,
but it is gathering.

The most recent war against us by Muslim fanatics
culminated in al Qaeda's September 11th attacks. But the
war began nearly a quarter of a century ago when Shiite
fanatics took power in Iran and seized American hostages.
It was their proxy, Hezbollah, which in 1983 attacked our
Marine barracks and embassy in Beirut. The rule of Iran's
theocrats has been an unmitigated disaster not only for the
victims of their terrorism, but for the Iranian people as well.
Now the outside world is beginning to notice what has been
chronicled by conservative scholar Michael Ledeen for some
months: The mullahs are beginning to lose control.

It is not only that Iranian students have been demonstrating against the regime, workers rioting, and the economy
collapsing. The ideology of Iranian theocracy is reeling, and
this is the trend to watch. Shiite theocracy today is where
Soviet communism was in the early 1980's: still in power,
but widely recognized as being rigid and unworkable.

Betraying Islam

When Ayatollah Jaladedin Taheri, the senior cleric for
Isfahan, resigned from the regime early in July, he not only
attacked the ruling mullahs for poor governance, he blasted
them for betraying Islam. On this point he joined the brave

Grand Ayatollah Montazeri, who has been under house arrest for five years and who recently issued a fatwah against suicide-bombers.

The ruling mullahs, who have never numbered more than a small percentage of Iran's Shiite clergy, are finding it harder and harder to get the police and even the Pasdaran ("Guardians of the Revolution") to repress the demonstrators; they have been driven to import Syrians and Palestinians to do dirty work. Knowing that the regime is dying, increasing numbers of the security forces do not want to attack fellow Iranians any more than Polish security forces wanted to attack Solidarity in the 1980's.

It should come as no surprise that Iranians have lost faith in the dysfunctional theocracy that rules them. Union of mosque and state has worked no better there than the union of church and state did in Europe. In the West, religious fanaticism wedded to state power produced, among other things, the Spanish Inquisition and the Thirty Years War. This bloody history created the conviction in the minds of Locke, Jefferson, and the others whose ideas shaped America that social peace requires the separation of church and state. In time, much of the rest of the world has learned the same lesson.

For almost all of its history Shiite Islam (although not Sunni) has been on the same side as Jefferson in this debate. Ayatollah Khomeini's 1979 innovation, Shiite theocracy, flouted religious tradition and turned Iran down an unaccustomed and disastrous path.

The strangeness of theocracy to the Iranian mind is probably one reason why the ruling mullah's implementation of repression and censorship, quite unlike the full-bore totalitarianism in neighboring Iraq, is brutal but not especially thorough. One major lesson from the history of revolutions is that economic privatization combined with sporadic and partial brutality quickens the pulses of the oppressed and turns them into committed rebels. Thus pre-Revolutionary conditions now exist in Iran.

One of the few public figures who noticed what's going on is President Bush. The White House issued a fine statement on these developments in Iran on July 12, to almost total press indifference. The Iranian regime responded with a pitiful pro forma anti-US demonstration by rent-a-crowds in Tehran and angry verbal blasts — sure evidence that the President struck a sore nerve.

By contrast, much of the American media and policy establishment and virtually all of Europe's leaders seem to have bought the notion that President Mohammad Khatami embodies the reform movement in Iran. At times his press in the West suggests that he may have retained the same publicists who sold the goofy idea in the early 1980s that KGB boss Yuri Andropov was going to reform the Soviet Union because he drank Scotch and listened to jazz. It is said that Mr. Khatami holds positive views about America's Founding Fathers. This may be true. Sadly, his behavior suggests that his favorite would be Cotton Mather, not Thomas Jefferson.

President Khatami has shown himself to be at best the ruling mullahs' poodle. At worst he is a coldly cynical participant in a good cop/bad cop act designed to give the Europeans an excuse to do business with Iran in spite of the fact that it exports weapons of mass destruction and sponsors terrorism.

A Choice

Mr. Khatami's second and final term as president is over in three years, so in the next year or two the ruling mullahs will have to make a big decision. They can try to find someone else they might palm off as an officially acceptable "reformer," but the students and real reformers almost certainly won't buy their choice. The mullahs will thus be driven to increase repression. Their other option is to follow the advice of Ayatollahs Montazeri and Taheri: Abandon the doomed attempt to marry the mosque to the state, and return all clerics to their traditional role outside government.

In the interest of avoiding bloodshed, we should hope that the ruling clerics retire gracefully. But if they continue to opt for deception, oppression, and terror, they will face a major crisis before long — one in which they are likely to lose everything, including their lives. If we maintain what President Bush rightly describes as moral clarity, we can help Iran take a major step toward changing the face of the entire Middle East. If theocracy dies in Iran as it has died in Afghanistan, then its remaining advocates — the Islamist terrorists and Saudi Arabia's Wahhabis — will be substantially weakened. It is vital that we let the Iranian people know we are with them in this struggle against theocracy.

(Mr. Woolsey was director of Central Intelligence, 1993-95.)

Victor Mordecai comments: The people of Iran (Persia) have traditionally always been the allies of Israel. Persian King Cyrus, who sent the Jews home to Israel after the Babylonian exile, is described as Messiah in the Bible. Esther and Mordecai were queen and prime minister, respectively, in the Persian kingdom of Artaxerxes. Our problem there was not with the Persians, but with the Arab Haman, a descendant of the biblically cursed Amalek. Once Haman was dispatched, everything was fine again between the Persians and the Jews.

In 614 AD, the land of Israel was invaded by the Persian Zoroastrian army and the Jews were liberated from Byzantine persecution.

Until the fall of the Shah in 1979, Iran was a strategic ally of Israel and West.

I don't hate the Iranians; I love them. They are people who were traditionally allies and blessed because they blessed us. This unfortunate kidnapping of the Iranian people by their fanatic Islamic leadership must be terminated. The Iranian people must be liberated from these Islamic tyrants.

On a recent TV show I did with Rev. Jerry Falwell, "Listen America" (October 28th, 2002), I answered his last question as to how I felt about US President George W. Bush. My answer was as follows: George W. Bush is an instrument of God. God used him to liberate the Afghanis from the crazy Taliban and al-Qaida in his first year of Presidency.

In the second year of his term, he will liberate the Iraqis from Saddam Hussein.

In his third year, he will liberate the people of Iran from the crazy ayatollahs.

And God willing, in his fourth and final year of his first term of office, he will liberate the North Korean people from Kim Jung IL, thereby defeating the "axis of evil" and delivering the hapless peoples in those countries from rogues and tyrants.

If he indeed succeeds in doing all these things, he will go down in history as the greatest President in US history.

PRIVATE INVESTIGATION

Bosnian Militants Turn US Allies to Enemies

Article by Yaroslav Trofimov, Staff Reporter of
The Wall Street Journal, on page 15 of
The Jerusalem Post, March 19th, 2002

Sarajevo, Bosnia-Herzegovina — Like nearly all Bosnian Muslims, Ali Ihsan grew up wearing Western clothes. She was taught that the Quran wasn't always to be taken literally. And while she celebrated some Muslim holidays, the 24-year-old Sarajevan was otherwise hard to distinguish from her Christian compatriots.

Now, as she sips Turkish coffee in a café here, Ms. Ihsan is shrouded head-to-toe in a Saudi-style black robe. In January, she joined hundreds of other Bosnian Muslims to protest the deportation of suspected al-Qaeda terrorists. The protest ended in a clash with police.

Ms. Ihsan is one of the thousands of Bosnian Muslims who embraced an ultraconservative strain of Islam after the country's bloody civil war. She's in a minority: Most Bosnian Muslims — about half of the country's four million people — practice their faith in a relaxed manner, if at all. They also link their political future to Europe's and regard the US as an ally. Yet, in recent months, Bosnia's new Islamist groups have provoked increasingly anti-American sentiments, raising fears of attacks on US troops and installations.

The seeds for this conversion to militant Islam were sown by Arab mujahedeen who flocked to Bosnia-Herzegovina as volunteer soldiers in the 1992-95 war against ethnic Serb and Croat militias. Some settled in the country, while others joined al-Qaeda bases in Afghanistan.

After Sept.11, the US pressured Bosnia to deport the remaining mujahedeen to clamp down on Arab charities and Islamist organizations. The Muslim protests that followed spread far beyond the Islamist fringe. "These Arabs have shed their blood for our country," complains Ms. Ihsan, who has a bachelor's degree in political science. "And now the government is betraying them just to please America."

Such bitter feelings are new in Bosnia — a country routinely held up by the US State Department as an example of America going to war on the Muslim side. Part of the problem, diplomats here say, is that the West sat by for years as Saudi and other Persian Gulf charities, often staffed by former mujahedeen, spent hundreds of millions of dollars to instill their puritan and anti-Western version of Islam.

The US did not help the Muslims by imposing sanctions on their principal enemy, the Serbs, and hitting Serb positions with air strikes toward the end of the war. But Islamists argue that when Washington intervened with a peace settlement after Muslim troops overran Serb lines, the move was designed to abort a probable Muslim victory.

The overwhelming majority of Bosnian Muslims maintain a staunchly secular lifestyle and identify themselves with the West. But the radical ideology of some Muslims, while a minority view, has succeeded in attracting some of Bosnia's more articulate and better educated young people. It has become almost a fashion on Bosnian campuses. Islamic youth groups have been largely nonviolent so far and are too small to bring dramatic change to Bosnian society, security officials say. Yet these officials see them as a reservoir of al-Qaeda supporters, and they are monitored by the Bosnian authorities and Western troops that enforce Bosnian peace.

The potential threat of Islamic fundamentalism in Europe and some American casualties persuaded the US and other Western nations to oppose the presence of foreign mujahedeen in Bosnia as part of the November 1995 Dayton peace agreements. The US- brokered agreements specifically call for the expulsion of all foreign fighters. But the Muslim-controlled Bosnian government circumvented the rule by granting Bosnian citizenship to several hundred Arab volunteers — and eliminating their "foreign" status — before the accord took effect. As of last year, many still lived in the country, often married to local women.

This tolerant attitude started to change after a new coalition of non-nationalist and moderate parties took control of the Bosnian government early last year. Then, after Sept. 11th, the country went into overdrive to address terrorist threats on its soil. "We don't want to be held hostage by our past, and that is why we want to clean out the stables," says Ivica Misic, the chairman of the Bosnia-Herzegovina Anti-Terrorism Team and the country's deputy foreign minister.

In the past six months, the government has revoked the citizenship of 94 former mujahedeen, prompting most of those still on Bosnian territory to go into hiding in recent weeks or abroad.

Until January, Bosnia's crackdown elicited little visible opposition. The government would quietly detain Arab mujahedeen, strip them of citizenship, and then hand them over to foreign countries, disregarding protests by human-rights groups such as Amnesty International.

Initially, the same scenario unfolded after the arrest of six Algerians accused of trying to blow up the US Embassy in Sarajevo and of contacting al-Qaeda's elusive military commander, Abu Zubaida, last year. Most of these Arabs worked at local branches of Persian Gulf-based humanitarian organizations, had Bosnian passports because of their participation in the war and were married to Bosnian women. All the detainees claimed innocence.

The legal proceedings were marked by confusion. Officials say the US had intelligence data that could have secured a conviction, but to protect sources, it wasn't shown to the Bosnian courts. The courts ruled that there were no grounds for prosecution and ordered the six freed. Bosnia's Human Rights Chamber, a state agency, issued an injunction to halt any deportation. The Bosnian government, which says it didn't receive the injunction in time, went ahead and handed over the Algerians to the US.

But on January 18th, the day of the handover, several hundred activists from Islamic youth organizations, including Ms. Ihsan, gathered at the Sarajevo jail. In video footage carried by local and Arab TV stations, Bosnian riot police clashed with the protesters, who lay in the snow and blocked police vehicles. The police eventually beat their way through the crowd. "On that day, I was ready to die for the name of Allah," says Ms. Ihsan, who says she received several truncheon blows.

The six Algerians were shipped to the US detention camp at Guantanamo Bay, Cuba, and President Bush publicly praised Bosnia's cooperation in his State of the Union address. The Bosnian Prime, Zlatko Lagumdzija, justified the decision by telling a local magazine called *Dani* that Bosnia's statehood "would have ended" and the country "would have been treated like Afghanistan" had it refused to give up these suspects.

But Mr. Lagumdzija's comments didn't quell the angry reaction of Bosnian politicians and intellectuals, which went on for weeks. Leaders of Bosnia's Helsinki Committee, the country's leading human-rights organization, said the government violated Bosnia's own laws. The cover of a popular magazine showed Uncle Sam urinating on Bosnia's constitution. Even Austria's Wolfgang Petritsch, the international community's high representative, who is the top arbiter of Bosnian affairs under the Dayton accord, remarked that "it remains to be seen whether [deportation decision] is up to the highest human-rights standards."

The deportations also produced an unlikely symbol for Bosnia's Islamists — Nadja Dizdarevic, the blue-eyed wife of one of the Arab deportees, Boudella Hadj. Ms. Dizdarevic, a 28-year-old mother of four and the sister of a well-known Bosnian lounge singer, used her contacts as head of a women's self-help organization to organize an all-night picketing of the jail. She has become a familiar figure on Bosnian television and Arab satellite networks.

"The fight against terrorism is justified — but it becomes senseless if you take it to innocent people," Ms. Dizdarevic says as she offers honey-soaked sweets in her Dobrinja apartment. The 94 former Arab mujahedeen who were stripped of Bosnian citizenship and deported or forced to flee have left about 300 Bosnian-born children behind. The wives often are denied health insurance and offered only about $12 a month per child in welfare payments, she says. "Who's going to maintain us — America?" Ms. Dizdarevic wonders, breaking into tears. "Every day, I keep asking myself, why did this happen to us?"

A far-fetched answer comes from posters plastered on the Sarajevo square facing the US Embassy. They show Mr. Lagumdzija wearing a skullcap during a visit to the Western Wall in Jerusalem and accuse him of being a Jewish agent "working to eliminate the last Bosnian Muslim." *Saff,*

Sarajevo's glossy Islamist magazine, published the same picture to accompany a story about the anti-mujahedeen campaign.

The new radicalism worries the traditional leaders of Bosnian Islam. They see growing tension between Bosnia's moderate Islamic establishment and the militant youths. Some of these youths beat up the mufti, or interpreter of Islamic law, of Sarajevo last month because they disapproved of his choice for a new prayer leader at a mosque. "I can't understand these people.... Maybe their kind of Islam can pass in the Middle East, but here it's just weird," says Jusuf Ramic, the Egyptian-trained dean of the Islamic Studies Faculty, the country's main Muslim religious academy. "This is Europe and a multidenominational place," he notes, and the militant youths "are a thorn in the eye... causing damage to the Muslims who live here."

[Victor Mordecai comments: Please see my February newsletter and article about "Bosnia: The Afghanistan of Europe."]

MILITARY INTELLIGENCE

US, European Intelligence Officials Wary of Hizbullah and Al-Qaida Cooperation

Article by *Jerusalem Post* staff on page3 of
The Jerusalem Post of July 1st, 2002

Hizbullah and al-Qaida are increasingly teaming up on logistics and training for terrorist operations, US and European intelligence officials and terrorism experts say.

According to a report in yesterday's *Washington Post*, the ad hoc and tactical cooperation is between mid- and low-level operatives, overcoming years of rivalry between the groups.

The cooperation runs the gamut from money laundering to weapons smuggling and acquiring forged documents, knowledgeable sources told the paper. The alliance is of great concern to US officials in Washington and intelligence agents abroad, who believe Hizbullah's assets and organization will help al-Qaida overcome damage suffered in American attacks on Afghanistan.

The new partnership has been discussed in the Senate and House intelligence committees, whose chairmen and vice chairmen are briefed by CIA Director George Tenet and FBI Director Robert Mueller. "Hizbullah is the A-team of terrorism," said Sen. Bob Graham (D-Fla.), the chairman of the Senate panel.

Analysts say there is an evolving pattern of decentralized alliances between terrorist groups and cells which share a desire to cripple the US and force it out of the Middle East, and Israel out of Palestinian territory.

"There's a convergence of objectives," said Steven Simon, a former National Security Council terrorism expert. "There's something in the zeitgeist that is pretty well established now."

A senior administration official said Usama bin Laden and his lieutenants have used the Internet to tell their followers to ally themselves with helpful Islamic-based groups like Hizbullah. The official said there is "no doubt at all" the two groups have been in communication on logistics.

Among the methods cited by counterterrorism experts are computer chat rooms, with operatives changing passwords when necessary and exploiting the chat rooms to plan operations.

However, some analysts believe that the fact that Hizbullah is a Shi'ite organization and al-Qaida operatives are largely Sunni Muslims means true cooperation is doomed to failure, according to the *Post* report.

"I just don't see it," said Kenneth Katzman, a Middle East specialist at the Congressional Research Service. "There's not a lot of commonality there."

However, testimony regarding just such an alliance

was provided by Ali Mohammed, a former US Green Beret who conspired with bin Laden to bomb US embassies in Africa.

According to the report, in October 2000, he testified about securing a meeting in Sudan "between al-Qaida... and Iran and Hizbullah... between Mughniye, Hizbullah's chief, and bin Laden." He said Hizbullah provided explosives training for al-Qaida, while Iran used Hizbullah to provide explosives which looked like rocks.

The report states that US and European intelligence operatives have had a hard time convincing their superiors of the new alliance until now.

"We have been screaming at them for more than a year now, and more since Sept. 11th, that these guys all work together," an overseas operative said in the report. "What we keep hearing back is that it can't be because al-Qaida doesn't work that way. That is [expletive]. Here, on the ground, these guys all work together as long as they are Muslims. There is no other division that matters."

[Victor Mordecai comments: Please see newsletter of May regarding Ali Mohammed's conspiring with bin Laden to bomb US embassies in Africa.]

Chapter XII
SEPTEMBER 2002 NEWSLETTER

Victor Mordecai's Monthly Message

On September 11th, 2002, the first anniversary of the "Pearl Harbor" of WWIII, we all remembered the martyrs of the Islamic attacks on the World Trade Center in New York City, the Pentagon in Washington, D.C., as well as the valiant passengers on the four hijacked jetliners who went to their deaths at the behest of crazed Islamic genocidal murderers and their leaders of Islam who have been preaching this message over the last few decades.

For over thirteen years, I have been traveling the world, especially the US, and investigating the movements and plans of Islamic terrorists whose goal is a global Islamic empire and the annihilation of all other systems. I started my travels, mostly in Texas at first, and accumulated testimonies in the churches from people who worked with the military, law enforcement, or other government agencies. These people had no reason to lie, but simply came forward with sincerity when telling me about Islamic attempts to infiltrate the US from Mexico. This is detailed in my first book, *Is Fanatic Islam a Global Threat?*

The first major terrorist infiltrations into the US that I heard about in Texas started in the 1982-83 period at about the time of "Operation Peace in the Galilee" (the Israeli incursion into Lebanon to terminate the PLO mini-state). These were Palestinian terrorists who came across the Rio Grande River at Boca Chica.

It was also at this time, just after the 1979 Islamic Revolution in Iran, that the Iranians started their invasion of the US, also with inimical plans for America. The two remaining Islamic revolutions which brought in terrorists were the defeat of the Soviets in Afghanistan which released tens of thousands of Al-Qaeda type terrorists to infiltrate the US plus the turning of Iraq into an enemy in 1990 with the invasion of Kuwait. More and more different and divergent groups of Moslems were now all aligning themselves together into one army of Allah with which to defeat the US.

With the election of Bill Clinton to the Presidency in 1992, a new ideology appeared known as "It's the economy, stupid." The purpose of this ideology was to subordinate all other ideologies to one important goal: economic growth and prosperity. There was no room for God or for gods of any kind other than money or "mammon" as it's known in the Bible.

Bill Clinton's thinking went like this: The only thing that interests Americans and the world is money. Wall Street must only climb. Therefore, Americans must be encouraged to invest. Investments only come about when the people have confidence in the economy. Any threat to that confidence will shatter the fragile economy. If there is a threat to the economy it can and must be bought off with money. (This, in Mafia terminology, is called "Paying Protection.")

When the World Trade Center underwent its first attack in February 1993, all the blame was placed on Sheikh Omar Abdul Rahman, an Egyptian cleric who preached Islamic Jihad or Holy War and the assassination of Egyptian President Anwar Sadat in 1981. Fourteen other co-conspirators were also given life imprisonment, but the "big fish," Ramzi Youssef, an Iraqi agent who built the bomb, got away.

It was easy for the American people to accept a "sealed and shut" case against 15 terrorists and leave it at that. But spreading the blame to include Saddam Hussein would have caused a no-confidence vote in Wall Street. Clinton succeeded in avoiding that.

In 1995, Timothy McVeigh and Terry Nichols were apprehended after the bombing at the Murrah Federal Building in Oklahoma City. All blame was pinned on McVeigh at first, and then, after his execution, the blame was extended to Nichols as well. But no one wanted to consider the Islamic or Iraqi connection to the blast. (See page 265 of my book *Is Fanatic Islam a Global Threat?* as well as my November 2001 newsletter.) I was in Tulsa, Oklahoma, on April 15th, 1991, during the blast in Oklahoma City and received information first hand about the Islamic involvement in the bombing.

An Oklahoma City investigative reporter by the name of Jayna Davis was working for NBC at that time and accumulated over 1,000 pages of evidence regarding the Iraqi involvement in the bombing. The FBI refused to accept the evidence. Why? Because: "It's the economy, stupid." The American people could accept two individuals like McVeigh and Nichols as being the guilty parties, but to extend this to include Saddam Hussein would "open up a bag of worms" which would threaten confidence in the US economy. Americans don't like bogeymen, and don't understand foreign ideologies. That was the thrust of the Clinton Administration from 1992 to 2000.

By the way, I recommend to all my readers to try to acquire or rent a copy of a video movie called *Arlington Road*. Without revealing too much about the movie itself, the movie shows how the media and the "agenda" almost always like to pin the blame on someone, anyone, and shut the case, because Americans don't understand terrorist groups or ideologies, and it is easy to pin the blame on patsies.

In 1996, a day before the TWA800 disaster, Saddam Hussein spoke in his national assembly in Baghdad and said: "Tomorrow is Iraq's National Day, and we are going to give the world a big surprise." On page 266 of my book *Is Fanatic Islam a Global Threat?* I give many proofs that the plane did not fall out of the skies because of a fuel injection problem, but was shot out of the skies by a missile, an Islamic Saddam Hussein missile. But the Clinton Administration ignored, or rather covered up this terrorist act by Saddam in order to prevent a panic in which Americans would become too afraid to fly. This in turn would lead to the collapse of the airline industry, as well as the tourism industry in America.

According to the book by Yosef Bodansky, *Usama bin Laden, The Man Who Declared War on the US,* he claims that Clinton paid bin Laden "Protection Money" to keep his terrorists away from American soil. This was exactly the manner in which the Saudis, Egyptians and Europeans behaved to "buy time, to buy protection" for their economies.

When the Texas cowboy George W. Bush became President in 2001, he claimed to be a born-again Christian, and definitely made no claims to pay off the terrorists.

To make a long story short, the deal which had served Clinton so well in the 1990's was now off. The chickens came home to roost with the 9/11 attacks.

Another aspect of my 13 years of travels to the US, Canada, Mexico, Europe, Russia and Israel was the constant gathering of information from all over the world about Islamic terrorism in all countries of the earth.

From the Israeli Army Spokesman's Office I received other information which together formed my opinions.

For example, in the early 1990's one of the Israeli army's iron-clad rules was that there cannot ever be a Palestinian State because the moment Israel gives up control of the heights overlooking the coastal Israeli Air Force bases or the civilian airports, Islamic Stinger, Sam or Strella anti-aircraft missiles would be able to bring down any and every plane taking off or landing. The last decade of Palestinian terrorism has shown anyone with any brains what the Palestinian plans really are. Therefore, there cannot be a Palestinian State, ever.

What I saw in the US was just how vulnerable US civilian airports are. That if the Moslems desired, they could shut down US airports just like Israeli airports and maybe with greater ease, because the Americans were not aware or prepared to deal with Islamic terrorism like the Israelis are. As I drove around the US, I saw that even a simple rifle, machine gun or RPG could bring down planes at the edge of the runways as planes were taking off or landing. I warned Americans in churches, synagogues, on radio and TV that this was a nightmare scenario. But for most who listened to me, it was too terrible to even think that what I was predicting could happen. I was branded a radical and an extremist for providing simple military intelligence information. But the cold hard facts were that one way to destroy the US economy was by destroying the airliners and tourism, causing a paralysis in the US population leading to an economic collapse.

In July 1994, information appeared about the counterfeiting of US $100 bills by Iran and Iraq, because in addition to enjoying extra greenbacks, the way to destroy the US economy was to cause a lack of confidence in the "greenback" — the US currency. This information appeared in the Israeli English language daily *The Jerusalem Post* and I quote these two articles on page 258 of my book *Is Fanatic Islam a Global Threat?*

Bill Clinton's response was the creation of a new currency, a new dollar bill. But Americans were only to know about this change in currencies two years later, in 1996. Again, why? Clinton did not want a panic. But he did know that Islam was trying to destroy the US economy, either by destroying airplanes and tourism, or the US currency. What was his solution? Buy off the Islamic terrorists, whether they were led by Usama bin Laden, Saddam Hussein, Yasser Arafat, or Ayatollah Khomeini. Another form of the solution was to back Moslem causes in Bosnia, Chechnya or Kosovo at the expense of the Christians, or to force Israel into an untenable situation with an Oslo "peace process," which would lead to the destruction of Israel and another holocaust of the Jewish people.

In 1998, the US embassies in Kenya and Tanzania were blown up by bin Laden's terrorists. In 2000, the USS *Cole* had a hole punched in its side by more of bin Laden's terrorists who committed suicide by driving their explosives laden dinghy into the side of the US Navy destroyer, killing 17 US sailors. What was Clinton's response? He shot a few Tomahawk missiles into empty tents in the Afghan desert as well as into a pharmaceuticals plant in Khartoum, Sudan.

According to US Rep. Rohrabacher, he twice knew the whereabouts of Usama bin Laden and begged that Clinton "take him out." But Clinton looked the other way, because attacking the US abroad was OK. Killing bin Laden would be "stirring up the hornets nest." The only thing that mattered was that there should not be attacks against the US on US soil. This was the deal with the Moslem terrorists so that the US economy would not be unhinged by a vote of no-confidence from the American people.

As we look at the economy of the US and of the world in September 2002, we see the economies of the world floundering because of the lack of investor confidence. There is also a recession which actually started during the last year of the Clinton Adminis-tration. President George W. Bush inherited a terrible legacy from Bill Clinton.

The attacks of 9/11, one year ago, were intended first to cause the simultaneous toppling of the two towers in New York City with the potential death toll reaching over 250,000 people. Praise God there was a miracle. Most people either were not in the buildings or succeeded in escaping. But the even greater plan of bin Laden was causing the towers to crash on Wall Street, literally a "crash on Wall Street." This would have destroyed the US economy and brought down the great Christian Satan (in the eyes of Islam).

Today, there is talk of nuclear fissionable materials on their way to Saddam Hussein. There is talk of biological and chemical weapons in the US and other Western countries in the hands of Islamic terrorists, backed by Saddam Hussein. What happens to the US economy if a nuclear or "dirty" bomb goes off in Manhat-tan? So this war is a religious war with the intent of destroying the economy of the enemy of Islam — the US.

The Judeo-Christian West must be destroyed by first toppling the US. The US must be destroyed by an economic crash brought on by Islamic terrorists with conventional, atomic, biological or chemical weapons. The first article in the "Current Events and Analysis" section is about the thwarted attempt to smuggle into Iraq nuclear fissionable material. But we will also see articles about more attempts at smuggling "shoe bomb" type dynamite onto civilian airliners in Europe, Islamic terrorism in Germany, Islamic terrorism in India/Kashmir, terrorism against Israelis in Los Angeles, Islamic terrorist connections to President Menem in Argentina and more.

The two most important terrible legacies President Bush inherited was the blinding and "dumbing down" of the CIA, NSA, FBI and the State Department, as well as local law enforcement and the military during the two Clinton terms. And secondly, Islamist radicalism and Islamic demographic growth worldwide are like cancers which are much harder to deal with today than they were in 1992 when Clinton came to power.

President George W. Bush's approach has been: Terrorism is the enemy, not Islam. Now, of course, I couldn't disagree more. Islam is the root cause of the terrorism. But his strategy has been to work with the so-called "moderates" such as Egypt, Saudi Arabia, Jordan, Pakistan, and Syria to root out the Al-Qaeda and those related to them and for that he needs the support and cooperation of the "moderates."

Unfortunately, however, I feel that these countries are part of the problem and not the solution. There are those in the US, Canada, Europe, Russia and even Israel who believe that the way to deal with rampant Islamic growth and conquest is to "do business with them."

My belief is that we all need to grab the bull by the horns and defeat global Islam. If you want to get rid of the mosquitoes, you need to drain the swamp. I do not see this happening in Washington, London, Paris, Berlin, Moscow or even Jerusalem. People still talk about the Islamic mosquitoes, but not the Islamic swamp which breeds the mosquitoes.

But the day will come, I believe, that 5/6 of the world's population will wake up and will deal with the 1/6 (Moslems) who want to destroy everyone else. It cannot be that 1/6 of the world thinks it can annihilate 5/6 of the world without itself being annihilated. They must realize the only answer is that Moslems must abandon that satanic ideology threatening humanity. They must realize that the so-called god Allah is not just another name for God. Allah is the opposite of God. Allah is Satan. This is a war between God and Satan. The good news is that God has already defeated Satan, and we are the victorious side if we remain loyal to the God of Abraham, Isaac and Jacob and recognize the above facts.

CURRENT EVENTS AND ANALYSIS

1. Turkish Police Seize Weapons-Grade Uranium

Article from *The Jerusalem Post* of
September 29, 2002

Ankara (Reuters) — Turkish paramilitary police have seized more than 33 pounds of weapons-grade uranium and detained two men accused of smuggling the material, the state-run Anatolian news agency said yesterday.

Officers in the southern province of Sanliurfa, which borders Syria and is about 155 miles from the Iraqi border, were acting on a tip-off when they stopped a taxi cab and discovered the uranium in a lead container hidden beneath the vehicle's seat, the agency said.

The incident happens at a time of mounting speculation the US could launch a military attack on neighboring Iraq for its alleged program of weapons of mass destruction.

US President George Bush has accused Baghdad of clandestine efforts to develop a nuclear bomb as his administration works to build international support for an operation to oust Iraqi President Saddam Hussein.

Officials at Ankara's Atomic Energy Institute would not confirm they had been notified about the material which Anatolian had reported.

"Our investigation on whether the uranium was destined for a neighboring country is continuing," a Sanliurfa police official was quoted as saying by Anatolian.

Police officials in Sanliurfa and Ankara declined to comment on the case.

Authorities believe the uranium came from an east European country and has a value of about $5 million, Anatolian said.

It was not immediately clear when the operation was carried out. Anatolian only gave the first names of the suspects, which appeared to be Turkish.

Smugglers use Turkey's porous eastern border to import drugs, and hundreds of thousands of migrants each year illegally cross the rugged frontier on their way to more affluent European Union nations.

Police in Istanbul seized more than 2.2 pounds of weapons-grade uranium last November that had been smuggled into Turkey from an east European nation. The smugglers were detained after attempting to sell the material to undercover police officers.

2. *"Shoe Bomb" Explosives Found on Moroccan Jet*

Article on page A11 of *The Jerusalem Post*
of September 27th, 2002

Paris (AP) — Explosives of the same type as found on alleged shoe bomber Richard Reid were discovered on a Moroccan jet after passengers left the flight at an airport in eastern France, authorities said Thursday.

Officials said there was enough explosive material to blow up a plane.

There was no detonator attached to the 3 ounces of explosives discovered in the passenger section of a Royal Air Maroc airplane on Wednesday night after it landed at the Metz-Nancy-Lorraine airport, according to police.

Judicial sources, speaking on condition of anonymity, identified the explosive material as pentrite and said it was the same as the substance Reid, a British citizen, allegedly tried to detonate on an American Airlines flight from Paris to Miami on December 22nd, 2001.

The airline refused immediate comment on the case.

The explosives found Wednesday were wrapped in aluminum foil, police said, indicating it might have been in transit for delivery. The Boeing 737 originated in Marrakech.

Judicial sources said they had been unable to find a fuse mechanism needed for detonation.

The explosives were found between armrests by dogs from the customs service as they performed a routine search of the plane. Anti-terrorism police were investigating the find, along with the counterintelligence agency known as the DST.

Pentrite is found in the plastic explosive Semtex, which was used in the bomb attack on Pan Am Flight 103 over Lockerbie, Scotland, in 1988 that killed 270 people.

Reid is charged with attempting to blow up the American Airlines flight with explosives hidden in his shoes. Passengers and crew members restrained him after he allegedly tried to light a fuse. The flight was diverted to Boston.

3. Witness Links Terror Suspects to Al-Qaida

Article on page A11 of *The Jerusalem Post*
of September 27th, 2002

Frankfurt (AP) — A witness at the terrorism trial of four Algerians accused of plotting to blow up a French Christmas market linked the group to Usama bin Laden for the first time, testifying yesterday that one of them boasted of a contact to the alleged terrorist leader.

The witness, Muhammad Saddiki, a former fellow inmate, said defendant Aeurobi Beandalis once told him the terror group's purported leader, Abdul Rahman of London, had "direct contact" with bin Laden.

Saddiki also said another defendant, Lamine Maroni, boasted of involvement in "terrorist activities" in London and said he was "on his way to an operation" when he was arrested in Germany in December 2000.

4. Israelis Advised to Stay Out of Egypt, Jordan

Article by Itim on page 4 of *The Jerusalem Post*
of September 4th, 2002

Israelis should refrain from visiting Egypt and Jordan, including Sinai, the Prime Minister's Office's anti-terrorism task force reiterated yesterday.

The recommendation was first issued in October 2000, just after the increase in Palestinian violence.

The Foreign Ministry adopted the recommendation, but said there is no legal bar to Israelis visiting the two countries.

5. Abdullah 'Working Closely' With Saddam

Article by Douglas Davis on page 5 of
The Jerusalem Post of August 4th, 2002

London — The Bush Administration has acquired evidence that Jordan's King Abdullah II, once a cornerstone of US policy against Iraq, is in fact working closely with Iraqi President Saddam Hussein, according to senior political sources here.

The sources declined to indicate the precise nature of the evidence, but they say it is damning and irrefutable.

Among the most sensational charges, they said, is that Abdullah has been passing sensitive American intelligence material to Saddam and that he has received substantial "gifts" from Baghdad.

The sources allege that Abdullah is also "very handsomely rewarded" by Saddam for facilitating the passage of illicit, Iraqi-bound cargoes that arrive in Akaba, and for purchases — ostensibly for Jordan, but in fact for Iraq — that are made by a select group of Jordanian businessmen.

In addition to Abdullah's intense relationship with Saddam, the sources said he also has a long-standing friendship with Saddam's sons, Uday and Qusai, with whom he spent most of his vacations during the 1990s before becoming king.

"But the friendship appears to be one-sided," said the sources. "Uday recently gave Abdullah a gift — three Porsches — but what he did not tell Abdullah was that the cars had been stolen. All three had been looted from Kuwait. It was a sign of Uday's contempt for Abdullah."

A leading businessman who acts as a courier between Abdullah and Saddam learned of the "gift" and bought Abdullah a brand-new, top-of-the-range Mercedes, urging him to dispose of the stolen Porsches. Abdullah accepted the Mercedes, said the sources, but continues to drive the Porsches.

The sources say that Abdullah insists on handling relations with Iraq personally, on one occasion ordering a top official to leave the room while he met with an intermediary to discuss his relations with Iraq.

According to the sources, Saddam has a fund of some $6 billion a year in cash — acquired from the sale of oil, either through the UN oil-for-food program or on the black market — which he uses to acquire weapons and for "gifts" and outright bribes to political figures throughout the region, "particularly in Saudi Arabia."

"It is no wonder," said one source, "that politicians throughout the Middle East are supporting Saddam."

The revelations of Abdullah's alleged duplicity are likely to seriously complicate his visit to Washington, where he was meeting with top administration officials, including President George W. Bush, yesterday.

They are also likely to upset the Pentagon's military planners, who had been relying on Jordan to play a pivotal role in the mooted US-led military operation to topple Saddam. Plans for Jordan's involvement are now expected to be radically reassessed.

Leaked Pentagon documents, which indicate the high level of trust the US once placed in Abdullah, suggested Jordan had been considered as a "jumping-off" point for an attack on western Iraq that would have involved up to 250,000 US troops, as well as forces from Britain and other participating US allies.

Jordanian officials denied the report and Abdullah has been cautioning against an attempt to mount a military operation against Baghdad, insisting that a resolution to the Israeli-Palestinian conflict must take precedence.

Another sign of Abdullah's affiliation with Baghdad became evident this week when, in an unprecedented display of family disunity, he condemned his uncle, Prince Hassan, for publicly siding with the Iraqi opposition in exile.

Hassan, who was dumped by the late King Hussein as his successor just days before his death, is revered by many Iraqis as the most senior member of the Hashemite royal family.

He caused a sensation when he made a personal appearance at a major conference, held here last month, of all the anti-Saddam groups that was convened by the US-backed Iraqi National Congress. INC leaders have been invited to meet with senior officials in the US administration in Washington next week.

In an interview with *The Times* of London this week, Abdullah represented his uncle as a dysfunctional political neophyte, when he declared that "Prince Hassan blundered into something that he did not realize he was getting into and we're all picking up the pieces."

He also told the paper that when he meets Bush he will demand full backing for Secretary of State Colin Powell against the Pentagon officials who are "fixated on Iraq," and he warned that US action against Iraq would open a "Pandora's Box" in the Middle East.

During visits to Paris, London, and Washington this week, Abdullah has strenuously sought to link the Palestinian and Iraqi issues, repeating the mantra with increasing stridency that Washington must first resolve the Israeli-Palestinian conflict before it contemplates action against Saddam.

On Sunday, he told CNN that it is "somewhat ludicrous" for the US to try to consider actions against Saddam without positive movement on the Israeli-Palestinian track.

And just hours before his meeting with Bush yesterday, he told *The Washington Post* that international leaders are deeply worried about US plans for war against Iraq, adding that it would be a "tremendous mistake" to ignore warnings from its allies.

"Everybody is saying this is a bad idea," Abdullah said. "If it seems America says we want to hit Baghdad, that's not what Jordanians think, or the British, the French, the Russians, the Chinese and everybody else."

He added that some US allies might have been reluctant to speak out because they believed the prospect of war was far in the distance: "All of a sudden, this thing is moving to the horizon much closer than we believed."

In what is regarded as a slap at Abdullah, US Undersecretary of Defense for Policy Douglas Feith offered a diametrically opposed analysis, arguing that the toppling of Saddam will create the opportunity for a diplomatic breakthrough.

He told the London-based *Financial Times* that "Iraq is purposefully and systematically aggravating Palestinian-Israeli relations" and said that the intensity of the Israeli-Palestinian conflict should not deter the US from seeking regime change in Iraq.

"[Saddam] may think that the more he can encourage terrorist bombings against the Israelis, the more the world is diverted from the issue of his tyranny, his weapons of mass destruction programs, his terrorist activities, and on to another agenda," Feith said.

6. Sudan Braces for More Fighting After Talks Fail

Article on page 5 of *The Jerusalem Post*
of September 4th, 2002

Nairobi (Reuters) — Sudan geared up for fresh fighting yesterday as the government and rebels traded blame over the collapse of landmark talks to end Africa's longest-running civil war.

Sudan's government suspended the negotiations on Monday and ordered a general mobilization of the army after rebels seized the strategic town of Torit, their biggest battlefield victory in two months.

The rebels, based in the south, which is largely animist with some Christians and Muslims, have been fighting since 1983 for more autonomy from the Muslim-dominated north.

"The government came more or less with an opinion to torpedo the talks," SPLA spokesman Samson Kwaje told a news conference. "They were not interested in negotiating seriously."

Sudan's charge d'affaires in Kenya, Ahmed Dirdeiry, accused the rebels of backtracking on an outlined peace agreement reached at a previous round of talks in July but said there is still a will to resolve the conflict on both sides.

Victor Mordecai comments: This politically correct report by Reuters fails to mention two things:

First, the reason for the civil war is the imposition of Islamic Sharia law throughout all of Sudan, including the south, which is not Muslim. The south is made up mostly of Dinka tribes who in the end will either be completely annihilated by the Moslems of the north, or will reach statehood, i.e., the south breaks away from the north.

Secondly, one of the outcomes of this civil war has been the annihilation of over 2,000,000 blacks in the south of the country. There are yet about 8,000,000 blacks left. The Sudanese government of Khartoum has even used biological and chemical weapons, gifts of the Iraqis and the Iranians, to kill the blacks en masse. It's interesting that Saddam Hussein is not branded as a war criminal even though he has killed over 2,000,000 of his fellow Moslems. Hassan Turabi and General Omar Bashir of Sudan have killed over 2,000,000 blacks in Sudan and they, too, are not branded and prosecuted as war criminals. Yet, Slobodan Milosevic, who killed 2,000 armed Albanian Moslem terrorists, was kidnapped by force and today is on trial in The Hague in the International War Crimes Tribunal. Rumors are that the same double standard will be applied to Israeli Prime Minister Ariel Sharon and other Israeli leaders and military officers. The same could apply to US military and soldiers for whatever happens in Iraq.

7. Singapore Leader Cautions Against Muslims' "Rigidity"

Article on page 5 of *The Jerusalem Post* of
August 19th, 2002

Singapore (AP) — Prime Minister Goh Chok Tong said yesterday that some of the city-state's Muslim minority have become "more rigid" in their religious practices, citing a recent flap over the wearing of Islamic headscarves to school.

Speaking at a national day rally, Goh said he is concerned that many Muslims worldwide are becoming more extreme and that "some Singapore Muslims too have become more rigid in the practice of their religion."

"The episode over the wearing of tudung in schools is one example," he said.

Many Muslim women wear headscarves in Singapore, but the government of this tightly controlled nation refuses to allow them in schools, saying the ban is intended to promote harmony and encourage students from all ethnic groups to mix.

Goh has repeatedly defended the decades-old restriction, saying that Singapore can ill afford racial division, especially in the wake of the 9/11 terrorist attacks.

Yesterday, Prime Minister Goh Chok Tong urged Singapore's Muslims to speak up against developments that threaten "the harmony of our multiracial, multi-religious society" and to "stand up against those who advocate intolerance and extremism."

Local Muslim activist Muhammad Latiff said in response to Goh's speech that most Muslims view the Islamic headscarf as a symbol of piety, not extremism.

The dispute has divided Singapore's minority Muslim community, which makes up about 15 percent of a predominantly ethnic Chinese population of about 3.2 million.

In February, the parents of four girls who defied the headscarf ban announced plans to sue the government, saying the measure is unconstitutional.

Victor Mordecai comments: It is very important to pay attention to this situation in Singapore. As the tension increases, Singapore could be threatened militarily by other Moslem groups or states. This will not go unnoticed or unpunished by Beijing.

The Chinese are fighting a war with the Moslems in the western Chinese province of Sinkiang. The Chinese have not forgotten the massacre of a half-million ethnic Chinese in Indonesia in the 1960's during the "time of troubles." Singapore is just another front in the global war of Islam. Islam needs to realize that the Buddhist world has a population of about 2 billion people, or one third of the human race. What do the Muslims want? Do they actually believe they can defeat the Buddhists and the Chinese in particular?

8. Bereaved Fathers of Kashmir Militants Vow to Fight On

Article by Munir Ahmad on page 5 of
The Jerusalem Post of June 19th, 2002

Lahore, Pakistan (AP) — Muhammad Aziz's oldest son Imam was killed in Kashmir in January, buried in the Himalayan region's thick forests by fellow militants fighting against Indian rule.

Aziz says he would not hesitate to sacrifice his remaining four sons for Kashmiri independence. And like many hard-liners, he is angry that President Pervez Musharraf has vowed to reverse Pakistan's long-time support for militant Islamic groups that send fighters into the Indian-ruled portion of the divided province.

"I feel proud that I am the father of a martyr," said the 65-year-old from Lahore, a city near the Indian border south of Kashmir. "By stopping our sons and brothers from waging jihad in Kashmir, President Musharraf has sold the blood of hundreds of freedom fighters."

In his anger, Aziz is not alone. He was among at least 10,000 people at a rally Sunday in Lahore, where hard-line political and religious groups vowed to continue fighting for Kashmir despite Musharraf's promise to stop militants based in Pakistan from crossing into Indian-controlled territory to stage attacks.

Militant groups that oppose Musharraf's crackdown and his support for the US-led war in Afghanistan have been blamed for a deadly series of attacks targeting foreigners or symbols of Western influence in Pakistan, including a bombing outside the US consulate in Karachi that killed 12 people this month.

Musharraf's pledges to stop cross-border infiltration have been made under pressure from the United States, which fears the Kashmir crisis could trigger a full-scale conflict between India and Pakistan — nuclear armed neighbors that have fought two wars over Kashmir since the dispute over the region began when they gained independence from Britain in 1947.

The two nations again approached the brink of war in the past month after an attack on an Indian army camp that killed 34 people.

India accuses Islamabad of funding and training the guerrillas who cross the Line of Control that divides Kashmir and carry out attacks on the Indian side, where tens of thousands of Indian troops, guerrillas and civilians have been killed. Pakistan says it only provides moral and political support for what it calls Kashmir's "freedom fighters."

Yesterday, Indian security forces said they killed four suspected Islamic militants in two separate gun battles in the Indian part of Kashmir. Police said two belonged to Hezbul Mujahedeen, one of the main militant groups fighting in Kashmir, and two to another Pakistan-based Islamic group, Lashkar-e Tayyaba.

9. Indian Forces Kill Three Suspected Islamic Militants

Article by Binoo Joshi on page 5 of
The Jerusalem Post of June 30th, 2002

Jammu, India (AP) — The Indian army killed three suspected Islamic militants yesterday after they crossed into Indian-controlled Kashmir from Pakistan, an army spokesman said. It was the first such incident since Islamabad promised to end such incursions last month.

Pakistani officials denied militants had crossed from Pakistan into Indian Kashmir.

The three men were killed during an hour-long exchange of gunfire in the Sagwari sector, half a kilometer from the Line of Control, which divides Kashmir between India and Pakistan, the army's spokesman said. The area is in Punch district, 210 kilometers northwest of Jammu, the winter capital of Jammu-Kashmir state.

The incident comes after Pakistani President Pervez Musharraf told US officials he would permanently stop cross-border infiltration by Islamic guerrillas. That promise – first made on May 27 and then repeated recently – pulled nuclear-armed India and Pakistan back from the brink of war.

On Friday, Indian Prime Minister Atal Bihari Vajpayee ruled out the possibility of war with Pakistan, but expressed doubts that Musharraf would keep his promise to permanently stop incursions by Islamic militants into Indian-controlled Kashmir.

10. India Blames Pakistan for Kashmir Massacre

Article on page 5 of *The Jerusalem Post* of
July 15th, 2002

Jammu, India (AP) — After weeks of relative calm, India again turned its anger yesterday on Pakistan and Islamic militants, blaming them for the massacre Saturday evening of 27 Hindu civilians in a slum on the outskirts of Jammu in Indian-controlled Kashmir.

At the base of the hill from which the heavily armed attackers emerged in the dark Saturday night, thousands of wailing slum residents yesterday furiously raised their fists and shouted frenzied slogans against Pakistan.

It was the deadliest assault in disputed Kashmir province since a May 14 strike by Islamic militants against a military base near Jammu that killed 34 people, mostly soldiers' wives and children – an attack that put India on a war footing with neighboring Pakistan.

11. Kashmir Candidate Targeted; 14 Killed

Article by Mujtaba Ali Ahmad on page 5 of
The Jerusalem Post of Sept. 29, 2002

Srinagar, India (AP) — Suspected Islamic militants blew up a vehicle carrying a legislative candidate in India's Jammu-Kashmir state yesterday, killing her father, two supporters, and one police escort, an official said.

The explosion hit the convoy of Khaleda Mushtaq, a member of the opposition Nationalist Congress Party, as she campaigned ahead of voting Tuesday in the Anantnag district, about 45 miles south of the state's summer capital, Srinagar.

In all, 14 people have been killed since late Friday in Jammu-Kashmir, where Pakistan-based militants fighting Indian rule have threatened to kill candidates and voters. The rebels say the elections are rigged to favor the ruling pro-India National Conference party.

Mushtaq was seriously wounded in the explosion, while her father, two of her supporters, and a policeman were killed, police said. Two passers-by were also wounded.

The blast left a seven foot crater in the dirt road and hurled Mushtaq's vehicle about 50 feet into a paddy field, police said.

Anantnag is one of four districts that go to the polls in the third round of voting scheduled for Jammu-Kashmir on Tuesday. The elections, which began this month, will end October 8th.

India hopes strong voter turnout will solidify its rule in the disputed region, which is split between India and Pakistan.

Al-arifeen, which India says is a front for the Pakistan-based Lashkar-e-Tayyaba militant group, claimed responsibility for the attack on Mushtaq's convoy in a call to a local news agency.

During the campaign, Al-arifeen has admitted it was behind the assassinations of government minister Mushtaq Ahmed Lone and independent candidate Sheikh Abdul Rehman, and several failed attempts to kill the state's tourism minister, Sakina Yattoo.

Also, yesterday, suspected guerrillas shot at the motorcade of Abdul Majid Mir, a National Conference party candidate in Shangas, 60 km. north of Srinagar, the police control room in Anantnag said. No one was hurt.

The attacks came as nearly 1,000 people blocked traffic, threw stones, and shouted anti-Indian slogans in Srinagar after an Indian security vehicle allegedly struck and killed Muzzamil Ahmad, a 19-year-old Muslim.

Police fired shots in the air to disperse the crowd, police said. Elsewhere in Jammu-Kashmir, police said at least eight suspected rebels and one soldier were killed in clashes that began late Friday.

Security forces clashed with separatists in the village of Sonarkalipora, about 15 miles southwest of Srinagar. Two suspected rebels and one paramilitary soldier were killed, police said.

Three rebels, including a district commander of the Jamiat-ul-Mujahedeen rebel group, were also killed in fighting overnight in the Gulgam Forest close to the India-Pakistan border, about 125 km. north of Srinagar, a paramilitary officer said.

Three more suspected guerrillas were killed in two separate clashes in the Kashmir Valley, the officer said. There was no independent confirmation of the police claims.

India accuses Pakistan of training and arming the rebels and helping them to cross over to Indian-held Kashmir to attack government targets. Pakistan claims it gives only moral support to the militants.

India and Pakistan have twice gone to war over Kashmir, which is claimed by both countries. The insurgents, fighting for Kashmir's independence from India or its merger with Pakistan, have killed two candidates and more than 160 political workers since elections were announced in Indian-held Kashmir in August.

The 12-year insurgency by separatist groups has left more than 60,000 people dead.

Victor Mordecai comments: Obviously, the above articles are the tip of the iceberg regarding tensions between the Moslems of Pakistan and the Hindus of India. The world has been very fortunate that a nuclear war has so far been prevented. But again, as in the case of the Chinese/Buddhists, the Hindus of India, over a billion of them, or 1/6 of the human population, are threatened with annihilation by the Moslems.

By the way, in my April and June 2002 newsletters I refer to the 120 medium-range CSS2 missiles the Saudis have in their Al-Solayil oasis base, courtesy of the Communist Chinese, and the nuclear warheads on those missiles, courtesy of the Pakistani nuclear program, funded, of course, by the Saudis. These missiles can reach the western parts of India, providing the Moslems with a second strike capability, in the event of a war between India and Pakistan. Please see Section D: Military Intelligence.

12. Pakistani Christian Gets Death for Blasphemy

Article by Massoud Ansari on page 5 of
The Jerusalem Post of July 2nd, 2002

Islamabad (AP) — Lawyers for a 25-year-old Christian sentenced to death because he converted to Christianity said yesterday they would challenge his conviction in the Pakistani High Court.

"We are confident that the higher court would set it aside," said Mahboob Ali Khan, a lawyer for the Human Rights Commission of Pakistan.

Aslam Masih was arrested in May 2000 and charged under Pakistan's blasphemy laws, which carries the death penalty for those convicted of defiling the Koran or blaspheming Islam and its founder, the prophet Muhammad.

Masih was born a Christian, but converted to Islam and then reconverted to Christianity.

The case started in early 2000 when Masih's employer, Rana Misah Ahmad, a member of the Sunni Tehrik religious militant group, told police that Masih said he only converted to Islam in order to marry a Muslim woman.

He then reconverted to Christianity and, according to Ahmad's statement, made derogatory remarks about the prophet Muhammad. Masih has been in jail since the accusations were made in May 2000. Masih, from a poor family, was provided a state, or "pauper's" lawyer to defend him.

Under Pakistani law, only the word of a Muslim accuser is needed to prosecute a non-Muslim defendant on blasphemy charges. Punishment, if found guilty, is death.

13. Pakistani Christians Mourn Massacre Victims

Article on page A11 of *The Jerusalem Post*
of September 27th, 2002

Karachi (Reuters) — Black flags flew over churches here yesterday, and hundreds of people staged demonstrations as Pakistan's small Christian community mourned the massacre of seven charity workers on Wednesday.

But sadness at the deaths at the hands of two unidentified gunmen was mixed with fear and widespread anger at the government of President Pervez Musharraf for not protecting them.

"Down with Musharraf," a group of around 200 protesters wearing black armbands chanted as they marched through the narrow lanes of a Christian slum.

Later in the day, about 400 protesters staged a sit-in outside the building where two gunmen burst into the office of a Christian charity and tied up and gagged the employees before shooting them in the head at point-blank range with a pistol.

14. Philippines Targeting Abu Sayyaf Chief

Article by Oliver Teves on page 5 of
The Jerusalem Post of June 24th, 2002

Zamboanga, Philippines (AP) — Philippines President Gloria Macapagal Arroyo has ordered soldiers to nab the chief of the al-Qaida-linked Abu Sayyaf group after one of its top leaders was believed to have been killed in a recent clash, a senior military officer said yesterday.

Maj.-Gen. Ernesto Carolina, the chief of the southern Philippines forces, said the military is now targeting Abu Sayyaf chief Khaddafy Janjalani and another senior leader, Ghalib Andang, known as Commander Robot.

Robot led the abduction of 21 people, including Western tourists, from a Malaysian resort in April 2000. All but one was released in exchange for large ransoms.

"The marching orders of the president are to get the others. The priority is Janjalani and Robot," Carolina said.

He said "Operation Daylight," which targets the remaining Abu Sayyaf leaders, includes rescuing three Indonesian crew members of a tugboat seized last Monday by gunmen believed to be Abu Sayyaf rebels and taken to Jolo Island, where Robot operates. The island is about 950 kilometers south of Manila.

Another Abu Sayyaf leader, Abu Sabaya, was believed to have been killed with two of his men in a gun battle on Friday off Mindanao Island. Sabaya spearheaded the kidnapping last year of 17 Filipinos and three Americans — missionaries Martin and Gracia Burnham of Wichita, Kansas, and Guillermo Sobero of Corona, California.

The guerrillas later abducted dozens more. Some, including Sobero, were killed; others escaped and the rest were freed, reportedly for large ransoms.

The kidnappings helped trigger the deployment of about 1,000 US troops to the southern Philippines for a counterterrorism training exercise with Philippine soldiers in the first expansion of the American war on terrorism outside Afghanistan.

The United States has offered a $5 million total reward for Janjalani, Sabaya, and three other Abu Sayyaf leaders. The Philippine government has also offered a reward for Robot and other leaders.

Yesterday, Carolina also showed reporters a videotape of two guerrillas, who were captured during Friday's gun battle, being interrogated. Both claimed they saw Sabaya fall into the sea after being hit by gunfire.

One of the rebels said Sabaya earlier had ordered another guerrilla to kill Martin Burnham if the group were cornered.

15. Suspected Islamic Extremists Kill 13 in Algeria

Article by Hassane Meftahi on page 5 of
The Jerusalem Post of June 30th, 2002

Algiers (AP) — Suspected Islamic extremists attacked a bus on the outskirts of the Algerian capital Friday night, killing 13 people aboard and injuring nine, the official APS news agency reported yesterday.

The attack came 24 hours after two people were shot to death and three injured in another bus attack near the coastal town of Bou Ismael, west of Algiers.

In the latest bus assault, five or six men attacked the bus with machine-gun fire in the town of Eucalyptus, 20 kilometers south of Algiers.

Eucalyptus, a small dusty town, is in an area known as the "triangle of death" because of the numerous attacks there in the early years of a 10-year-old Islamic insurgency that has left an estimated 120,000 people dead.

The area and the Mitidja Plain to the south were long controlled by the radical Armed Islamic Group, blamed for large-scale massacres in the region. Security forces were thought to have largely cleaned up the area over the past two years.

The Friday night attack was the third deadly assault on a bus in the last three weeks, and there is speculation it might signal a new strategy by the Armed Islamic Group's new leader, Rashid Abut Turab, demonstrating the group's ability to continue killings.

On Thursday, two young men armed with pistols boarded a bus at a stop near Bou Ismael, 45 kms. west of Algiers, killing the driver at point blank range and firing on the passengers, killing one and injuring three, according to press reports.

Eleven people were killed in an attack June 11 on a bus in Medea, south of Algiers at the foot of the Mitidja Plain.

Buses are widely used by Algerians in the hot summer months to head to beaches, but mixed swimming is condemned by the extremist Muslims.

Abu Turab replaces Antar Zouabri, killed in February in an attack by security forces on his hide-out in nearby Boufarik.

16. Morocco Arrests Al-Qaida Operative

Article by John J. Lumpkin on page 5 of
The Jerusalem Post of June 20, 2002

Washington — Moroccan authorities have arrested a senior al-Qaida recruiter known as "The Bear" who is suspected of plotting attacks against Western interests in Morocco, US officials say.

Another 13 people suspected of plotting to attack targets in Saudi Arabia were detained there, Saudi authorities said Tuesday. The 11 Saudis, an Iraqi, and a Sudanese man planned to shoot down a US military plane taking off from a Saudi air base, the government said through the official Saudi Press Agency.

US officials said Abu Zubair Haili, who was arrested in Morocco early last week, is considered among the top 25 al-Qaida lieutenants of Usama bin Laden.

Before September 11th, Haili ran some of bin Laden's training camps in Afghanistan. During the US-led war against the Taliban and al-Qaida, he helped evacuate al-Qaida operatives from the country, officials said.

It was not clear when the Saudi, who weighs more than 135 kilograms earning him the nickname "The Bear," came to Morocco, officials said.

Haili was a close associate of Abu Zubaydah, the senior al-Qaida operations chief whom US authorities captured in Pakistan in March.

Like Abu Zubaydah, Haili was central to al-Qaida's international recruiting network, accepting recruits into training and placing them in overseas cells, officials said.

Haili has not been tied to specific past al-Qaida terrorist operations, but officials said his knowledge of al-Qaida operations and terrorist cells would be useful to interrogators. US authorities are believed to have access to whatever information Haili is providing his interrogators. His arrest is the latest in a series of breaks in the US war on terrorism, both in Morocco and elsewhere.

On Monday, three alleged Saudi al-Qaida members were charged in connection with a plot to bomb US and British warships crossing the Straits of Gibraltar between Morocco and Spain.

Last week, Moroccan authorities said the suspects planned to sail a dinghy loaded with explosives from Morocco into the strait to attack the vessels.

Another al-Qaida senior lieutenant, Abd al Rahman Nashiri, is suspected of organizing the plot.

Nashiri, one of the alleged masterminds of the 2000 bombing of the USS *Cole,* remains at large, officials said. Haili's arrest was separate from those linked to the Gibraltar plot.

In Saudi Arabia, the US-allied government announced its first arrests linked to bin Laden, the Saudi exile whose first cause was the overthrow of this Muslim kingdom.

One of those arrested, Abu Huzifa of Sudan, has admitted he fired a surface-to-air missile at a US warplane near Prince Sultan Air Base, south of the Saudi capital of Riyadh, according to a US official, speaking on the condition of anonymity. The missile apparently missed; the launch went undetected.

The missile launch tube was found last month by patrolling guards.

Abu Husifa is suspected of being an al-Qaida cell leader, the official said. He was detained by Sudanese authorities in his home country, and turned over to Saudi Arabia.

However, Saudi authorities said they will not allow foreign security personnel to interrogate its 13 detained al-Qaida suspects, a government-controlled Saudi newspaper reported yesterday, describing a policy that could strain US-Saudi relations.

The daily *Okaz* said access to the suspects will be limited to Saudi authorities because "the crimes that they committed or planned to carry out occurred or were going to take place on Saudi territories."

The Saudi Press Agency provided only sketchy details on when or where the suspects were arrested.

The alleged plotters "were planning to carry out terrorist attacks against vital and important installations in the kingdom, by using explosives and two (surface to air) SA-7 missiles, smuggled into the kingdom and hidden in different places around the country," the agency said.

17. EU Tries to Defuse Morocco-Spain Tensions

Article on page 5 of *The Jerusalem Post* of
July 15th, 2002

Brussels (AP) — The EU yesterday called on Morocco
to find a quick diplomatic solution involving the removal of
its soldiers from a small uninhabited island claimed by both
Spain and Morocco.

Following the landing on the island four days ago,
Spain sent three war vessels to two of its enclaves on the
Moroccan coast. A frigate arrived in Ceuta and two corvettes
arrived in Melilla. The 12 Moroccan soldiers who landed
on Perejil set up two tents and raised two of their country's
flags, Spanish officials have said. Morocco said it occupied
the island to fight illegal immigration from Morocco to Spain
and continental Europe.

In a short statement, the EU said it is "very concerned"
over Morocco's occupation of Perejil island, which has been
claimed by Spain since 1668.

18. Moroccan, Spanish Foreign Ministers
Discuss Disputed Islet

Article by Susan Linnee in *The Jerusalem Post*
of July 23, 2002

Rabat, Morocco (AP) — The foreign ministers of
Morocco and Spain opened talks yesterday centered on the
thorny issue of sovereignty, two days after Spain withdrew
forces from a tiny Mediterranean island claimed by both
countries.

Discussions between Foreign Minister Muhammad
Benaissa and his counterpart, Ana Palacio, were restricted
to implementation of an "understanding" set out in a July 20
letter by US Secretary of State Colin Powell, and arranging

further talks, the Spanish Embassy said.

Powell was credited with unblocking a 10-day stand-off between this Arab Muslim nation and Spain.

Yesterday's encounter was made possible by the US-coordinated withdrawal of Spanish Legionnaires from the islet 200 meters from the Moroccan border, called Leila, or Night, by Morocco, and Perejil, or Parsley, by Spain.

The official Moroccan newspaper *Le Matin* suggested that the status of Spain's two enclaves on the Moroccan coast, Ceuta and Melilla, as well as a sprinkling of other islands that run east from Ceuta to the Algerian border, would also come up for discussion.

This was the highest-level meeting to take place between Morocco and Spain since Morocco abruptly recalled its ambassador from Madrid last October. It came about after a round of telephone diplomacy by Powell involving Moroccan King Muhammad VI, Benaissa, and Palacio.

A handful of Moroccan gendarmes set up camp on the contested island on July 11th, on the eve of the public wedding of Muhammad VI. Spain and the European Union protested loudly about a violation of Spanish sovereignty, and Spain set several warships and helicopters to encircle the island. Early on the morning of July 17th, Spanish Legionnaires from Ceuta landed on the island, briefly detained the half dozen Moroccans, and planted two flags on the island's rocky crest.

Morocco said it would only agree to talk about the island's future if the Spanish troops withdrew. As the sun was setting on July 20th, the last of the Legionnaires left.

Opposition newspapers in Morocco have openly questioned the reasons for Morocco's initial action, which officials called a routine periodic check on the smuggling of drugs and clandestine immigrants from Morocco to Spain across the narrow Strait of Gibraltar.

But, said the socialist *Liberation*, "even though the pretext was not very serious, it nevertheless succeeded in broaching a state of affairs that is much more serious for both countries."

L'Opinion, owned by the nationalist Istiqlal Party, said the fate of Western Sahara would also be discussed. Morocco has occupied the former Spanish territory since 1975 and intends to hold on to it.

19. Report: Islamic Extremists Plotted Attack on Church

Article on page 5 of *The Jerusalem Post* of
June 24, 2002

Rome (AP) — Suspected Islamic extremists were plotting an attack on a northern Italian church that has been the subject of protests by Muslims in the past, a newspaper reported yesterday.

The Milan daily *Corriere della Sera* said the San Petronio basilica in Bologna was targeted apparently because it contains a 15th century fresco that depicts Islam's prophet Muhammad in Hell, being devoured by demons.

Last year, a group of Italian Muslims appealed unsuccessfully to the Vatican to have the fresco by Giovanni da Modena removed or parts of it covered, arguing that it offended Islam. The group, the Union of Muslims in Italy, yesterday denied any link to the plot to attack the church and questioned the report's veracity, president Adel Smith told the Associated Press.

Corriere said Italian Carabinieri para-military police learned of the plot by intercepting phone conversations as part of a larger investigation into Muslim extremists operating in Italy.

That investigation led to the convictions earlier this year of seven Tunisians in Milan who were accused of providing logistical support to al-Qaida recruits passing through Europe.

The Tunisians were also accused by prosecutors of links to the Salafist Group for Call and Combat, a dissident faction of the Armed Islamic Group, Algeria's most radical insurgency movement. The United States has branded the Salafist group a terrorist organization and ordered its assets frozen.

The wiretaps indicated that starting in February, members of the Milan cell began plotting an attack on the Bologna church on orders of Salafist leader Hassan Hattab, *Corriere* said. Specific details, however, were never discussed.

Over the course of the investigation, authorities learned details of a Libyan in Italy, identified only as Amsa, who allegedly was sent by Usama bin Laden's al-Qaida network to coordinate activities of the various cells operating in the country, *Corriere* said.

20. FBI Probing LA Airport Terror Attack

Article by Janine Zacharia on page 2 of
The Jerusalem Post of September 4th, 2002

The FBI has decided to investigate the July 4th shooting at the El Al ticket counter at Los Angeles International Airport as an act of terrorism.

El Al ticket agent Victoria Hen and passenger Ya'acov Aminov were killed in the attack, which the FBI was initially reluctant to classify as an act of terrorism.

"While no final conclusion has been reached, our Los Angeles office has opened this case as a terrorism investigation," the FBI wrote to Congressman Eliot Engel (D-NY).

Engel had written in late July to the FBI to say he was "deeply troubled" by the agency's refusal to consider the shooting a terrorist act. Hesham Muhammad Ali Hadayet, an Egyptian, opened fire at the counter before being gunned down by an El Al security guard.

21. Shooter at the El Al Counter Confessed in the Past: "I Am a Terrorist"

Article by Eitan Amit on page 12 of the Hebrew
Israeli daily *Yediot Ahronot* of Sept. 26th, 2002 —
Translated by Victor Mordecai

A terrible mistake in the US by the INS: The Egyptian
who three months ago shot and killed two people at the El
Al counter at Los Angeles International Airport (LAX) confessed in the past to having been accused of being a member
of a terrorist organization — but this was never checked out,
and he was not deported.

Hesham Muhammad Hadayat arrived on July 4th,
2002, at the El Al counter at LAX and shot to death the
ground hostess, Vicki Hen (25), and a traveler, Ya'acov
Aminov (46). An El Al security guard rushed him and killed
him.

The *New York Times* revealed yesterday that in 1992,
Hadayat submitted a request for political asylum in the US
claiming that he was persecuted by the Egyptian authorities. A year later, as part of his request, he filled out forms
in which he admitted that the Egyptian authorities accused
him of belonging to the "Jamaah Islamiyah" group — an
extremist group which appears on the State Department's list
of terrorist organizations. Hadayat indeed said that he had
confessed to membership in this organization, but claimed
that the confession had been extracted by force and against
his will.

INS officials ignored the statement, and did nothing
to check this out, even though his asylum request remained
pending for another 2 1/2 years. In 1995, Hadayat received
a negative answer, and at the end of that year, an indictment
was prepared against him that he was illegally in the US. In
spite of the fact that Hadayat did not appear for his trial and
disappeared, he received a year later a temporary working

permit, and in 1997 he and his family even received the status of permanent residents, after his wife won the Green Card lottery.

According to the *New York Times,* Attorney General John Ashcroft was "red with rage" when he heard of this shortcoming, and demanded to know if steps were taken against those responsible. Following this disclosure, Ashcroft demanded that all requests for political asylum in the last 12 years be reviewed, fearing that terrorists slipped into the US in this manner.

[Victor Mordecai comments: It took the "politically correct" media and agenda three months to finally admit their mistake. This was not a hate crime. It was terrorism.]

PRIVATE INVESTIGATION

1. New York Times: Iran Behind '94 Buenos Aires Bombing

Article by Melissa Radler on page 1 of
The Jeruaslem Post of July 23rd, 2002

New York — Iran is responsible for the 1994 bombing of the AMIA Jewish center in Buenos Aires that killed 85 people and wounded more than 200, according to a secret, 100-page, sealed deposition by an Iranian defector that was obtained by *The New York Times.*

According to the deposition, a transcript of which was provided to the *Times* by Argentine officials frustrated that the investigation into the attack remains unsolved, Argentina's president at the time of the attack, Carlos Menem, was paid $10 million by the Islamic Republic to deny Iran's involvement.

Menem, who served two terms as president from 1989 to 1999, is considered a leading contender in the upcoming primaries for the country's next presidential elections, to be held next year.

In Israel, senior officials in the Prime Minister's Office said they were not surprised by the report, and called upon the United States to act on it immediately.

"It's no secret that Iran has developed a terrorist network around the world as part of its foreign policy," one top official said. "The US should use all the measures at its disposal, including economic pressure, to stop Iran from supporting terror and causing instability in the Middle East." The Prime Minister's Office said Iran was intimately involved in supplying the weapons on the *Karine A* arms ship and has provided Hizbullah with 9,000 rockets and missiles.

"The report is an ominous development that the intelligence services of Western countries and Israel have been monitoring for quite some time," the official said. "This only further proves the need to curb Iran's terrorist capabilities." Although Iran has repeatedly denied any link to the AMIA bombing and a similar bombing of the Israeli Embassy in Buenos Aires in 1992 that killed 28 people, the *Times* article cites a high-level defector from Iran's intelligence, identified as Abdolghassem Mesbahi, describing Iranian efforts to woo Menem, who is of Muslim ancestry, to their cause.

Mesbahi, who defected to Germany in 1996, said that the July 18th, 1994, attack was planned by the cultural attaché at the Iranian Embassy in Buenos Aires, Mehsen Rabbani, and supervised by a high-level official from Iran's intelligence service, Hamid Neghashan.

According to the *Times,* Mesbahi said that two cells were involved in planning the attack on the Jewish center. The first focused on "cooperating with members of the Argentine police, corrupting them or threatening them to collaborate with the attack," and the other cell focused on obtaining explosives in Brazil.

After the attack — the worst in Argentinean history — was carried out, Iran's supreme leader Ayatollah Khamenei publicly praised it, and Menem sent an emissary to Teheran to negotiate a pay-out to the Argentinean leader for his silence. The $10 million was deposited into an account number provided by Menem from a $200 million Swiss account held jointly by Iran's then-president, Hashemi Rafsanjani, and a son of the late Ayatollah Ruhollah Khomeini.

2. Argentina's Elections Are Israel's Business

Article by Eliahu Salpeter on page 5 of English edition
of *Ha'aretz* of Aug 2, 2002

As expected, the former president of Argentina — and possibly its future one — Carlos Menem, has denied a detailed *New York Times* report, based on testimony by an Iranian deserter from its intelligence services, that Menem received $10 million from Iran to hide Iran's responsibility for the explosions that destroyed the Israeli Embassy in 1992 and the Jewish community center in Buenos Aires in 1994.

There are many reasons to believe the Iranian agent, as Jose Harcman, president of Delegacion de Asociaciones Israelitas Argentinas (DAIA), declared last week. But it's also worth remembering a few points that mitigate the chances of ever proving the accusations against Iran and Menem.

It has been a decade since the bombing of the embassy and eight years since the Jewish community center was bombed, and there are no signs the government is moving with any more intensity to solve the cases than was done in the past decade. The most recent report by the American Jewish committee says that "clearly," some of the people who could have shed light on the attacks, "delayed, obstructed and undermined" the investigation "for political reasons."

The investigating judge, Jose Galiano, has admitted to destroying evidence. The trial against 20 junior police officers, which did finally begin, is dealing with marginal issues and doesn't approach the main suspicions. As time passes, evidence is disappearing and witnesses have a tendency to say they can't remember. Dr. Israel Singer, chairman of the World Jewish Congress, has vehemently criticized the trial's management. He says that 43,000 pages of trial transcript and testimony given by 3,185 witnesses have not been able to identify even a single prime suspect.

The civilian government that replaced the anti-Semitic military government has not made an effort to neutralize the anti-Semitism on the far right. The Jewish community, which in the beginning of the 1990's numbered nearly 250,000, has not recovered from the two blows of the explosions. That has certainly contributed to how the community, once one of the most stable and wealthy in Latin America, has been reduced to poverty by the economic crisis in Argentina.

Argentina has a large community of immigrants from Arab countries (Menem himself is of Syrian origin) and it's reasonable to assume that the Iranians, including some diplomats who hurried out of Argentina immediately after the embassy bombing, first went to the local Arab community to look for accomplices for its terror plans.

Claudio Lifshitz, a former aide to Investigating Judge Galiano, claims the judge had evidence linking Iran to an underground network in Buenos Aires. He says that early on the judge had evidence of suspicions that Menem received $10 million from the Iranians to cover up their involvement. Lifshitz essentially confirms the rumors that have long existed in the Jewish community about Menem's role in the cover-up. He says that "Galiano himself asked the Swiss authorities to investigate the movement of monies" in Menem's numbered account.

The Swiss government has now confirmed it is investigating Iranian money transfers through numbered accounts, but says the investigation is still ongoing. Menem admitted last week he has a Swiss bank account, but claims he received the money as compensation for his time spent in prison during the military regime. It takes a large measure of naivete to believe that a military regime, or the one that followed it, would hand out millions of dollars in "compensation" to political prisoners.

This is all important regarding Menem's past, his connections, and credibility, and for understanding the terrorist nature of the Tehran regime. Two elements buttress these issues: Washington decided last week to give up its support for the "reformist" president in Tehran, Muhammed Hatami, because it reached the conclusion that he is less moderate than claimed and because he is incapable of passing any of the few reforms he promotes. Hatami's supporters say that blaming the Buenos Aires bombings on Iran strengthens the American campaign to change the regime in Iran.

The second issue that makes the issue important is that Menem has announced that he's running for president again in next year's elections. His supporters say that the *New York Times* report about the alleged $10 million bribe was meant to undermine his chances for reelection. That also requires, of course, a large measure of good will (or bad) to believe the *New York Times* would publish information without checking it first in order to intervene in an Argentine election.

Israel cannot pretend that all this is a domestic Argentine matter. Observers believe that the economic crisis will send most Argentines to the polls to vote for Menem whether he took Iranian bribes or not. That means Israel must make the effort to find out as soon as possible answers to the following questions: Did Menem indeed take the bribe, and if so, what for — a declaration that Iran was not involved or a guarantee to foil the investigation of the bombings?

As a country whose embassy was bombed and the perpetrators have yet to be identified, and as a state that claims to defend Jews in danger the world over, Israel must find out who really is the man who purports to lead Argentina once again.

MILITARY INTELLIGENCE

1. India Seeking Israeli Help to Bolster Air Power

Article by Arieh O'Sullivan on page 2 of
The Jerusalem Post of June 30th, 2002

India's defense minister said over the weekend that his country is seeking to strengthen its air defenses by buying Israel's Arrow anti-ballistic missile system.

In a rare reference to India's growing military relations with Israel, Yogendra Narain said India has already acquired the Arrow's Green Pine radar, capable of detecting incoming missiles from up to 500 kilometers away.

"After discussions for the past three to four years, we have acquired a 'Green Pine' radar," Narain was quoted as saying in the *Times of India.*

Israel has never officially confirmed any arms deal with India.

Without the Arrow interceptors, Narain said, the Green Pine radar is currently used for "advance research."

The radar system is a mobile ground-based radar capable of tracking incoming missiles. It would have great strategic value along the Indian-Pakistani border, as it could cover all of Pakistan's military bases between Islamabad and the Indian frontier.

The system reportedly lets India track Pakistan's nuclear centers and missile sites.

The daily said India is also looking into the Russian S-300 anti-missile system, which is not yet operational. Israel and Russia are India's two main arms suppliers.

India also wants to acquire the Phalcon airborne early-warning radar. Sale of both the Phalcon and the Arrow missiles would require US approval.

India already has Searcher Mark II drones manufactured by Israel Aircraft Industries; one was shot down in Pakistan earlier this month.

2. Let India Have the Arrow, Too

Article by Ilan Berman on page 6 of
The Jerusalem Post of September 29th, 2002

As another war in Iraq seems to approach, Israelis can feel considerably more secure from missile attack than they did in 1991, when 39 Iraqi Scuds landed in Israel. The reason is the substantial improvement in Israeli missile defenses, an improvement that other nationals understandably are seeking for themselves.

Among the first in line interested in Israel's Arrow Theater Missile Defense system is, not surprisingly, India. Though the debate over whether to allow the purchase to go forward has not been given much attention, it could have momentous consequences for both American missile defense plans and US strategy in South Asia.

The debate first surfaced this July, when the Indian government — citing ongoing tensions with neighboring Pakistan — publicly floated a request to Jerusalem for the Arrow system.

India has good reason for its interest. Pakistan, thanks to Chinese and North Korean assistance, is fast emerging as a major missile power.

According to recent reports, Islamabad's "Shaheen-3" rocket, touted as one of the world's most advanced missile systems, is about to enter testing by the country's armed forces. And in recent months, as tensions with India have escalated, Pakistan has conducted high-profile tests of its "Hatf-III" short-range and "Guari" nuclear-capable medium range missile in an unmistakable signal to its regional rival.

For New Delhi, the lack of any comprehensive protection against Islamabad's burgeoning arsenal has made missile defense a top priority. Just days before stepping down, outgoing Defense Secretary Yogendra Narain publicly outlined his government's plans for a "sharp and visible" acceleration of anti-missile efforts.

Domestically, this has taken the form of an ambitious program to develop indigenous defenses. And internationally, India has initiated a serious dialogue with its newest strategic partner — Israel. The centerpiece of these discussions is New Delhi's acquisition of the Arrow, the world's only operational, fielded theater missile defense system.

But the proposed sale of the Arrow is politically contentious. The system, jointly developed by Israel with the United States, requires American approval for export to third countries. Pentagon planners, who view India as a critical component in Washington's planned international missile defense architecture, are pushing hard for the sale. Foggy Bottom, however, has other ideas.

The State Department is concerned that a green light for the sale could ratchet up tensions between New Delhi and Islamabad, and might encourage a South Asian arms race. So US diplomats are now lobbying New Delhi to drop its bid to acquire the system.

So far, the White House appears undecided on the Arrow issue. But Washington's wavering could turn out to have far-reaching consequences.

For one thing, other missile defense suitors — like Russia — are waiting in the wings. Russian President Vladimir Putin's upcoming December trip to India is expected to entail a major effort to expand the military relationship between Moscow and New Delhi. On the agenda are proposals for the construction of an integrated national architecture for India based around Russia's S-300VM air-defense system. Such a development could decisively take India off the table as an American missile defense ally.

Even more significantly, Indian officials are increasingly making clear that they view the Arrow issue as a barometer of the emerging strategic relationship between Washington and New Delhi. As one Indian policymaker recently put it to the Far Eastern Economic Review, "What does this new relationship consist of if the US does not deliver in areas of interest to India?"

A good question and one with important ramifications for the US. Approval of the Arrow sale could put New Delhi squarely in Washington's corner, not only on missile defense, but on larger regional security issues as well.

In addition, arming India with the Arrow — given New Delhi's deepening ties with Jerusalem — could mark the start of just the international missile defense architecture that the Pentagon is hoping for. A perceived American ambivalence to Indian defense needs, on the other hand, could torpedo hopes for a warmer strategic relationship, much to the detriment of US plans in the Asia-Pacific. It might also strike a serious blow to the Bush administration's long-term plans for a layered global missile shield.

For President Bush, arming India with the Arrow would go a long way toward making his campaign pledge to protect the US and its allies from ballistic missile attack a reality. With so much at stake, the decision should be an easy one.

(The writer is vice-president for policy at the American Foreign Policy Council in Washington, DC.)

3. Why Isn't Democracy Necessary for Pakistanis, Too?

Article by Brahma Chellaney in the
International Herald Tribune of Sept. 3rd, 2002

New Delhi — The more justifications George W. Bush puts forward to launch military strikes on Iraq, the more he exposes the contradictions in his foreign policy and risks needlessly stoking anti-US sentiment in the world.

Bush is right that Saddam Hussein, a leader who gassed members of his Kurdish minority, epitomizes evil. He is also right that Saddam's ouster, by whatever means, is essential to resolve the 11-year humanitarian crisis confronting Iraqis and bring their country back into the international mainstream. If Iraq were reintegrated with the world it would send oil prices tumbling, benefiting oil-importing nations.

But Bush is wrong in seeking to impose a unilateral solution. He mistakenly believes that his foreign policy can apply different standards in pursuit of politically expedient, short-term objectives without damaging America's global leadership.

His differential calculus in foreign policy is most evident on the key issues of democracy, terrorism and weapons of mass destruction. Even as he builds a case for declaring war on Iraq for democracy's sake, he has openly winked at the latest action by the military dictator Pervez Musharraf in proclaiming 29 constitutional amendments in one stroke to crown himself virtually the emperor of Pakistan.

Musharraf's continued export of terror has kept his country perilously close to war with India.

Asked to comment on the constitutional assault, Bush did not utter a word in criticism. He praised Musharraf for being "still tight with us on the war against terror." He promised, disingenuously, to "continue to work with our friends and allies to promote democracy."

If democracy is good for Iraqis, why is it not good for Pakistanis? If Bush really wants South Asian peace and stability, he cannot overlook the fact that every Pakistani military ruler has waged war with India and that the only occasions when the two neighbors have come close to peace have been during the shorter periods of democratic rule in Islamabad.

The more power Musharraf has usurped, the more unpopular at home and the more dependent on his army he has become. That makes it more likely that he will ratchet up hostilities with India.

With cross-border infiltration of Islamic extremists from Pakistan into India rising and Musharraf making belligerent statements on Kashmir, the danger of a full-fledged war between the two nuclear-armed neighbors is again growing.

No ruler in the world has benefited more than Musharraf from the terrorist attacks on the United States nearly a year ago. Yet he presides over a country that is the main sanctuary of Al Qaeda, Taliban and Kashmiri terrorists.

Bush insists that Iraq poses a continuing nuclear threat. But he has not said a word about Pakistan's clandestine nuclear and missile cooperation with the Communist regimes in China and North Korea that US intelligence continues to track.

The Musharraf dictatorship overtly employs nuclear terror to shield its export of terror. When earlier this summer it again used nuclear blackmail against India, how did the Bush administration react? Far from penalizing Islamabad, it urged India to exercise restraint.

Bush's message to India is that the world's largest democracy should not strike, even in retaliation, at state-sponsored terrorism and nuclear blackmail. To stop that possibility, Washington has since the Dec. 13 terrorist attack on the Indian Parliament supplied Musharraf with more than $175 million worth of military equipment, including badly needed replacement parts to get the Pakistani F-16 fighter jet fleet back in full service.

In doing so, Washington has validated Prime Minister Atal Bihari Vajpayee's public admission that he erred in not seizing the moment after Dec. 13 to launch military reprisals. The air force was ready the following day to inflict punitive blows on the Pakistani terror infrastructure and its guardians. A wider ground war would not have followed quickly because the rival armies were not mobilized. But the air force waited in vain for the political green light.

Consistency is a virtue in foreign policy, especially when America's unprecedented primacy in the world calls for responsible leadership and prudence. Bush can hardly strengthen US global leadership by demanding democracy in enemy states while lubricating friendly dictatorships.

(The writer, a professor of strategic studies at the privately funded Center for Policy Research in New Delhi, contributed this comment to *The International Herald Tribune.*)

4. War With Iraq Risks Israeli Use of Nuclear Weapons

Article on page 11 of *The Jerusalem Post*
of September 27th, 2002

Hong Kong (AP) — A US-led military campaign against Iraq could escalate into a broader Middle East war that would risk tempting Israel into using nuclear weapons, a former chief UN arms inspector said yesterday.

Israel refrained from retaliation after Iraq fired 39 Scud missiles at Israeli cities during the 1991 Gulf War.

Richard Butler, an Australian who headed the UN special commission (UNSCOM) to disarm Iraq from 1997 to 1999, said he believed Washington was unlikely to be able to dissuade Israel from responding if it is attacked again.

"My deepest fear is that if that conflict occurred and if the war escalated, that Israel would use its nuclear weapons," Butler said.

"If that happens, this world will have been changed beyond recognition," he told a gathering of business executives in Hong Kong. "And I would fear, too, that if that happened, the State of Israel would cease to exist. It would have lost the moral authority that supported its creation."

On Tuesday, an Israeli newspaper reported that messages had been sent to Baghdad through "diplomatic channels" that Israel did not intend to join any American offensive against Iraq but would not sit idly by if attacked itself.

The Israeli government has not commented on the report.

Iraqi President Saddam Hussein shattered a UN Security Council consensus for action against Baghdad last week when he agreed unconditionally to the return of UN weapons inspectors after nearly four years.

Butler has urged the United States and Russia to make another joint effort to get Iraq to agree to serious weapons inspections. Inspectors have not been allowed to return to Iraq since 1998.

US President George W. Bush dismissed Saddam's offer as a stalling ploy, and recommended a new resolution aimed at authorizing force against Iraq should Baghdad ignore existing resolutions on inspections.

Butler also expressed skepticism. "Why not throw open your doors and allow the world to prove you have no weapons of mass destruction?" he said.

Butler termed the last of a UN consensus on Iraq "a crisis in the management of global security." If the UN Security Council does not act, "the US will take the action required," he said. "It will happen and it will happen soon."

[Victor Mordecai comments: The above four articles I have used make the point that Israel and India, both nuclear powers, are asked to show restraint while anti-democratic Islamic countries are free to do whatever. Saudi Arabia is a country whose CSS2 Chinese missiles, tipped with Pakistani nuclear warheads, are a threat both to Israel and India as well as the US, but it seems Saudi Arabia is a "Holy Cow" for Washington, DC, and this emboldens these Islamic countries to think that they can do whatever they want and that Israel and India must be sacrificed for the proverbial barrel of oil. This bodes ill for peace in the world — and brings the threat of international nuclear holocaust much closer.]

<u>CONCLUSIONS</u>

In his book, *The Clash of Civilizations and the Remaking of World Order,* Harvard Professor Samuel Huntington describes what many feel is the historical trend by which the United States of America, like all great empires, is now sliding downwards and within fifty years will no longer be World Power #1.

Professor Huntington speaks of the different forces at play. Mandarin Chinese is spoken by twice as many people as "Anglo-Saxon Westerners" who speak English. Another rival cultural group is the Hindus with a population of over a billion human beings. And, of course, the group that concerns me personally is the Muslim population of over a billion — some say a billion four hundred million — because it is their religion which calls for the annihilation or conversion of all non-Muslims to Islam. But also, what concerns me most is their motto: Kill the Saturday people (the Jews) on Saturday. Kill the Sunday people (the Christians) on Sunday. We Jews have experienced enough holocausts in the last two millennia.

It is in light of Huntington's teachings that I remember another historian, Alexis De Tocqueville, who wrote his famous book in 1820: *Democracy in America.* He said: "America will be the greatest country on earth because the American people are a good people, and their pulpits are on fire for the Lord."

Though today I live in Israel, I feel I was shaped first and foremost by the greatness of American democracy, on the permanent emancipation from slavery, equality for women, as well as a long list of the liberties and rights to the pursuit of happiness which make America and Western Civilization greater than any other, and if this is threatened by other systems, then all efforts must be made to defend all these advancements and achievements over the last four thousand years of Judeo-Greek-Roman and -Christian civilization.

The Islamic attacks on America on 9/11/2001 were intended to topple the economy of the "Great Christian Satan America." I have been speaking about this since my first trip to the US in November 1990. I even predicted that "They would take American airliners and crash them into the twin towers of the World Trade Center." I said this on July 11th, 2001, two months before the attacks. This was committed to tape and CD by Chuck Missler and his Koinonia House ministry.

People looked askance for many years as I spoke about these horrible plans of world Islam to destroy Christian America. In my first book, *Is Fanatic Islam a Global Threat?* I quoted an article on page 96 of my book from the Israeli daily newspaper *Yediot Ahronot* from 1995 about how the first class of Islamic Kamekaze pilots had graduated from flight school in Iran and had been already dispatched to different countries.

I mentioned the WTC five times in that book. Also mentioned was the *Jihad in America* video of Steven Emerson produced in 1993-94 predicting such Islamic terrorist attacks on the US. Instead of receiving the Congressional Medal of Honor, Steven Emerson was basically "put on the blacklist" by the supposedly prestigious National Public Radio (NPR). The Clinton Administration period was a black hole in US preventative law enforcement. Anyone who dared to swim against the current regarding the truth about Islam was blacklisted.

As I write this, my third book, in the year 2003, I look back with great frustration at how hard I had to work to self-publish my books and to print only 53,000 of the first book and 20,000 of the second. Had I sold 53 million of the first and 20 million of the second, there would not be so many people opposing the US in its wars of liberation, first in Afghanistan, second in Iraq, third and fourth hopefully in Iran and North Korea respectively.

Without attacking the duplicity of the Belgians, French, Germans and Russians regarding the war against Saddam Hussein, I cannot help but remember Professor Samuel Huntington's admonitions that the Judeo-Christian West was sinking, and instead of backing the US, the four above-mentioned countries were playing into the hands of those cultures, especially Islamic and Mandarin Chinese, which seek to replace the Judeo-Christian system with their own totalitarian systems. These two totalitarian systems were perfecting the "divide and conquer" techniques on the Christian West. But it was still the US which had to do the "dirty work" for persecuted peoples of Afghanistan, Iraq, Iran and North Korea, just to mention a few.

I have said many times in the churches of the US that God almighty had anointed the US in its formation. We must never forget the persecuted minorities that fled from all over the world to the freedom of the 13 colonies and after 1776, this new republic which had room for anyone and everyone with absolute freedom to believe in God, or not to believe in God. To go to this house of worship or that house of worship or to none at all.

We must never forget that the United States was always an isolationist country. It really did not want to get involved in the affairs of other countries. It did not start WWI. That was a European mess. The US did not want to enter this war, but in 1917, had no choice. In the end, the US had to save the world from the mess started by the Europeans.

WWII was also not started by the US. The US did not want to get involved. It was started by the Japanese in the Pacific region, particularly, Korea, Manchuria and China; the Germans and Italians in Europe and in Africa. All of this was already happening in the 1930's. When Germany finally started its war with Poland in the summer of 1939, this was when Britain and France officially entered the war.

Russians, by the way, were allied with the Nazis in this attack on Poland as part of the Molotov-Ribbentrop pact. The Americans succeeded in maintaining neutrality until December 7th, 1941, when surprised by the Japanese "sneak attack" at Pearl Harbor, Hawaii. But the Americans did not start this war either. Again this was a European mess compounded by Japanese expansionist ambitions in the Pacific theater.

Again, as in 1917, the Americans were anointed by God to enter the fray, to save the world from itself and finally, to rebuild devastated Europe and devastated Japan. The US undertook to rebuild Europe and Japan with the Marshall and McArthur plans respectively. The Americans had NO intentions to remain, or to conquer foreign lands, but to get the job done and bring home the GI's.

Immediately after the end of WWII, there was now a new threat — that of the Communist Cold War. It was only the US that could save the world from this imperialist expansionist threat. And praise God, America succeeded and was vindicated in its efforts.

My frustration for the last 13 years has been to warn America and the Judeo-Christian West that it is not yet over. Now the last and greatest threat is looming — that of Islam. It is only Judeo-Christian America that can lead the world in defeating this anti-Semitic, anti-Christian, anti-Hindu, anti-Buddhist, anti-democratic, anti-women and slavery of blacks system which is responsible for the deaths of tens of millions of people in the last three decades.

In my opinion, the attacks on 9/11 were the "Pearl Harbor" of WWIII. Unfortunately, there is no appreciation from the Belgians, French, the Germans, or Russians for anything that the US has done for Europe and the world in the last hundred years.

As I write this book, the US is in position to finish off Saddam Hussein, and to capture or kill Usama bin Laden, but this is not the end of the problem. Contrary to what US President George W. Bush has said, this IS a war against Islam. It will not end until Islam or everybody else is gone. That is the reason for the writing of my first two books as well as this third and hopefully, fourth, fifth and sixth books, etc. This is a long haul, because it is not easy to terminate a religion like Islam. But this has to happen or 5/6ths, perhaps 6/6ths, of the human race will be destroyed.

Here are some highlights of the information contained in this book:

1. The Moslems have a plan for the annihilation of all the Jews in Canada. Moslems in every city will be responsible for killing the Jews in every city. (October 2001 newsletter — "The Edmonton Revelation")

2. Saddam Hussein's Involvement in the Bombing of the Murrah Federal Building in Oklahoma City on April 19th, 1995. (November 2001 newsletter)

3. Islamic Infiltration Into the US Along the Mexican and Canadian Borders. (December newsletter)

4. Use of Bio-Chemicals in Palestinian Homicide Bombs. (December newsletter)

5. Palestinian Smuggling of Weapons of Mass Destruction into Palestinian Autonomy Areas by the *Karine* A Gun Smuggling Ship. (January 2002 newsletter)

6. Islamic Persecution of Christians in the Palestinian Autonomy Areas. (January 2002 newsletter)

7. Bosnia, the European Afghanistan. (February 2002 newsletter)

8. New Islamic Movement Seeks Latino Converts in the US. (March 2002 newsletter)

9. Moslems Murder Driver Registration Licensing Official in Tennessee. (March 2002 newsletter)

10. Secret Saudi Missile Base at Al-Solayil Oasis in Saudi Desert. (April 2002 newsletter)

11. Saudi Funded Terrorism in Florida. (April 2002 newsletter)

12. Saudis Pledge Up to $20 Million for Clinton Library.

13. America Continues to Close Its Eyes to Hamas Terrorism. (May newsletter)

14. Islamic Cyber Attacks. (June newsletter)

15. Saudi PR Sullies US, Saudi Arabia's Captives, Saudis Boycotting US Goods, Saudi Arabia Considering Free Trade Agreement with Iraq. (June newsletter)

16. Army Intelligence Expert Warns of Nuclear Equipped Iran. (June newsletter)

17. Syria Preparing Long-Range Scud Rocket. (June newsletter)

18. Geostrategy London: Concerns of Saudi Missiles Hitting UK. (June newsletter)

19. Egyptian Suppression of Democracy. (July newsletter)

20. Imprisonment of Syrian Democracy Proponents Upheld. (July newsletter)

21. Chemical Biological Attack Feared in Turkey. (July newsletter)

22. Thailand Suspects Islamic Group in Train Bombing. (July newsletter)

23. Dutch Lawmakers Call for Survey of Muslims. (July newsletter)

24. Moroccans Arrested in Cyanide Plot. (July newsletter)

25. Islamic Terrorist/Professor Sami Al-Arian. (July newsletter)

26. Louis Farrakhan Launches Anti-Israel Lobby. (July newsletter)

27. Syria Secretly Purchasing Weapons for Iraq in Eastern Europe. (July newsletter)

28. Ticking Time Bomb in Saudi Arabia. (August newsletter)

29. The Coming Revolution in Iran. (August newsletter)

30. Bosnian Militants Turn US Allies Into Enemies. (August newsletter)

31. Turkish Police Seize Weapons-Grade Uranium. (September newsletter)

32. Various Articles on the Important Role of India in the Struggle With Islam. (September 2002 newsletter)

33. Articles on Iran's Role in Islamic Bombings in Argentina 1992 & 1994. (September 2002 newsletter)

34. Singapore Leader Cautions Against Islamic Rigidity. (September 2002 newsletter)

35. Philippines Targeting Abu Sayyaf Leader. (September 2002 newsletter)

36. War With Iraq Risks Israeli Use of Nuclear Weapons. (September 2002 newsletter)

Of course, there is yet much more in the newsletters to be gleaned about globalist Islamic plans for world domination. There is, of course, even much more information that I must have missed because of the myriad of countries and myriad of Islamic groups active in all the countries of the world. I have tried my best with the limited resources available to provide a faithful mirror of what Islam is doing today throughout the world.

I pray that this book will succeed even more than my first two books, and that I will be able to come out after October 2003 with "Islamic Threat Updates Almanac #2 - 5763" with the following year's collection of articles and information pieces. Even with the defeat of Saddam Hussein and Usama bin Laden, we have not seen the last of the Islamic threat. There is much more yet to come and we must document this, in order to defeat the next stages of the Islamic plan, primarily in Iran, Saudi Arabia, Syria and Pakistan.

Victor Mordecai